The Complete

MASTER KEY SYSTEM

The Complete
MASTER KEY SYSTEM

*Using the Classic Work to Discover
Prosperity, Joy, and Fulfillment*

WILLIAM GLADSTONE,
RICHARD GRENINGER, AND
JOHN SELBY

JEREMY P. TARCHER/PENGUIN
a member of Penguin Group (USA)
New York

JEREMY P. TARCHER/PENGUIN
Published by the Penguin Group
Penguin Group (USA) LLC
375 Hudson Street
New York, New York 10014

USA · Canada · UK · Ireland · Australia
New Zealand · India · South Africa · China

penguin.com
A Penguin Random House Company
Copyright © 2010 by Waterside Productions, Inc.
Tapping the Source was first published by Sterling Publishing Co., Inc. in 2010. First Tarcher/Penguin
paperback edition, entitled *The Complete Master Key System*, published in 2014.

Most Tarcher/Penguin books are available at special quantity discounts for bulk
purchase for sales promotions, premiums, fund-raising, and educational needs. Special books
or book excerpts also can be created to fit specific needs. For details, write:
Special.Markets@us.penguingroup.com.

ISBN 978-0-399-17182-6

Printed in the United States of America
1   3   5   7   9   10   8   6   4   2

CONTENTS

FOREWORD BY MARK VICTOR HANSEN   xi

INTRODUCTION   xv

Part One: Getting Started

  1: WHO WAS CHARLES HAANEL?   3

  2: WHO ARE RICHARD, WILLIAM, AND JOHN?   9

  3: HOW TO USE THIS BOOK   18

  4: RICHARD'S BACKGROUND AND INSIGHTS   21

  5: WILLIAM'S BACKGROUND AND INSIGHTS   36

Part Two: Activate Your Inner Potential with John Selby

  6: REBIRTHING THE HAANEL VISION   49

  7: UNIVERSAL CREATIVE MIND   69

  8: ENTERING INTO CREATIVE SILENCE   82

  9: SHIFTING INTO RECEIVE MODE   104

10: CLARIFY YOUR CORE DESIRES   116

11: TAP THE CREATIVE SOURCE   131

12: MANIFEST YOUR HIGHER PURPOSE   142

Part Three: Achieve Genuine Fulfillment

13: APPLY THE DAILY ATTRACTION PROCESS   161

14: DISCOVER THE SECRET OF GIVING   181

15: ACHIEVE ENDURING ABUNDANCE   189

16: HEAL YOURSELF AT CORE LEVELS   201

17: RADIATING SPIRITUAL INTENT   213

Part Four: Practice Makes Perfect

18: FINAL WORDS FROM CHARLES HAANEL   225

AFTERWORD BY JACK CANFIELD   235

ACKNOWLEDGMENTS   237

ADDITIONAL RESOURCES AND ONLINE PROGRAMS

    Online Training, Inspiration, and Reinforcement   239

    Advanced Coaching and DVD Programs   240

    Live Seminars and Conferences   240

READING GROUP QUESTIONS   241

APPENDIX: THE MASTER KEY SYSTEM   249
    by Charles F. Haanel

DAILY MANIFESTATION PROCESS

Step 1: Remember to Remember
"I choose to focus enjoyably inward."

Step 2: Quiet Your Mind
"My mind is quiet . . . I am now in the Silence."

Step 3: Enter into Receive Mode
"I am open to receive guidance from my Source."

Step 4: Feel Your Core Passion
"I know what I want."

Step 5: Tap into Manifestation Power
"I feel connected with creative power."

Step 6: Focus upon Your Higher Intent
"My vision is right now perfect and complete."

Step 7: Manifest Your Goal
"Each new moment is manifesting my dream."

We are always in the presence
of an Infinite and Eternal Energy
from which all things proceed.

A single idea may be worth millions of dollars,
and these ideas can only come to those who are
receptive, who are prepared to receive them,
who are in a successful frame of mind. Is it
not worthwhile to make the effort?

—CHARLES HAANEL,
The Master Key System

FOREWORD

What a treasure you have in front of you in *Tapping the Source*. I know something about manifesting and thinking on a large scale. My Chicken Soup book series has sold more than one hundred and fifty million copies, and I have encouraged and taught tens of thousands of ordinary people just like you to live their dreams and become successful authors and speakers. In *Tapping the Source*, you now have the formula for manifesting your own dreams, whatever they may be. You may be working in the real estate industry, or working as an automobile mechanic, or taking care of your children as a stay-at-home parent. It really does not matter what or if you have a profession because *Tapping the Source* is the key to your true fulfillment and happiness in life. That's right. This book you hold in your hands is all you need to start living the life of your dreams.

Richard Greninger, whom I have worked with as a friend and colleague for more than twenty years, has done us all an enormous service in rediscovering the Master Keys of Charles Haanel and teaming up with William Gladstone and John Selby to create an immediate action plan for twenty-first-century readers not just to read the original keys, but also to implement them. The Focus Phrases and exercises in *Tapping the Source* are unique. No other self-help book gives you these simple exercises that capture the wisdom of the ages and allow you to not just understand how to manifest but also *feel* the energy of manifestation in your very own body.

In studying with my mentor Buckminster Fuller, I was exposed to cutting-edge thought and a mind that was capable of dreaming big dreams. From Bucky I learned to dream big, to dream differently, and to overcome obstacles. With the tools you now have in *Tapping the Source*, I encourage you to dream big, to dream differently, and to overcome the obstacles in your own life. I know you can, and I know that the process of doing so will bring you great joy.

We are living at a unique time in human history. All the technology and building blocks necessary for creating a world that works for everyone already exist. The missing ingredient has been human will and dedication to a larger vision. That larger vision has actually been with us for hundreds of years. Charles Haanel was the first modern thinker to see how to use this ancient wisdom to manifest abundance and happiness. One of my favorite quotes from the Master Key System of Charles Haanel is: "Large ideas have a tendency to eliminate all smaller ideas so that it is well to hold ideas large enough to counteract and destroy all small or undesirable tendencies. This is one of the secrets of success: Think big thoughts. The creative energies of mind find no more difficulty in handling large situations than small ones."

My advice to you is that you use the tools you now have before you in *Tapping the Source* to "think big thoughts." Start with big thoughts and build big dreams. Make them real and share them with humanity. You are here to make a difference.

With my sincere wishes
for your highest success,
Mark Victor Hansen

INTRODUCTION

Everything you ever wanted can be yours. Everything. Not just wealth, health, and material abundance but also true eternal happiness.

How can we know this? How can we offer such assurance? What is the source of our knowledge and confidence that this is true?

This book will reveal these secrets in accessible language with easy-to-follow exercises that have proven to be effective. But where did this information come from? Why should you trust that this book is the true guide to all you have been seeking?

In all areas of your life you must always examine the source. This book is not just the creative output of three successful and widely divergent intellects. *Tapping the Source* is first and foremost a modern-day presentation of the ideas provided to the world by an extraordinary individual named Charles Haanel.

Charles Haanel lived from 1866 to 1949. During his

lifetime, Haanel created a great fortune and dedicated himself to teaching others his secrets of manifestation. Haanel combined the unique skills of being both a practical businessman and a metaphysician interested in esoteric beliefs and esoteric practices. He was one of the first individuals in America to believe in meditation and manifestation through concentrated focus and discipline. Haanel believed in hard work, but he also believed in something more: the ability of each individual to tap into the Divine Source of knowledge and wisdom that permeates the universe. Of the many books Haanel wrote, his most famous and useful, *The Master Key System*, was published in 1912, almost one hundred years ago. This book went on to influence Ernest Holmes, Napoleon Hill, and many other authors and individuals through to the present day, including the creators of *The Secret*. Anywhere you go on the Internet, you will see the links between Charles Haanel and *The Secret*.

The Master Key System, as a book and correspondence course, sold in excess of two hundred thousand copies at a time when America had perhaps only one-tenth the reading population it has today. One of those readers was a gentleman named Napoleon Hill. Hill is famous for his classic work *Think and Grow Rich*, which has sold tens of millions of copies and is widely regarded as the first and most useful self-help book ever published. He went on to create the Napoleon Hill Institute, which remains robust and active today, still touching the lives of millions of individuals focused on creating material wealth.

Hill wrote a letter in April 1919 in which he gave full

credit to Charles Haanel and his Master Key System as the source for his own books and teachings. At this time, Hill had already published the first edition of his book *The Law of Success* and was also publishing his *Golden Rule* magazine, both precursors to *Think and Grow Rich*. In today's world of self-aggrandizing self-help teachers and gurus, this is a truly gracious letter of recognition:

My dear Mr. Haanel:

I believe in giving credit where it is due; therefore, I believe I ought to inform you that my present success and the success which has followed my work as President of the Napoleon Hill Institute is due largely to the principles laid down in *The Master Key System*. I shall cooperate with you in getting your course into the hands of the many who so greatly need your message.

Cordially and sincerely,
Napoleon Hill

Hill was not just a powerful self-help author. He practiced the principles he learned from Haanel and amassed one of the largest fortunes in America through *Golden Rule*, consulting agreements with business titan Andrew Carnegie, and the creation of his own publishing empire. Perhaps even more importantly, he focused on philanthropic activities and sharing his knowledge with others. Indeed even his act of acknowledging Haanel can be interpreted as part of the wisdom imparted in the Master Key System itself. The true power of the Law of Attraction and other laws of abundance that are at the center of the Master Key System is about constantly giving to others and acknowledging the role of others in everyday success on every level of our lives.

Many books, such as *The Law of Attraction* by Jerry and Esther Hicks and *The Secret* by Rhonda Byrne, have taken an idea here and there from the writings of Napoleon Hill and Charles Haanel, but there has never been a book that goes back to Haanel's original words and provides the full context of what his principles and laws really are and how to implement them. Part of the reason for this may be that times have changed since his work was first published, and some of the insights provided are no longer as timely. This in fact is not the case. Though his writing may seem dated, his ideas are timeless. There is not a single principle or law in the original Master Key System that is less relevant today than when originally published. *The Master Key System* is truly a book of timeless wisdom and insight. The modern world has progressed in many areas in one hundred years, however, and one of the areas of such progress has been specifically in how to use meditation and focused concentration to reach alpha states for peak performance. Books have been written, such as *Flow: The Psychology of Optimal Experience* by Mihaly Csikszentmihalyi and *Zone Tennis* by Jay P. Granat, about how to be "in the flow" or "in the zone" and reach maximum physical and mental potential at all times. *The Secret* hinged on just one of Haanel's principles, but in fact *The Master Key System* illustrates that a single principle from the full twenty-four presented is not sufficient for success.

In *Tapping the Source*, we have gone back to Haanel's original words and principles and have added specific easy-to-follow exercises that enhance your ability to implement Haanel's recommendations. In the original Master Key System, Haanel provided a powerful principle, such as focusing on your connection to the source of abundance in the universe, and then told his readers to sit quietly and meditate on that idea. In *Tapping the Source*, John Selby has developed specific Focus Phrases that mirror Haanel's instructions so that you have a practical guide that will enable you to more thoroughly and more quickly capture the experience of not just understanding but *feeling* what it means to be centered and connected to your ultimate and unlimited potential.

We are humbled to serve as your guides to the wonderful wisdom of Charles Haanel. This is a magical book that will change your life—not just in helping you achieve your own material and emotional desires, but also in helping you help others achieve their goals as well. At the heart of *Tapping the Source* is the awareness that all life is interconnected and that the true secret of happiness is connecting to others and helping them connect to the same Source from which all is manifested. In so doing we all have the potential to live our lives to our fullest potential and to create the conditions for humanity as a collective whole to also reach its highest potential.

As you read *Tapping the Source*, remember to breathe and enjoy.

Part One

GETTING STARTED

CHAPTER 1

WHO WAS CHARLES HAANEL?

It is hard to overstate the magic and wisdom of Charles Haanel's lifework. He was a living example of the synthesis of both Western and Eastern philosophies, a man who appreciated material abundance but who never lost sight of the importance of inner calm and inner peace. Haanel was a man with a healthy ego and concern for his own well-being but also a man with tremendous compassion and interest in helping others. He had an innate ability to penetrate the true meaning of world religions and an awareness of the ability of each and every human being to have a direct relationship with the Divine Source of intelligence and abundance that created the universe.

Charles Haanel (pronounced *HAH-nell*) was born in Ann Arbor, Michigan, on May 22, 1866, to Hugo and Emeline Haanel. Hugo, like many Americans of his generation, was born in Europe and arrived first in New York City. He relocated to Maryland before moving to Michigan shortly after his discharge from military service in 1862.

Hugo married Emeline Fox in 1865, and Charles was born a year later. The family moved to St. Louis, Missouri, when Charles was four years old. Hugo's family was not wealthy and neither was he, but he attended college in Michigan and became the principal first of the Picker School and then of the North School of the Church of the Holy Ghost, both in St. Louis. Hugo and Emeline had four other children, all of whom were brought up in St. Louis. We can deduce from Hugo also having served as a minister that Charles was raised with religious training in the independent Evangelical Protestant traditions of these schools.

Charles was educated in St. Louis, and it was there that he started his business career, quite modestly, as an office boy and then as a clerk for the St. Louis Stamping Company, a Company that perfected the manufacturing of cooking pans. Although records are not definitive, it seems Charles started his work life before the age of fourteen. It is believed he worked for the St. Louis Stamping Company for fifteen years, and by the time he was twenty-nine, he was also president of his own publishing company. At thirty-five, he became the secretary of the Oaxaca Coffee Culture Co., and just four years later—at not yet forty years of age—he was appointed president of the Continental Commercial Company. Continental was a good-sized company with ownership of many sugar, coffee, grape, and cattle plantations spread throughout California and Mexico. At the same time, he was also secretary of the Mexico Gold and Silver Mining Company.

Charles married, at the age of twenty-two, Esther Smith,

who bore four children before her untimely death in 1904 at the height of Charles's business success. Charles married Margaret Nicholson of St. Louis in 1908, and Margaret bore him two additional children. Charles died in 1949 at the age of 83, Margaret in 1951. Throughout his business career, Charles maintained an interest in esoteric subjects and was a member of the Keystone Lodge, the Shriners, the Masons, and the Missouri Athletic Club. He was a Republican and a firm believer in the basic family values that he and his family supported throughout their lives.

This seemingly prosaic biography is important for what it doesn't recount: Charles Haanel was a true American. He was not someone who took advantage of others. He was not someone motivated by amassing wealth alone. He understood the common man and woman. He was an entirely self-made business success and rose through the ranks after many years of hard work. He did not just write down his goals and expect them to magically come to fruition. He focused and was disciplined in seeking knowledge and working one day at a time toward success. Nor was he immune to tragedy—not only did his first wife die prematurely, but one of his daughters also died while still a child.

Throughout his life, however, Haanel was obsessed with learning and sharing information with others. He started his first publishing venture while still in his twenties and perhaps while still working as a clerk for the St. Louis Stamping Company. It was during this time that Haanel developed, first as a correspondence course, the Master Key System that is the inspiration for *Tapping the Source*. Haanel went on to write many other books, some of them related to his interest in meditation and Eastern religions. However, none of the books written after *The Master Key System* come close to the power contained in those courses and the eventual book first published in 1917.

Some have speculated that the Master Key System was first created to be shared only with elite business leaders and those with the sophisticated educational background that Haanel himself did not have. We do not believe that was the case, though clearly it was not until Napoleon Hill and others started to publicly acknowledge their debt to the Master Key System that Haanel became a popular public figure. However, even before the Master Key System was published as a book accessible to all, Haanel had already achieved a position of prominence and esteem in St. Louis society.

Writing in *St. Louis: The Fourth City* (St. Louis: S. J. Clarke Publishing Company, 1909), author Walter B. Stevens introduces us to Haanel, stating:

> Charles Haanel is largely associated with the business interests of the city, being affiliated with a number of enterprises of acknowledged financial worth. . . . Mr. Haanel is in every sense of the word a self-made man, having risen in the commercial world to his present situation of worth and prominence by the utilization of his own natural resources.

This is not from an obituary, but from a book about the history of St. Louis at a time when Haanel was not yet forty-five years old. This was also written at a time when very few, if any, people knew of the Master Key System. This is important, since so many of today's self-development and get-rich-quick gurus are getting rich only on the advice they are providing and not on the actual experience of creating real value in agriculture, manufacturing, mining, and industry as Haanel had prior to ever writing about or sharing his secrets to wealth creation.

Stevens concludes his entry on Haanel for the 1909 publication with perhaps the most succinct and complete overview of Haanel ever written:

> He is a man of mature judgment, capable of taking a calm survey of life and correctly valuing its opportunities, its possibilities, its demands, and obligations. He has wisely sought success along the lines of least resistance, and yet, when difficulties and obstacles have confronted him, he has displayed a force of character that has enabled him to overcome them and continue on the pathway to prosperity. Many a man whose life is one of untiring industry does not win success for he lacks the complement to industry a laudable ambition which prompts the individual to reach out into other fields and eagerly grasp the opportunities that are presented. In these qualities Mr. Haanel is richly endowed and has thus attained his present enviable position in financial circles.

The key points for us, as advocates of Haanel, is to recognize that he was a truly self-made man and one whose "laudable ambition" prompted him to "reach out into other fields and eagerly grasp the opportunities." We do not believe from examining Haanel's life and work that these ambitions were limited to financial interests only. Why would a man who, at the age of forty-four, had already achieved such remarkable financial success and recognition dedicate so much of his time and energy to creating the Master Key System and sharing his success secrets with others? In part it could be just good business practice, for, as Haanel has written in the first explanation ever formulated of the Law of Attraction, giving to others is the key to attracting, but it seems more likely that Haanel's having achieved a high level of material and emotional happiness in his own life was sincerely motivated by an altruistic impulse to help others.

Because this book is called *Tapping the Source*, it is essential that you know the source of the information you are reading. Haanel, in our opinion, is an impeccable source. And, just as you have read, it is not just our opinion, but also the opinion of Napoleon Hill and many other self-made millionaires and self-development teachers. For many, Haanel is considered to be "the Father of Personal Development," and we as authors of *Tapping the Source* fully agree. But before you go forward in your reading of our presentation of the modern, up-to-date, enhanced-power version of the Master Key System that *Tapping the Source* is meant to be, you should also know something about Richard, William, and John, your guides to the brilliant teachings and techniques of Charles Haanel.

CHAPTER 2

WHO ARE RICHARD, WILLIAM, AND JOHN?

Okay, so Charles Haanel was an extraordinary and extraordinarily accomplished human being. But what does that matter to you? Well, it so happens that the techniques that Haanel developed actually work and have worked for millions of people over the last one hundred years. Even more important, there are profound and practical insights Haanel shares that will help you no matter what your position in your life, your educational background, or your personality type. This is what is truly extraordinary. Most self-help authors and teachers provide information and techniques that are useful for certain types of individuals and certain types of thinking. Haanel's Master Key System, unlike any of the other dozens of systems we three authors have ever studied or used, is truly universal.

You could not find three more divergent personalities than your author team of Richard Greninger, William Gladstone, and John Selby. Each of us has been extremely successful in aspects of our lives. Each of us, upon studying

Haanel's Master Keys, achieved personal mastery in our own lives when we followed the guidance provided in his book. And based on what we know now, we have come together to share what we each believe is the simplest and most powerful guidance any human being can have toward living a happy and successful life.

RICHARD GRENINGER

Richard Greninger never thought that he would be an author or teacher. Richard attended the prestigious Art Center College of Design in Pasadena, California, which is known the world over for developing famous world-class photographers, filmmakers, and automobile designers. Richard's commercial career began in 1970, and he was a commercial producer in Hollywood for some fifteen years. As his career progressed, he became familiar with the personal development field of production. He was introduced to Berny Dohrmann, founder of CEO Space and a visionary in transforming people's way of thinking, and was asked to create live videos for a self-help seminar called IBI. IBI was about teaching people how to create multiple streams of income. Among the speakers who spoke at these seminars were the creators of the Chicken Soup for the Soul book series, Mark Victor Hansen and Jack Canfield, and many other self-help gurus and inspirational speakers. As it turned out, Richard had a wonderful ability to capture Mark and Jack's presentations and their audiences in a way that grabbed people's attention. Word spread, and soon Richard was the go-to videographer for Tony Robbins, T. Harv Eker, and many other motivational speakers.

Richard's videography business thrived, and along the way Richard could not help but notice that the basic messages of many of these speakers were similar and that the people attending were not coming just to increase their incomes, but also to be inspired and motivated to live happy and fulfilling lives. The energy at many of these events was extraordinary, and Richard was able to observe firsthand the near-miraculous transformations and successes of many who had attended. But Richard also observed that in many cases the same people would return again and again, even after achieving success, still seeking more profound results or simply because they enjoyed being in the energy created at these events. Why was that so?

Richard, being someone who wants to know why things work, started to study on his own. In the process, he came upon the work of Haanel and his Master Key System. Haanel was a revelation for Richard. Here, in one small book, were all the keys that all of the other self-help teachers were talking about. Richard became so motivated that he created his own very basic video version of the Master Key System and started living the principles in his daily life. Although the video series did not take off at that time, Richard felt and saw the powerful success these tapes had with those who viewed them. He vowed then that, when the time presented itself, he would find a way to bring the wisdom of the Master Key System to millions of people through a book and a new and better video series. Of course, one of the major problems for Richard was that he was not an experienced writer. And so he waited.

WILLIAM GLADSTONE

As John Lennon wrote, "Life is what happens when we are busy making other plans." One of Richard's other plans was to work on a promotional video for a novel by a friend of Mark Victor Hansen's, William Gladstone. The novel was called *The Twelve*, and part of the assignment included flying to New York City to shoot some subway scenes with William. In the process, Richard and William became good friends. Shortly after the promotional video for *The Twelve* was completed, Richard drove down from his home and studio in Newport Beach, California, to William's home and office in Cardiff by the Sea, California, to go over the final cut and make some tweaks. The meeting turned into lunch, and after lunch Richard mentioned to William that his own dream—much like the writing of *The Twelve* had been William's—was to write and publish a major book acknowledging Charles Haanel and his Master Key System as the most powerful self-help guide ever written.

William was busy with many other projects in addition to promoting his novel. As the founder and active president of Waterside Productions, a major literary agency, he was personally representing best-selling authors such as Eckhart Tolle and Neale Donald Walsch. However, William could not ignore the enthusiasm with which Richard raved about Haanel and his Master Key System. Finally, with some reluctance, William gave in. "Okay, send this Master Key System to me and I will see what I can do. We will need to bring in a writer to update the story for twenty-first-century readers, but if the original is as strong as you say it is, I am sure I will be able to find a writer."

A few days later, the manuscript of the original Master Key System arrived. William was too busy to do more than spend about five minutes with it, but he thought a local writer he was meeting with that very day might be ideal to rewrite the text. So William gave this writer the manuscript with the hope that he would be inspired to become part of the project. The writer took about a week before responding to William, and though he was excited by the material, he had another project that required his immediate attention. It looked unlikely that he would be able to even consider becoming the coauthor of a book about the Master Key System for another five or six months. That was just too long to wait, so William had the writer return the manuscript and decided he would take it with him the following weekend when he went to Kauai, Hawaii, for his annual spring vacation.

William is not your ordinary literary agent. He grew up in a wealthy book publishing family and wanted to be a writer before his father persuaded him that writing was an unlikely profession if he ever expected to support a family or maintain the highly affluent lifestyle he had experienced as a child. William had obtained an advanced degree in cultural anthropology at Harvard University before entering the world of business, and from his first days as a film producer working with Rod Serling and NBC Television, and then as an executive editor for Harcourt Brace Jovanovich Publishing, it was clear William had a unique talent for selecting and managing creative talent. William is always focused, disciplined, and a hard worker. Utilizing these Haanel-like qualities, as well as his natural openness to "synchronicity" and "good fortune," William soon built his own multimillion-dollar literary agency, Waterside Productions, which not only represents book authors but entire companies, including mid-level mergers and acquisitions up to $30 million in individual transactions. William is a busy guy but believes in living a balanced life that includes playing golf and taking frequent visits to his second home in Kauai.

JOHN SELBY

One of the friendships William had developed in Kauai was with an author named John Selby. John is an accomplished writer and has worked with a number of literary agents in order to build his résumé, which includes more than twenty books with more than a million copies sold in total. The relationship between William and John sometimes included some agenting, but William is not John's primary literary agent and their relationship is based more on having children with similar interests and both having received Ivy League educations (William went to Yale as an undergraduate, John to Princeton).

John knew William was coming to Kauai that May and

had invited William to dinner soon after he was due to arrive. A funny thing happened to William on the plane ride from San Diego to Kauai. He read Haanel's original *The Master Key System* cover to cover. He couldn't believe the manuscript. He later commented to Richard and John, "I felt that I was reading a manuscript that I could have written myself. I have been living these principles in my work for the last twenty-five years. Haanel's Master Keys are literally the keys to my own career and financial success."

Well, the dinner with John took a very different course than just talk about the kids and John's latest marvelous video products, which were designed to help people sleep better and reduce stress. "John, you have got to read this manuscript. I need a writer to bring this up to the twenty-first century, and in my gut I know you would be great for the task," William suggested, almost before dinner had started.

John replied, cheerfully but firmly, "Well, I'm super busy with my new video production and I have another agent who is offering me a book deal, so I really just don't have the time. I'm sorry, but at this stage of my life I really want to focus exclusively on my own projects."

Never one to give up on creative talent without a second or third attempt, William simply looked at John as he handed him the manuscript. "I understand," William said, "but please at least skim this and let me know if you can think of someone else on the island I might meet with. I know this is powerful and deserves a great writer like you."

"Okay, I can do that at least," John responded as he took the manuscript and noticed that it was the work of Haanel.

"Funny you should hand me this. My grandfather was a major cattle rancher and owned the largest ranch in what is today Ojai, California, and he used to rave about Charles Haanel and his Master Key System to me when I was a boy. I never paid much attention at the time, but I did come across his work later when I was doing my studies in cognitive psychology at Princeton. It will be good to spend an hour or two getting reacquainted with Charles and his Master Keys. Must be more than thirty years since I looked at his stuff."

Dinner in John's Kauai "writing shack" was even more pleasant than usual that evening, with great barbequed steak prepared by John and exotic, organic Hawaiian vegetables, grown and prepared by John's wife, Birgitta. When William woke up the next day, he was pleased but not altogether surprised when John called, almost shouting, "This is unbelievable. In the last thirty years, my entire life's work has been on helping people focus and overcome addictions and stress. Now I see that I have been missing one major ingredient in my own teaching, and Charles Haanel has had that secret for me all these years. There is no question. I was meant to write this book. My heart is racing just thinking about what a powerful message we can bring to others and how I can use my expertise in teaching breathing meditation exercises to fully complement what Charles Haanel has been recommending for more than a hundred years. I know I have the missing ingredient that will enable people to immediately use the Master Keys in a way that they never could before. When should we get started?"

And of course John was 100 percent correct. The book you hold in your hands is the result of the unique gifts of three different authors. We are certain that what you will discover is the most inspiring and practical advice you will ever read anywhere: the original and streamlined wisdom of master thinker and manifester Charles Haanel.

CHAPTER 3

HOW TO USE THIS BOOK

As three very different authors with different learning styles of our own, we recognize that not all readers should necessarily read books in the same way. For those of you who are able to immediately start working with the core material from Charles Haanel and can jump into the meditation and breathing exercises provided, go directly to part two, "Activate Your Inner Potential." Just read along page by page through to the end, making certain to actually do the exercises in the order they are presented. John Selby has helped tens of thousands of people with exercises similar to those provided, and the unique context of Haanel's Master Keys and insights will ensure success if you follow the program John has created.

For those of you who are hurried for time or just not ready to sit down for a long read that includes doing the exercises, it is fine to start with the insights provided by Richard and William. In fact, for some of you, that may be all you need—just a reminder in simple language of what really matters in life and how to be happy and successful (and rich in financial terms as well, if that is important to you).

Those of you interested in business may just want to start with chapter 5, which has the distilled business principles William first wrote about in his own business autobiography, *Be the Deal*, which he later recognized as resonating so closely with the Master Keys of Haanel.

Other readers—especially those who have been exposed to concepts such as the Law of Attraction, the Law of Abundance, and other principles Richard writes about based on his own interpretation of Haanel's Master Keys and what he has learned from his decades-long association with Tony Robbins, Mark Victor Hansen, Bob Proctor, and other teachers—may want to start with chapter 4, immediately following this section.

Some of you may want to jump to part four, "Practice Makes Perfect." Although these are in fact the final words, they are also a synthesis of the key phrases and insights from Haanel's Master Key System. John, William, and Richard have found a way to represent these teachings in a way that will be immediately useful to your everyday lives. If you do nothing more than read and reflect upon these final ten pages of *Tapping the Source*, you will have received more than your money's worth from purchasing this book. And if you are able to absorb the incredible wisdom and put into action the insights from these ten pages of "final words" from Haanel, consider yourself ready to become a guide and teacher to others as well.

Of course, most people will benefit greatly from reading and implementing John's Focus Phrases. John's phrases and meditation teachings are the secret missing ingredient. So, if you are like most people, simply read the rest of the book exactly as we have written it. Our authentic desire in writing *Tapping the Source* is to help you and others create a better world. We are living in a time of both individual and collective crises, and *Tapping the Source* is designed to be but one of many resources to help you respond to the challenges that may face you and those you love.

John was the primary writer for parts two and three of *Tapping the Source*. He sometimes writes in the first person, and sometimes not. Conceptually and editorially, *Tapping the Source* is a collaborative effort on every level, and all three authors have incorporated their unique knowledge into the material that awaits you.

CHAPTER 4

RICHARD'S BACKGROUND AND INSIGHTS

Since 1989, I have been privileged to work with the top masters of the personal development world as a producer of their large seminars and video media: Tony Robbins, Mark Victor Hansen, Jack Canfield, Bob Proctor, and so many other great intellects. One of my jobs was to interview attendees for the all-important "testimonial moment" in each video. It struck me that I kept interviewing the same people over and over again. And so I asked myself, "What did they miss at the last event that they felt they needed to attend the same program again?"

These programs promised participants newfound wealth, fame as an author or speaker, and a great career as an entrepreneur in the world of business. Some promised a new and exciting connection to their primary relationship, and maybe even finding a true soul mate. So what did each of these individuals hope to find? Did they really want to travel the hard road of becoming an author, or risk everything to start a new business, or trade in their current relationship for a new model? Why were these people exploring these workshops for information they could use to change their lives for the better? What were they *really* looking for?

What I discovered is that they all had one thing in common: They wanted to be happy and content. All the aforementioned desires were just a means to that end: to be happy and have time to enjoy their life with some sense of balance. That is why *Tapping the Source* was written: to give you a road map to the destination of personal happiness.

My goal is to bring you and your loved ones a new point of view on how to achieve happiness. When you think that happiness is a state of mind, then why can't we just be happy? If you look at people around the world, they find happiness with or without money, power, and prestige. People are happy most everywhere, and they don't necessarily have a financially free life. They work, eat, and find happiness in their everyday lives. Quite frankly, having millions in the bank is less important to me than living like a millionaire. I would be pleased if this book generates millions of dollars, but trust that I will not allow managing additional wealth to take my time and energy away from the things that have proven to be my true source of happiness. Having time to share with loved ones and do the little things with them can be worth more than a million bucks!

If you follow the path that John, Bill, and I have laid out, while gleaning the amazing wisdom of Haanel as your GPS to destination happiness, I can promise that you will find what you are looking for. I am not guessing. This is an absolute guarantee. You can and will find happiness. All I ask is that you pass this book on or, better yet, buy several and give them to your friends; that way they will be with you when you arrive at destination happiness. Good luck!

USING THE LAW OF ABUNDANCE

Abundance. Well, I have to tell you that I am tired of hearing about all the abundance in life when around me is lots of lack of it, or so it seems. You have to ask yourself, "If there is so much abundance, then where is it? It isn't in my bank account!"

Therein lies the problem: Abundance never shows up in the form of paper. It shows up as satisfaction, smiles, happiness, pride, and prestige. The paper stuff is just a calculator of your abundance, and not necessarily the real thing.

Money fundamentally represents the fruits of your labor, what you actually love to do. Your passion is what drives you and moves you to your finest moments. This personal movement creates success and fame, and the resulting output is wealth in all of its forms. If you chase money for money's sake, the result may be paper money, but that money may not track with true abundance.

The Law of Abundance shows itself at work everywhere. It is wise to stop and take a look at what is really around you. Glance at nature, billions of stars, millions and millions of trees, flowers, plants, animals, fish, and people. There is no shortage here, and even if there were, nature can replenish and reproduce at will.

The shortage we are feeling can be corrected by carefully using the laws of nature to bring to you what you truly desire. Haanel stated it this way: "The law is that THOUGHT is an active and vital form of DYNAMIC ENERGY which has the power to HARMONIZE AND CORRELATE with the mind's vision and creations. Then it brings out from the invisible world; substance from which all things are created and then ultimately delivered into the visible or physical world." It is pretty powerful and exact, not a lot of guessing going on in the universal design.

As you look at the broad landscape of life, you soon will come to the realization that all this came from somewhere, and it wasn't purchased at the local mall. Every material possession you own—your car, your house, your golf clubs—comes from the infinite invisible where everything exists in a form of moving energy. I recently did a Google search for "images of atoms," and there they were, moving atoms under a powerful electron scope. Energy is the substance from which all things are created, and that includes you, your future, and the things that support you. The law operates on vibrations, and that is why you must have the convincing emotion and desire in your body and mind to harmonize with the Law of Vibration, which will bring forth your desires as your vision has created them. Dream on!

USING THE LAW OF VIBRATION
IN YOUR DAILY LIFE

The most mysterious and profound event of all time had no apparent cause. Nothing in science or language can adequately describe what occurred in that first hundred-millionth of a second when the majesty of an intelligently designed universe suddenly came into being.

Everything that exists in the universe, even the cold vacuum of empty space, vibrates in a kind of never-ending cosmic dance.

Whether we can see it or not, everything is constantly shimmering, jiggling in its own rhythm. This includes humanity's magnificent ancestral home. The earth and everything on it continuously pulsates to its own unique vibration. Everything that exists vibrates.

Let me see if I can clearly demonstrate to you how all this works in our real world. When you turn on a radio, your antenna attracts the station that you want to listen to. In reality, your antenna transmits the same pulse that the large radio station on the hilltop transmits. These radio pulses harmonize when they bump into each other, just as two instruments vibrate when they are in tune. This signal is called the carrier signal.

Amazingly enough, when the two radios are connected with the carrier signal, you can send messages from one station to the other by pulsing the carrier. It sounds a little complicated, and it is. However, if you step back you can see that your body is like the radio, looking for a connection to the great radio in the sky, your Creator.

Your unique vibratory rate can connect with your Creator, and you download what you need to create your vision. Metaphysics in a nutshell! Does it take a leap to go with it? Sure, just like it does to believe your cell phone is talking to a local cell site 24/7 from your pocket—unbelievable but true. So, may I suggest that it is just a nice way to move through life? You connect and you receive . . . why not?

USING THE LAW OF WEALTH
IN YOUR DAILY LIFE

It is essential to understand the nature of wealth, how it is created, and what it depends on. Understand that success is contingent upon a higher ideal than men and women accumulating riches. True wealth depends upon man's creative ability and the application of these abilities in the real world.

It is valuable to understand that premature wealth, the type sometimes experienced by a lottery winner, can be the forerunner of personal and financial disaster. This disaster usually happens because the receiver has not understood the Law of Wealth, and the results are obvious.

Wealth is a product of labor. Capital is an effect, not a cause; a servant, not a master; a means, not an end. Money is a result of work, and when there is no work involved, the value of the capital has no reference point, and that is the case with premature wealth.

Hence, wealth should never be desired as an end, but simply as a means of accomplishing an end result. Success is contingent upon a higher ideal than a mere accumulation of riches, and those who aspire to such success must formulate an ideal for which they are willing to strive. Another way to say this is: If you have a big enough "why," then the "how" will be provided naturally.

The power to create depends primarily upon spiritual power. Idealization, visualization, and materialization are three essential steps in this process. Thought always precedes any action, and that action is always a result of thinking. How you act is a result of how you think, and as you think, you become. Therefore, it is critical that your thoughts remain under your control, and these thoughts will guide your actions until you achieve your desired goal.

We can form our own mental images without regard to any limitations of budget, place, circumstances, or the like. These building blocks must be protected from the negative thoughts that surround each of us every day. These negative thoughts always enter our mind through the five senses of the body. Environment, chance, and fear of failure are powerful negative energies that should be contained and kept out of the creative process.

If we can form our own mental images via our process of thought, regardless of what others may think, of exterior conditions, or of environment, then we can control our own destiny, body, mind, and soul—all this by exercising the power of the mind.

Therefore, to control thought is to control circumstance, conditions, environment, and destiny. This is the key to creating wealth. These natural laws work in a perfectly natural and harmonious manner; hence, everything seems to "just happen."

So, if you wish to bring about the realization of a desire, form a mental picture of such by repeatedly visualizing and, most important, feeling your desire. Feel what it is like to be there now, and, like the antenna on a radio, send out to the invisible world a request to provide you with what you need to create that worthwhile desire.

THE POWER OF THINKING—
WHAT A THOUGHT!

It has been said that thinking is what separates you and me from all the other people in the world. Thinking is unique to each of us, somewhat like a fingerprint. Did you know that even identical twins from the same egg have different fingerprints? They say that your fingerprint is the unique spiritual address of your mind—what a thought!

The question is, how do we embrace all the wonderful opportunities that the world has to offer and at the same time be a unique individual? Each of us has many of the same goals as others, so how do we achieve without becoming just another face in the sea of humanity? How do we climb above it all to reach what we see as our destiny? The answer is clear: Use the power of your perfect mind.

Haanel was the personal teacher of Napoleon Hill, who wrote *Think and Grow Rich*. To quote Haanel, "How we think is who we become." Therefore, it is vital to respect our thoughts as a creative force for our future. Everything ever made in the world came from a thought. Thoughts are things and must be treasured as such.

Creating a fulfilling life is much like driving a car. There are rules of the road, and if you obey the rules you will probably have fewer accidents than if you chose to ignore them. Our Creator has seemingly created some very clear rules that drive each of us on a moment-by-moment basis. There are many laws of nature, including the Law of Attraction, the Law of Wealth, the Law of Health, the Law of Power, the Law of Morality, the Law of Spirit, and the Law of Vibration.

Knowing how these laws operate will affect your personal journey. Achieving a balanced life is a product of using nature's laws to your advantage. Again, these are nature's laws, not some personal or organizational law that will change; these are fixed, permanent laws. Test it out for yourself: Try to change, say, the Law of Gravity. See what I mean?

Each of us has a brain, which is a physical organ of the body. The brain receives signals from your nervous system and gives you messages as to whether you are on the smooth path of life or on a path that leads to anxiety and turmoil. The Law of Morality will be the first red light indicator on the dashboard that will get your attention when you divert from an honest and worthwhile direction.

Tapping into the source of your creation is essential for you to receive the power and insight from your Maker. I would imagine he or she or it is perfect in all ways, so it would seem to me that if that same life force made you and me, then you received everything you need to discern the marvelous possibilities that are all around us. We can take control of our natural gifts and power to make our hopes and dreams come true. Your thinking is what will guide you to your destiny, and *Tapping the Source* is the perfect road map to your great adventure. Let's go!

YOUR SPIRIT: A CHOICE POINT

Throughout history, mankind has been seeking a true purpose for being here on planet Earth. We have been seeking, creating, hoping, praying, kneeling, envisioning, and for that matter dreaming of a place that makes everything worthwhile and fulfilling.

I believe that we as humans have what I call a "choice point." We have an opportunity to play the game, join the crowd, mingle with the believers—or not. The "or not" part is pretty scary, since 90 percent of all humans seek solace in a higher power. You can venture down the path of life with the faithful or choose to make it on your own.

I think I would recommend the choice point of spirit. My father is ninety years old as I write this, and he is a non-believer. I say to him, "Dad, if you are right and there is nothing after this, then who cares? If you are wrong and there is a great afterlife when we pass on, then you probably would have wished you had chosen a different path."

The point is, there is no downside to choosing a spiritual path. Beliefs in a spiritual world have been around a very long time, and that alone has to be something to look into. If you feel more comfortable looking toward a third-party entity such as Jesus, God, Buddha, Allah, or any of the hundreds of images we choose to follow, or you are more inclined to a metaphysical belief in which you are part of the Creator, then fine.

Make a choice and enjoy the benefits that come with being part of a group of like-minded people, most with good intentions and a view of a better life ahead. Don't worry about proving to yourself that "this is it"—sometimes looking for proof is a waste of time. Like your radio, you don't need to figure out what makes it work; just turn it on and enjoy it, and you probably won't go wrong.

Having a spiritual connection opens many doors. Haanel said this about spirit:

> Spirit, whatever else it may or may not be, must be considered as the essence of consciousness, the substance of mind, the reality underlying thought. And as all ideas are phases of the activity of consciousness, mind or thought, it follows that in spirit, and in it alone, is to be found the ultimate fact, the real thing, or idea.

Spirit is creative in its purest form, and we humans have the one thing that separates us from all other creatures on the planet: We are creative. Spirit is the ultimate creative force and exemplified by our existence. So, to bottom line it, I say, "Go with it!"

MANAGE YOUR OWN MEDIA

In the last several decades, new forms of media have invaded our daily lives. First there was television, then two hundred channels of cable, interactive fiber-optic cable, streaming media from computer networks, and now iPods are connected to every ear in America. Blogs, Twitter, MySpace, and Facebook keep us all connected in some form or another. Every moment seems to be documented, talked about, and viewed by strangers for one purpose or another.

Certainly these wonderful technological discoveries are extraordinary and have brought a world of entertainment and information to every facet of society. Celebrities seem to guide our buying habits, our political views, and even our personal dreams and aspirations.

Society seems to live vicariously through *The Oprah Winfrey Show*. We wake up to Regis and Kelly so we can prepare what we will talk about around the water cooler at the office.

We are glued to news of Britney and Jessica, as their lives make radical turns to the altar or the bedroom, and then off to the courtroom.

The nightly news puts us to bed with seemingly unending chaos, human tragedy, and heart-wrenching hopelessness.

The question I ask is, What about you? What about your life? What does this barrage of information and images do to inspire, motivate, and uplift your life in a world that is already difficult to navigate?

How do you become sensual and passionate while body bags are being counted and RPGs are mutilating our eighteen-year-old soldiers on the flat screen above your bed?

How do you feel accomplished when there are images everywhere idealizing the latest hot car, sprawling estate, outrageous destination, or beautiful men and women made even more unattainably so by the magic of Photoshop?

How do you move forward in your personal life when it seems that everyone has already arrived—and become a millionaire?

I think you get the point, and the point is: It is time that you lived for *you, your* life, *your* dreams, and *your* rewards.

Often, the source of satisfaction and dissatisfaction is comparison. What we compare ourselves to is critical to our personal happiness meter. If you compare your financial success to that of Bill Gates every morning, I can assure you that you will feel like a pauper even if in reality your financial profile is one to be admired. Again, if you compare yourself to Naomi Campbell or Tom Cruise in the looks category, well, you will have to spend a lot of time at the gym and in front of the mirror with little satisfaction.

Tapping the Source teaches that you can start a process of listening to your inner self, your true partner in life. Begin to use this deliberate form of communication, which is not really new, but an approach you might have put on the shelf a long time ago.

We can begin this journey with the suggestion of shutting off, unplugging, and disconnecting. Go offline. What a thought! It almost sounds like treason these days.

Think of it: simply being with the one you love in a calm and quiet atmosphere. Maybe you have a nice light dinner, with candles burning, and you sit next to each other with absolutely no expectations, just sit with each other, in the silence . . . simply being together. You don't have to be cute or charming or smart or sharp or witty or funny. Just try to be with each other.

You will find that it is an eye-opening and maybe even sensual experience of the highest quality. When you tap your inner source, you will find an extraordinary place to create memorable moments that you can develop and share with your loved one. A new form of communication will appear that will touch each other's hearts—that is, if you don't touch the flat screen remote. Try it. I think that if you manage your media intake, you might just save your life.

YOUR SOURCE OF YOUR HEALTH IS YOU

Understanding that your physical body reacts to your mental state helps to develop a lifestyle that is healthy. Thoughts can bring about an emotional vibration that can be helpful or harmful to the physical body's response.

The life force process is carried on by nutrition, secretion, and elimination. This process includes the complexities of the how, why, and what of food and drink. How is the food prepared and emotionally ingested?

How does eating relate to your hunger, fuel, health, and emotional habit? What to eat and drink brings the thought vibration into the body. Creating nurturing feelings, thoughts, and food can bring your senses to a state of well-being and an emotional vibration of wellness.

Every mental action is a vibration. Any given vibration, therefore, immediately modifies every atom in the body affecting every life cell.

The objective mind has certain effects on the body that are readily recognized: laughter, tears, or blood rushing to the face when angry or embarrassed. It is amazing how the mental state affects the body through the emotional vibration of joy, sadness, fear, and elation.

The action of the subconscious mind differs. When wounded, thousands of cells begin the work of healing at once. A surgeon sets a broken bone, but it is the subconscious mind that restores the bone. The subconscious mind will build a wall around an infection to facilitate healing. Using the vibration of perfection and wellness, the subconscious mind is aided by the superconscious mind to restore perfection.

Thoughts make a difference. Each cell in the body carries intelligence. Cells are known to respond to thought, and positive thought can enhance healing. Every element of the human body is the result of the rate of vibration. Mental action is a rate of vibration. A higher rate of mental vibration governs, modifies, controls, changes, as well as destroys a lower rate of vibration. Therefore, understanding the power of the mind can allow us to be harmonious with the always present natural laws. Everything in the universe is what it is by virtue of its rate of vibration. Everything and everyone is using this power to sustain life.

You can enhance becoming your ideal self by connecting with the Originating Mind that forms, upholds, sustains, and creates all there is. This is the essence of *Tapping the Source*.

CHAPTER 5

WILLIAM'S BACKGROUND
AND INSIGHTS

In 1998 I wrote a book titled *Be the Deal*. This book was written in ten days and never edited, but was immediately rushed to print within thirty days of having been written. *Be the Deal* was the first individually authored book ever to be published by ToExcel, the forerunner of iUniverse, which is now part of Author Solutions. We believe that *Be the Deal* may be the first book ever published using print-on-demand technology, and the purpose of the book was actually to prove the concept that print on demand could be used effectively to create commercially viable books cost effectively. *Be the Deal* convinced potential investors of the viability of ToExcel, and shortly after publication the company received $28 million in financing.

When I wrote *Be the Deal*, I was not concerned with the actual content of the book. I had a specific goal, which was to prove the concept of print on demand and help my cofounders of ToExcel achieve our investment goals to launch the company. However, I wanted to provide a useful book that would have integrity and interest for readers. The quickest book I could write to do that was my business biography, and that is what *Be the Deal* became.

Interestingly, in writing my business biography, I wrote in some places almost word for word the philosophy and concepts that Haanel had written almost a hundred years before. At first this may seem surprising, but when you analyze the true nature of wealth creation and the basic Law of Abundance and the other laws that Haanel, and now John and Richard, have written about in *Tapping the Source*, it is not surprising at all. Truth is truth, and effectiveness is effectiveness. Haanel had figured out the true keys to wealth and happiness. Fortunately for all of us, Richard brought this wisdom to my attention, and then through synchronicity I happened to be visiting Kauai, where John Selby lives, and John had the ideal writing and scientific background to bring the secret wisdom of Haanel to the widest possible audience. John's background as a cognitive psychologist was an extraordinary synchronicity. Richard and I could have found many other writers to help with the re-creation of the words in modern prose, but I truly believe only John had the necessary knowledge to in effect provide the "missing manual" for the actual exercises that Haanel mentioned but did not elaborate upon in his original text.

At first I was going to provide some additional insights and comments, as Richard has, but in rereading *Be the Deal*, I realized that even though it was written quickly and without editing, the concluding chapter, titled "Putting It All Together: The Seven-Step Program for Creating Your

Own Good Luck in Business," closely follows the wisdom of Haanel. For those of you with a specific interest in manifesting money and abundance through business activities, these may be the final words for you to put into practice in your daily business activities.

Like Haanel, I believe that the universe contains unlimited abundance and that each and every human being has the capacity to fulfill every material, emotional, and creative desire just by connecting with or, as this book says, tapping the Source. The most important principle to creating true wealth is to be of service to others. Somehow I stumbled onto this truth at a very young age and in the process created a business, Waterside Productions, which has brought great happiness and wealth not only to me and my employees and clients and book publishers but also to the hundreds of millions of people who have read books "birthed" through my direct and indirect efforts. My work life has been an experience of pure joy, and the seven steps for creating luck, described on the following pages, are really the seven steps for tapping the Source and living a life of integrity and purpose. This is what I hope for each of you who reads these words. Of course, if you want to know more about the specific business techniques and experiences that led to these seven steps, *Be the Deal* is available to read in whole from iUniverse through Amazon and other book outlets.

Remember, these seven steps are complementary to the wisdom of Haanel that John and Richard share. They are my individual mantras for success, and I encourage you to formulate and share your own.

THE SEVEN STEPS TO CREATING YOUR OWN GOOD LUCK IN BUSINESS

(Adapted and abridged from William Gladstone, *Be the Deal*, pages 137–141)

Step One: Aptitude

If you are going to create your own luck in business, it is absolutely essential that you have an aptitude for business and for deal making. This does not mean that you must be an instinctive deal maker, or that you were born thinking business, business, business. But at a minimum, you do need a basic aptitude for business and basic enjoyment of the rough-and-tumble nature of the business world. If you do not have this basic aptitude for business, you should probably not pursue business at all, as you are unlikely to be able to create your own luck or have any true enjoyment in your business life. This does not mean that you couldn't have a wonderful career as an artist, technician, teacher, or other professional for which you do have a basic aptitude and sense of enjoyment.

Step Two: Attitude

Once you have established that you have an aptitude for pursuing some aspect of the business world, you must develop a positive, can-do attitude. Part of your ability to create luck is your belief that you really are entitled to unlimited abundance and good fortune. You should cultivate this positive attitude by helping others and focusing on your accomplishments and personal gifts of health, energy, enthusiasm, and willingness to work toward your goals. By cultivating these qualities and acting as if you can take on any problem and contribute to any situation, you will start to see positive results in actually accomplishing these goals. Miraculously, you will begin to cultivate your own ability to be in the right place at the right time and to generally create your own luck.

Step Three: Application

Having a positive attitude and a basic aptitude for the specific area of work you have chosen will get you headed in the right direction, but you still must apply yourself. There is no substitute, particularly at the beginning of an endeavor or a career, for hard work. You need to be focused and ready when opportunity knocks, and you cannot be ready unless you are extremely well prepared in your field of specialization.

You need to know the vocabulary of your field and the basic structures and formulas that apply in your industry. You need to apply these principles whenever you can and learn from them so you know, almost intuitively, what is likely to work and what won't, at least based on industry standard experience. Just applying the principles of the past is never enough, but you can't begin to know when to deviate from the tried and true unless you understand the norms. You must know what the norms are, and, as in most pursuits, the deviations are not the norm by definition. Creating your own luck often will depend upon nothing more than observing trends and knowing what is likely to happen next.

I can't emphasize enough, however, the importance of applying yourself and obtaining a firm grounding in the fundamentals of your field. Picasso was an extremely accomplished realistic painter before he created modern techniques that defied the norms of his art. The same is true for innovators in other fields. Very rarely does it make good luck to step up to the plate not even knowing what kind of ball is going to be thrown at you, or without truly knowing the rules and logistics of the game.

Step Four: Acceptance

Accept yourself as you are, both your strengths and weaknesses of personality and character. You will be surprised to learn that no single attribute or quality you possess is ever in and of itself either a strength or weakness. There are always situations in which a quality that is normally a virtue can be a hindrance. Whether a quality is a strength or weakness for you depends upon the environment in which you are acting and the specific situation that presents itself to you.

Perhaps you are extremely bright and able to make quick decisions, and you believe that this is your greatest virtue. In most cases it probably is, but in instances in which your superiors do not want a quick decision made, you risk alienating an entire negotiation by coming up with too facile a solution. You may seem out of place or too ambitious and destroy an opportunity to succeed that a slower-thinking colleague would not risk.

In order to create your own luck, you must accept not only your own givens, but also the vagaries of the business world. You must be willing to accept risk and change and failure. Someone who never fails is not pushing the envelope far enough and will never reach their full potential. Good luck is less likely to visit the cautious than the brave, and it is only by accepting all that comes before you—even your own fears—that you can move into the space of courage, which will draw good luck to you.

Step Five: Awareness

Heightened self-awareness and awareness of your environment are essential to drawing any good luck to you, as is realizing that what I call magic is always in the air if you are ready for it and aware of its signs. Having an aptitude, cultivating a positive attitude, applying your skills and knowledge, and accepting yourself and your environment without resistance are keys to heightening your awareness.

Anyone who is fully aware can start to anticipate events and perfect his timing and strategize deals. Having the right energy and the right sense of timing automatically improves your odds of success and draws luck to you. There are a number of psychological techniques for increasing your awareness, but perhaps the easiest technique is to simply cultivate your breathing. Some people are born with greater capacity for awareness than others, but anyone can improve their awareness. It is partly a matter of courage. Don't stick your head in the sand and ignore potentially painful or embarrassing situations.

It is only by confronting situations head-on, for good or bad, and looking clearly at the past, present, and probable future that you will be able to take advantage of silver linings in clouds and miraculously turn lemons into lemonade. Every situation has the potential for profit, or at least self-improvement. If you are aware of your own needs and those of others, you will see and feel the magic that others ignore. They will wonder at your good luck in surviving what on the surface might appear to be disastrous situations or even boneheaded mistakes. You will know that you created those lucky exits yourself.

Step Six: Abundance

Once you have experienced in a consistent pattern the five previous steps, you will begin to experience the feeling of abundance in your work life. This abundance will probably be manifested by greater earning capacity and a greater inflow of money to you. The key to abundance consciousness, however, is much more fundamental than having additional money. In my own life, having a lot of money in the bank was never as important as having the expectation of receiving a lot of money in the future. In practical terms, I would rather have $100,000 rolling in a month with debts of $500,000 than $1 million in the bank, no debt, and no prospects for generating additional revenue. Since the guarantee of future revenues is always subject to some doubt, my abundance consciousness is really more dependent on my self-confidence and belief in my ability to generate future income than actual receivables. This abundance consciousness really can be learned and actually reflects the true nature of reality. There really are, on a universal basis, unlimited resources. You really can have everything you want on a material level, because there really is a finite limit to what material items you can desire, consume, or appreciate.

At a very basic level, money is merely energy, and the universe contains limitless energy. You need to cultivate an appreciation of the abundance of energy in the universe and your own role in cycling and recycling energy. Even if you have limited money at a particular moment in time, you have limitless enthusiasm, limitless joy, and limitless insights to share with others. By sharing your gifts with others, you restore your own personal store of energy and experience the truly abundant nature of the universe. Once you truly integrate this abundance consciousness, you will be even more open to the magical good fortune that is trying to reward you every day if you will only allow it to.

Step Seven: Appreciation

Even with a full implementation of the preceding six steps, you will not maximize the good luck in your life unless you also take time out to show and share your appreciation for the good fortune that is yours. Almost all successful entrepreneurs in the later stages of their development show their appreciation for the good fortune that society has bestowed upon them by giving back, whether it be by mentoring others or making billion-dollar gifts to the United Nations, like Ted Turner did. Even Bill Gates recognized that his main job now is giving away his fortune, through the Bill and Melinda Gates Foundation, not continuing to double or triple it every year.

But it is not enough to show your appreciation at the end of your life. You need to show it every day from the very beginning. You can show it in small ways, including private prayers of thanks, smiles to your employees, words of thanks to your colleagues, or sincere gratitude expressed to those who have helped you. There is no person among us who can succeed without a nurturing universe, and we should give thanks whenever possible. Good fortune smiles on those who appreciate their good fortune and who realize that their good fortune is not for their enjoyment alone, but for the betterment of the planet and of others. I would venture that anyone who has enjoyed good luck for any length of time, and even those who practice the six previous steps, would not long continue their string of good luck if they were not consciously appreciative and grateful to the universe for all that they have been given.

Part Two

ACTIVATE YOUR INNER POTENTIAL WITH JOHN SELBY

CHAPTER 6

REBIRTHING THE
HAANEL VISION

Charles Haanel never claimed to have invented the process of manifestation that he taught. In fact he often refers to classic sources in the Judeo-Christian heritage and Greek and Eastern traditions to highlight the ancient wisdom he's drawing from and expanding upon. But beyond classic parallels, his personal vision appears to be uniquely inspired with new psychological insights and remarkably clear elucidations of the core principles that drive our everyday lives:

> What you and I desire, what everyone is seeking, is happiness and harmony. If we can be truly happy, we shall have everything the world can give. If we are happy ourselves, we can make others happy.

One of the primary differentiating qualities of Haanel's vision is that he's not fixated on material possessions or giant bank accounts or a fleet of fancy cars in the garage.

Yes, he does fully support abundance, but he bases his teachings on the fact that what we really want deep down is to feel genuinely happy and in ongoing harmony with ourselves and the world. As he says:

> Harmony and happiness are states of consciousness, and do
> not depend upon the possession of things.

After all the ongoing New Age media hype that has fixated overmuch on manifesting material possessions and making money as one's primary intent, I was relieved to see Haanel stating the psychological and spiritual fact that the fulfillment we seek to manifest is ultimately an inner feeling, not an external situation.

> It is our attitude of mind toward life which determines our
> experiences; if we expect nothing, we shall have nothing;
> if we demand much, we shall receive the greater portion.

Haanel was one of the first American writers to state core psychological facts that cognitive science would later "discover" in the 1960s and the New Age movement would fixate upon in the 1980s. Indeed, our chronic thoughts, attitudes, and beliefs do strongly and predictably determine what we manifest in life. Therefore, learning to consciously manage our thoughts and attitudes is the primary act in our search for fulfillment.

THE POWER TO MANIFEST

> Creative power does not originate in the individual, but in the Universal, which is the source and foundation of all energy and substance; the individual is simply the channel for the distribution of this energy.

Here we find the foundation stone of Haanel's vision: that our personal manifestation power comes from a source beyond our individual ego identity. Furthermore:

> The only real power which you can have is the power to adjust yourself to divine and unchangeable principles. You cannot change the Infinite, but you can come into an understanding of Natural laws.

Power does lie at the heart of Haanel's writings, because manifestation of any kind requires power. But his understanding of power extends considerably beyond our usual ego definitions of personal force. As this quote establishes, the natural laws of human manifestation are understood to function in harmony with the creative principles of the universe and beyond. Therefore, we gain individual power only to the extent that we adjust our thoughts and intent with universal laws. This is a giant difference from all the get-rich-quick manifestation programs claiming we can push our will upon the universe to get whatever we want. For Haanel, we must first adjust ourselves to universal principles if we are to access manifestation power.

The implications of this statement are profound, suggesting that in order to attain the deeper harmony and happiness we all desire, we must first access, understand, and adjust our personal attitudes and actions with the deeper reality of nature and the universe.

THE LAW OF ATTRACTION

One of the natural laws that imbues all of Haanel's writings and that will prove vital to this discussion is called the Law of Attraction. And right at the beginning, let's be clear on how Haanel equates the relationship among thought, attraction, and love:

> It is love which imparts vitality to thought and thus enables thought to germinate. The Law of Attraction, or the Law of Love, for they are one and the same, will bring to thought the necessary material for its growth and maturity.

Haanel historically was one of the first Americans to talk about the Law of Attraction—and in this book Richard, Bill, and I hope to clarify Haanel's expanded vision of how this underlying law operates. Notice, for instance, that in the above quote, love itself is the force that gives our thoughts their power to manifest. This essential integration of creative thought and harmonious feelings lies at the heart of Haanel's vision.

DESIRABLE THOUGHTS

Thought may lead to action of any kind, but whatever the action, it is simply the thought attempting to express itself in visible form. It is evident, therefore, that if we wish desirable conditions, we can afford to entertain only desirable thoughts.

The science of cognitive psychology has proven that our thoughts do carry the power to generate creative physical action. This is how something new comes into being in our lives. We first have a desire or passion for something (emotion), which leads to a creative thought (vision), which leads to physical action expressing that thought in visible form (manifestation).

Haanel was one of the first to clarify that if we want to increase desirable conditions in our lives (as we all do), then we must assume full responsibility for continually focusing our thoughts in desirable directions. As we'll see in this book, this is easier said than done, and a pragmatic daily method for maintaining desirable thoughts must be learned and applied.

Thought ordinarily leads outwardly in evolutionary directions, but it can be turned within, where it will take hold of the basic principles of things, the heart of things, the spirit of things. When you get to the heart of things it is comparatively easy to understand and command them.

Notice here that for Haanel, thought is a cognitive phenomenon that we can turn where we want to—and the key direction to turn our thoughts is "within" rather than "outwardly." For most people most of the time, thoughts run on autopilot, without conscious direction. Haanel's challenge is to take charge of your mind and aim your thoughts purposefully inward so that you "get to the heart of things."

Do you know how to do this? Do you do it often? Do you want to learn how to manage your thoughts more effectively? You might want to pause and reflect for a few moments on what we've talked about thus far, so that already in this program you take time to aim your attention inward, to your own source of inspiration.

REDEFINING ABUNDANCE

Haanel was definitely an advocate of abundance. He was a successful businessman in several large ventures, and he acknowledged that material possessions often help us to feel happy and fulfilled. He was also an advocate, as mentioned before, of becoming a person of power, explaining that in order to manifest, and to be of service to others, we must receive and expend power. But he put curious twists to the abundance theme, such as the following:

> Self-denial is not success. We cannot give unless we get; we cannot be helpful unless we are strong. If we wish to be of service to others we must have power—but to get it we must give it; we must be of service.

In the quote above, we find a primary law of manifestation and fulfillment—that power (and wealth itself) is not a static possession. It is an energetic charge that flows through our lives and equally the lives of those around us. This means that if we aren't busy giving and serving others, we won't receive power. It's that simple—yet far too often people focus on possessing power, not on sharing it.

MIND AND SPIRIT

It's important to understand that Haanel often uses the words "Spirit" and "Mind" interchangeably in his teachings.

Spirit is Mind, because Spirit is intelligent.

Haanel was not, from my understanding, an esoteric man; he was in fact an early advocate of scientific examination, of logical deduction based on as much information as he could gather. But he constantly pushed beyond the known limits of science, in trying to understand the deeper ways in which the individual mind interacts with the Universal Mind.

At some point before he wrote *The Master Key System*, Haanel almost certainly had a revelatory spiritual experience, because his writings express a vision that transcends our normal logical boundaries and reveals a reality in which the intelligence, compassion, and creativity of one's individual mind arise from the intelligence, compassion, and creativity of the Infinite Mind that created and permeates the universe.

Reflecting this expanded understanding, in which our material universe continually emerges from a higher creative source, he wrote:

> The essence and soul of all things is spiritual; the spiritual is the real, because it is the life of all there is; when the spirit is gone, the life is gone.

Haanel strongly differentiated between "spiritual" and "religious." For him, "religious" referred to a cognitive set of belief systems created by the human mind based on past history and future projection, whereas "spiritual" referred to the direct present-moment experience of one's creative communion with the Infinite Divine.

Haanel insisted that he didn't want any new religion to emerge based on his spiritual and psychological insights (even so, several religions, notably the Church of Religious Science, did come into being based on his teachings). Instead, he aimed attention away from external theologies, beliefs, and social institutions and toward a regular shift of attention inward to one's Source, where direct encounter with the Divine is experienced:

> The great fact is that the source of all life and all power is found within. This means that the insight, strength and power to answer our needs will be found within.

Many New Age manifestation programs are focused outward on what people think will bring them happiness—more money, lovers, stocks and bonds, physical health, tropical getaways, and so on. Haanel refreshingly insists that we must learn how to focus within, toward the true source of our power, in order to manifest.

Unfortunately, most people have a deucedly difficult time shifting their focus away from external things, toward their internal universal core of power and being. This is where I hope to add process to Haanel's vision. Specifically I would like to teach you how to employ a set of newly developed Focus Phrases, inspired by Hannel's teachings, that will help quiet your thoughts and aim your focus of attention inward—to where your power and happiness are awaiting your attention.

THE POWER OF GIVING

The more we give, the more we shall get; we must become a channel whereby the Universal can express activity. The Universal is constantly seeking to express itself, to be of service, and it seeks the channel whereby it can find the greatest activity, where it can do the most good.

The entire universe for Haanel is a magnificent infinite creative flow of intelligent harmonious energy; in this regard his vision closely matches that of Einstein, who was his contemporary. When Einstein stated that "the intent of the experimenter influences the outcome of the experiment," he was expressing a core element of Haanel's manifestation methodology: that "everything influences everything."

Every transaction must benefit every person in any way connected with the transaction—because the individual is a part of the Universal. The welfare of each part depends upon a recognition of the interest of the whole.

To be honest, far too much of the New Age movement has been focused on selfish intent. But for Haanel, "the interest of the whole" must permeate our thoughts about manifestation, not because of any moralistic dogma, but because that's simply how the universe operates.

UNIVERSAL MIND

The Universal Mind is the totality of all mind in existence. The universe must have been thought into shape, before it could become a material fact. And we find our thoughts taking form, just as the universe took form. It is the same mind, operating through the individual.

Throughout his writings, Haanel makes clear that the inflow of what he calls Spirit or Universal Wisdom or Infinite Intelligence and other names is the true source of our power and inspiration, connecting our individual consciousness with the Architect of the Universe.

By the way, if it helps you to think the word "God" when Hannel says "Universal Mind" or "Creative Source" or whatever, please feel free. Terms such as "Allah," "Tao," "Yahweh," the "Naguah'l," and so forth found throughout our world cultures are all labels for the one infinite, compassionate creator of our universe and beyond. All words can do is point our attention toward shared experiences. That's communication—and Haanel used carefully selected words that resonate deeply with common human experience and expanded spiritual realization.

AFFIRMATIONS AND FOCUS PHRASES

Haanel is considered one of the originators of affirmations. But note the difference between his affirmations and most of the affirmations that are popular today.

> The affirmation "I am whole, perfect, strong, powerful, loving, harmonious, and happy" will bring about harmonious conditions. The reason for this is because the affirmation is in strict accordance with the Truth, and when Truth appears every form of error or discord must necessarily disappear.

As I discovered on my own a couple of decades ago, and as Haanel clearly shows here, affirmations have no power if they are not grounded in reality, in "Truth," as he calls it. To possess power, they must be "in strict accordance" with natural laws, with unselfish desires, with the higher good.

The Focus Phrases that I'll be teaching you throughout this book, in the last section of each chapter, are based on this employment of carefully worded, reality-based sentences used as mental tools to point your attention in directions that connect you with the Universal Mind, by whatever name. In so doing, these Focus Phrases will help bring you into resonance with the natural laws that sustain your life and nurture your goals.

"I am whole, perfect, strong, powerful, loving, harmonious, and happy."

Does this statement reflect your own deeper potential? From Haanel's perspective, it is indeed true that we are right now "perfect" beings—because God's entire creation is perfect and we are an expression of that perfection once we put aside self-judgment. Likewise we are "whole" when we allow ourselves to realize our true oneness with our Creator. We're certainly "strong" and "powerful" when we reconnect with our infinite power source. We're "loving" when we learn to focus our attention habitually in positive compassionate directions. And we're "harmonious" and "happy" when we master the fine art of holding our focus inward to our true infinite unity with the Universal Mind.

Similar to Jesus saying, "Be ye therefore perfect, even as your Father in heaven is perfect," Haanel insists that you and I are already perfect whole empowered beings—except for our negative judgmental thoughts that separate us from our true infinite nature. If we learn to successfully manage our thoughts and focus regularly toward connecting with our true nature, we are in fact one with our Creator—not sometime in the future, once we improve ourselves, but right now.

Well-crafted affirmations and Focus Phrases are mental tools for redirecting attention in successful directions. My rule in generating Focus Phrases is that they must aim our attention in directions that we all naturally desire but too often forget. They must resonate with the higher laws and aim toward the higher good. And they must be powerful in eliciting an immediate inner response.

Because the thoughts you hold in your mind determine what happens in your life, it's vital to assume conscious responsibility for your thoughts. This is the basic logic of Haanel's teachings. When you've finished reading this book, you'll have learned a set of Focus Phrases that will be of primary assistance in managing your mind to your higher advantage.

PASSION AND WORK

A thought's vitality depends upon the feeling with which the thought is impregnated. If the thought is passionate and constructive, it will possess vitality; it will have life; it will grow, develop, expand; it will be creative; it will attract to itself everything necessary for its complete development.

This quote expresses a major aspect of Haanel's manifestation process, and indeed of his deeper philosophy of life: that thought without feeling is nothing. An idea without passion is powerless. Desire and yearning are the driving force of an idea, and without them no idea will achieve success.

In fact, for Haanel, the passion must come first, then the thought. First you identify what you hunger for, what you are yearning to achieve or experience or own, and if this passion resonates with your higher Mind and the natural laws of the universe, inspired thoughts will come flowing into your mind with creative ideas and insights into how to manifest your yearning and passion in the physical domain.

> Every success has been accomplished by persistent concentration upon the object in view.

Again from Haanel there comes a primal challenge: In order to manifest what your desire in life, you must make a persistent effort to focus your attention directly toward what you want. Work will still be required, following the vision. You must continue to hold your mind's awareness toward your ultimate goal.

Accomplishing this focusing goal can prove difficult without the proper mental tools. This is where most of us encounter what we consider failure in achieving our goals. We tend to lack discipline and focus. Therefore, I'll be teaching you the most effective focusing methods so far devised, based on the integration of ancient meditative techniques and potent new insights from cognitive psychology.

YOUR SOLAR PLEXUS

Over and over again, Haanel returns to the question—where does this Universal Wisdom by whatever name actually enter into our personal bodies and awareness? His answer surprised and enlightened me: He insists that insights and empowerment from our Universal Source flow into human consciousness not directly to the brain, or the heart, but rather through the solar plexus—that energetic center of our organism where heartbeat and breathing function in intimate harmony to maintain personal vitality and creativity.

> The solar plexus is the point at which the part meets with the whole, where the Infinite becomes finite, Universal becomes individualized, Invisible becomes visible. It's the point at which life appears, and there is no limit to the amount of life you can generate from this solar center.

Having focused for many years mostly on my heart center as the locus of spiritual and energetic inflow, I found this statement challenging. We usually think of inspired insight flowing into our brains, or perhaps into our hearts. In this book I'd like to explore with you this dictum, by teaching you an "open to receive" meditation that might truly change your life.

MENTAL ATTITUDES

In the mid-1960s at the University of Pennsylvania, a psychology professor named Aaron Beck formally launched a new division of experimental enquiry called cognitive science, in which the attitudes and beliefs we inherit as children and advance as adults are the determining dynamic in all that we accomplish in life.

There is actually very little to be found at the core of cognitive psychology and its highly successful offspring, cognitive therapy, that Haanel didn't clarify fifty years earlier. Indeed, ancient yogic masters such as Patanjali in ancient India very clearly laid out the same insights: that our attitudes determine our thoughts, our thoughts stimulate emotions, and our emotions motivate actions that determine what happens in our lives.

Haanel taught that by aligning our personal attitudes with the natural laws of the universe, and by opening to receive insights that further advance our attitudes in successful directions, we can transform our lives in positive ways and attract the material environment that we desire to make us feel happy and harmonious:

> If we desire material possession of any kind, our chief concern should be to acquire the mental attitude which will bring about the result desired. This mental attitude is brought about by a realization of our spiritual nature and our unity with the Universal Mind, which is the substance of all things. This realization will bring about everything which is necessary for our complete enjoyment.

Within the scope of this book you will be encouraged to take a concerted look at your existing mental attitudes. You will discover which ones serve you and which ones that hold you back—and, as Haanel encourages, throw out the ones that hold you back. You're also going to learn to master the process of cognitive shifting, in which you actively redirect your attention toward attitudes that powerfully serve you.

SILENCE

Over and over, Haanel points our attention inward to experience a state of consciousness he calls the Silence:

> It is in Silence that you get in touch with the omnipotent power of the subconscious mind from which all power is evolved. Intuition usually comes in the Silence; great minds seek solitude frequently. Silence is the condition required for all great purposes.

Throughout all meditative traditions, learning how to enter regularly into inner silence has been a primary tool. Why? Because quieting the mind does predictably lead to contact with the Divine. In the Old Testament, for instance, we find the remarkable contemplative challenge: "Be still, and know that I am God."

The human mind tends to generate a nonstop habitual stream of consciousness that dominates one's focus with seemingly random thoughts and images, memories and imaginations, worries and daydreams. Only when we learn to quiet the nonstop chatter of our ego minds can we begin to listen to the deeper voice that speaks to us beyond our mental chatter. That inner voice comes to us quite effortlessly in the midst of moments of silence, when we suddenly know our true spiritual nature directly. And as Haanel points out, from this inner infinite knowingness emerge all of our sudden flashes of insight that in turn point us toward creativity, harmony, manifestation, and happiness.

THE PROCESS

Whether you desire a new love mate or a new job, better health or a better backhand, higher grade scores or higher spiritual harmony, and regardless of the type of manifestation, big or small, that you seek in life, here's the pragmatic procedure that I've found most effective.

First you need to learn a method to temporarily silence the nonstop mental chatter that usually runs through the back of your mind with all sorts of chronic fixations and worries. There are new cognitive methods that enable you to quickly quiet your thoughts.

Once you quiet your ego's nonstop monologue, you enter into the Silence and begin to open up and listen to your deeper inner voice, to realize what you need in your life to feel happy, healthy, and in harmony. Tune in, be honest with yourself, and experience insight.

Here's how Haanel expresses this power of entering into the Silence where we can "truly think":

> For the realization of conscious power, we should seek the Silence frequently. Power comes through repose; it is in the Silence that we can be still, and when we are still, we can truly think, and thought is the secret of all attainment.

And once you become clear as to what you truly desire to manifest, then you will need to bring your focus of intent regularly to your goal, day in and day out, so that you channel power and insight, strategy and action, in directions that manifest your dream.

Logically, based on the insights that Haanel puts forth and that have inspired this book, there exists a natural psychological process that you can identify, explore, master, and apply often to maximize your effectiveness in life. Here's the seven-step procedure that we'll be learning in this book:

1. Remember to pause and turn inward.
2. Quiet your mind and enter into the Silence.
3. Open inwardly to receive insight from your Source.
4. Identify a primary need or desire you want to fulfill.
5. Through focusing on your solar plexus, connect with the infinite manifestation power of the Universal Mind.
6. Focus devotedly upon your vision and your goal.
7. Continue to employ the "power of attraction" process so that you act step by step to manifest your dream.

This is the core manifestation session that we will encourage you to master and move through each new day, so that you stay tuned into your connection with the Universal Manifestation Force.

As mentioned before, you can do several of these manifestation sessions each day, to meet your various needs. You can also pause for a couple of minutes, perhaps three to six times a day, to refocus upon an inner manifestation intent, so that your mind continues to nurture the manifestation process as your life progresses. That's the full daily routine that will generate the results you want.

We heartily welcome you to this exploration and awakening of your personal potential to tap your inner source of creation, harmony, and happiness. By looking to the core of your needs and desires, and then actively focusing on manifesting the harmony, abundance, love, and fulfillment that you hunger for and fully deserve, you'll achieve the life mastery that Haanel so lucidly encourages.

As a gentle beginning step in the direction of acting to fulfill your current and long-term needs, large or small, see what you experience in the next moments if you put this book aside. Tune into your breathing for a few relaxed inhales and exhales, and then see what comes effortlessly to mind as you ask yourself the following questions: What is it that I really want to bring into my life? How do I want to change or advance my current situation so as to make me feel truly happy and fulfilled?

CHAPTER 7

UNIVERSAL CREATIVE MIND

This is a reality-based book about your manifestation powers and how you can learn to activate, manage, and express those powers at a higher level. You don't need to "believe" anything in order for this program to work for you—all you need to do is open yourself to actual experience and discover for yourself the results of the process.

At the heart of this program is the understanding that there exists a Universal Manifestation Power, a pervading nonphysical consciousness, that willingly and in fact eagerly chooses to flow in when invited into our personal consciousness.

The Universal Mind is the intelligence which pervades all space and animates all living things. The ability of the individual to think is his ability to act upon the Universal Mind and convert it into dynamic mind, or mind in motion.

What is the nature of this Universal Mind, and how does Haanel's vision of our Creator fit into our culture's existing spiritual, philosophical, and scientific understandings of the nature of the universe and beyond?

I remember a sunny springtime morning about twenty-five years ago, when I was sitting in the dining car of the Vienna-Berlin express, sipping a strong coffee, and flipping through the pages of a *Scientific American* magazine I'd bought at the train station. I became quickly engrossed in a discussion of string theory and several other new scientific visions of the universe that daring members of the "new physics" were proposing. What struck me especially strongly was the emerging theory that there simply must be more than four dimensions to the universe in order to explain new discoveries in physics.

Somehow, reading that statement in a revered scientific journal made me sigh with relief—finally science and religion seemed to be coming to the same conclusions about the nature of the universe. As I stared out the train's window at the onion-shaped spires of Austria's traditional churches, I reflected upon Christian beliefs based on the existence of dimensions entirely beyond the space-time continuum—in the realms of nonphysical transpersonal Spirit.

I also found myself remembering the inspired words of a Buddhist spiritual teacher from Burma back in the late 1960s in San Francisco. Thakin Kung had likewise insisted, from his deep meditation experience, that there exist without question numerous "consciousness dimensions" beyond the scientific dimensions of physical volume and chronological time.

Thakin taught that consciousness itself, the very thoughts that run through our minds and the imaginations that spring into being inside our heads, exist in a dimension outside of the space-time continuum, in a fifth dimension within which we spend our entire lives, like fish in water, without even noticing.

Haanel also posits a fifth dimension of consciousness that we all live within and are sustained by. This dimension is the intelligent energetic glue that holds together the space-time continuum, and through it the transcendent power of intuitive thought can flow into our personal bubbles of awareness and thus influence our physical world. Haanel often calls this fifth dimension the Universal Mind:

> The Universal Mind is not only Intelligence, it is substance, and this substance is the attractive force which brings electrons together by the Law of Attraction so that they form atoms; the atoms in turn are brought together by the same law and form molecules. This Law of Attraction, which is also the Law of Love, is the creative force behind every manifestation—not only of atoms but of worlds, of the Universe, of everything of which the imagination can form any conception.

For Haanel, this entire physical universe is made up of Universal Mind, and that's why we can employ the power of consciousness to manifest what we desire in life. As we saw before, Haanel believes (along with the ancient Hindu masters and many other spiritual teachers) that before the creation of our physical universe there existed a primordial power and Consciousness utterly beyond the imagination of our mortal minds. And this Universal Mind somehow simply "thought" our material universe into being during the nanosecond of the Big Bang.

The creation equation is clear for Haanel: First came the desire (passion). Then came the thought (imagination). Then came the physical expression (manifestation).

I remember as a child reading and rereading one particular sentence in the New Testament's Gospel according to John: "In the beginning was the Word, and the Word was with God, and the Word was God." So we find in the Judeo-Christian tradition the exact same creative vision that drives Haanel's manifestation process. "The Word" is another term for Thought. Thought was present before and at the beginning of our universe. Thought is the Creative Force ("and the Word was God").

In case you missed the following primary Haanel quote I offered in the previous chapter, here's his creation dictum:

> The universe must have been thought into shape, before it could become a material fact.

Haanel is with this quote doing the one thing that materialist scientists cannot: He's looking back to before the Big Bang creation event and describing how the Big Bang was actually generated—by the power of thought emerging from the Universal Creative Mind. There pre-existed an infinite intelligence, a vast power, a loving being, that through thought brought our universe into mind, and thought the universe into existence.

Here's the key point that animates this book: That same pre-existing infinite dimension that created our material universe (the dimension of infinite creative thought) continues to permeate our universe and to animate and instruct and inspire our own creative thoughts. And our individual thoughts, when inspired by the Universal Mind, are a chip off the old block in that they also hold unlimited power to create:

> The unlimited creative power of the Universal Mind is within control of the conscious mind of the individual. We can have the inspiration of the omnipotent Universal Mind on demand at any time.

Haanel was adamant that each of us is a perfect expression of our Creator, and that we can tap into our Creator's power at will. Of course, Jesus himself spoke heretically when he said, "This which I do, and even more, you can also do."

It is this direct link between our Creator and our own creative minds that lies at the heart of Haanel's teachings and the manifestation method being taught in this book. This is why we're beginning our discussion focused upon the Universal Creative Mind—because if you habitually deny your own ability to tap the power of your Creator, you in essence don't have that power. You must recognize your higher nature and regularly turn your attention directly toward this inner Source of infinite creation if you want to access creative vision and manifest your higher desires.

There are always limitations blocking our success when we fixate upon these limitations. Haanel instead insists that we discipline our minds to focus upon our infinite oneness with the Universal Mind, so that we break free from limitations:

> The Universal Mind is unconditional; therefore the more conscious we become of our unity with this Mind, the less conscious we shall become of conditions and limitations, and as we become emancipated or freed from conditions, we come into a realization of the unconditional. We have become free!

This is a massive statement, one to be pondered deeply until it becomes lucid in our minds. Haanel is welcoming us emphatically to move in the direction of being conscious of the fact that, even right now, we are not separate from the infinite creative force of the universe. Indeed, we are in an active state of "unity with this Mind."

You must of course decide for yourself what you think about all this. As we'll see in chapters to come, Haanel doesn't insist that you believe his vision; he insists that you learn how to enter into the Silence, quiet your mind, and discover for yourself as a direct experience the reality of what he's describing. And I entirely agree.

Don't continue to generate new and bigger beliefs based on what you hope might be true. Instead quiet all your ego imaginations, look honestly at what's real, focus within to your Source, experience what's true, and, as Haanel encourages, surrender and align your beliefs with the truth, and throw out any fantasy, no matter how sacred, that is not in perfect resonance with God's creation, with the Universal Mind itself. This is the path to power.

> The Universal Mind is the live wire. It carries power sufficient to meet every situation which may arise in the life of every individual. When the individual mind touches the Universal Mind it receives all the power it requires. This happens in the world within.

Our challenge is to make sure that, on a regular basis, our "individual mind touches the Universal Mind." We must somehow remember to remember that we are more than the mental and emotional programmings that we inherited from our parents and our community and culture. It's so easy to slip back into relative unconsciousness, and a major part of this book and process is the development of new habits that help us remember that we are in constant control of where we choose to focus our attention. And everything in our life is determined by where we focus our attention, moment to moment.

To begin the pragmatic part of this book, let's explore the power of just one carefully tuned Focus Phrase that almost instantly re-aims your attention exactly where Haanel recommends aiming it: toward your own inner center of being, where you in fact encounter the Source that will empower this entire process of manifestation.

If you can remember to regularly refocus your attention

inward in a joyful spirit, you'll regain that essential mental posture that in turn will enable you to advance through the full manifestation process.

STEP 1: REMEMBER TO REMEMBER

Always the first step in a daily manifestation program is remembering to pause and move through the program. If you don't remember to pause, you'll probably continue to run on autopilot and not make progress. So it's time to introduce the first step of practical action that you can take, inside your own heart and mind, to shift your attitudes and inner experience in directions that will promote active manifestation of your dream.

What's the first step to manifestation? To regain a positive emotion in the process of aiming your attention directly inward, toward the experience of Universal Mind deep within your consciousness.

One of Haanel's assumptions is that turning your attention toward God, toward the Universal Mind, does make you feel better, in and of itself. As we've already seen, he also insists that if you don't feel good inside your own skin, you're not going to manifest a good-feeling dream. Let's take another look at what we quoted Haanel saying earlier:

> What you and I desire, what everyone is seeking, is happiness and harmony. If we can be truly happy, we shall have everything the world can give.

Do you agree with this statement?

The word "happiness" has become as overused as the word "love" in our society, to the point where we've perhaps lost touch with the power of the term. I hope that you rediscover the term's power in this book, because it's vital to openly admit to our core intent of somehow learning to feel happy, rather than unhappy, in daily life.

It's the same with the term "inner harmony." For Haanel, this quality is the foundation of happiness and success in life:

> Harmony in the world within will be reflected in the world without by harmonious conditions, by agreeable surroundings, and the best of everything. Inner harmony is the foundation of health and a necessary essential to all greatness, all power, all attainment, all achievement, and all success.

To manifest more harmony and happiness in your life, Haanel urges you to regularly return your attention toward positive thoughts and harmonious emotions. Focus on what you want to manifest—that's the primary act! But often it seems impossible to even attempt to do this because there's so much negative stuff in one's life.

Haanel doesn't deny the negative. He simply recommends that you turn your attention regularly away from all the negative stuff and choose to focus on what you want to manifest, which ultimately is feeling good and in harmony, and enjoying each new moment—which ultimately means feeling tuned into your inner source of life and love and good feelings.

Okay, here's the Focus Phrase that will instantly help you shift your focus toward the ultimate source of feeling better:

"I choose to focus enjoyably inward."

There you have it—the statement of intent that in turn generates the ultimate refocusing of attention. Your challenge is to silently say this clear, powerful statement of intent regularly to yourself, so that you hold this key focus in your mind and heart as you go about your day.

Say it. Do it! Choose to focus enjoyably inward. And make this choice often during each new day.

MASTERING THE FIRST STEP

Let's examine this core statement more closely. Notice first of all that by saying this Focus Phrase, you are clarifying that there is a choice to be made—and you're making it right now.

"I choose . . ." And what are you choosing? To focus inward to make contact with your infinite wellspring of harmony and joy—toward pleasure rather than pain, brightness over darkness, joy instead of depression. Each moment, there is this decision: what to focus on. And you are exercising your power to choose positive over negative, and to focus on inner spiritual experience rather than external mundane fixations.

Almost everyone wants to feel good, not bad. Given the choice, you want to experience creativity and harmony, not stagnation and conflict. Furthermore, almost everyone prefers to be in tune with their spiritual core of being, rather than feeling disconnected.

What you're doing with this first Focus Phrase is shifting from being passive to being active in determining your inner condition. You're making a choice, and acting on it!

How does such a seemingly simple statement of positive intent generate action? It's cognitive science 101:

When your guiding ego voice states its intent, the rest of your being immediately responds.

In this case, you focus your attention inward, toward the ultimate fountain of happiness, and in so doing you stop fixating on all the external things that might make you feel bad.

Each new moment, it's your choice to decide whether you're going to enjoy this moment or remain stuck in thoughts and fixations that dampen your spirit and weaken your power to manifest what you want.

As mentioned earlier, one of Haanel's driving points concerning the human dilemma is that you're continually choosing where you're going to focus your all-powerful attention—on negative or positive thoughts. When you run mostly on habit and instinct, you remain a victim of habitual mood swings, of external events, of the ups and downs at work, or of your lover's whims.

Only when you act so as to be more conscious can you choose where to focus your mind's attention and thus choose your own moods.

Look at this a bit more closely. At any given moment, there are usually a dozen things present in your mind, emotions, or environment that, if you focus on them, will make you feel bad. You might have an ache or pain somewhere physically that you can fixate on and suffer. You can remember something terrible that happened to you in the past, relive the terrible event, and feel horrible. You can worry about something that might happen in the future and generate any sort of negative feeling. That's your choice.

Likewise there are almost always quite a great number of things to focus on that will immediately boost your mood and make you feel happy. Right now you can remember something enjoyable from the past, you can imagine something beautiful in the future, you can tune into where you feel especially good in your body, or you can focus on any number of positive sensory or social or intimate experiences around you, and thus bring happy feelings into your life.

But the source of all good feelings is found beyond sensations, beyond bright ideas and feelings about your external life, and in this first Focus Phrase, "I choose to focus enjoyably inward," you're instantly aiming your attention where you know you'll find good feelings.

Whatever else you're doing each moment, you can remain tuned into your inner source of happiness and harmony.

Therefore I strongly encourage you to develop a new

habit: holding this potent beginning Focus Phrase in your mind as much as you can, regardless of what you're doing, and letting it effortlessly aim your attention toward feeling bright, empowered, and inspired by your inner infinite Source.

This is how you can predictably optimize happiness and positive manifestation in your life. The statement leads directly to a response throughout your being.

And yes, practice does make perfect. Perhaps you'll feel very little in the way of positive mood uplift the first few times you say this elicitor statement, but continue to memorize and master the inner process for a few days and you'll develop a fond addiction to holding this statement of positive intent in the back of your mind as you move through each new day.

This Focus Phrase will become your lifeline for breaking out of old negative mood habits and passing through Haanel's "joy portal" into a transforming life experience—over and over again!

Right now, if you want, I encourage you to take a breather from reading and shift into experiencing. Say the Focus Phrase again silently to yourself as you exhale, and then as you inhale be open to a new experience:

"I choose to focus enjoyably inward."

CHAPTER 8

ENTERING INTO
CREATIVE SILENCE

We saw clearly in the last chapter that the path to successful manifestation and joy in life is to focus toward the inner source of that joy and success. As Haanel puts it:

> When the individual mind touches the Universal Mind, it receives all the power it requires to manifest. This happens in the world within.

In order to understand the process through which your individual mind can touch the Universal Mind, let's see what Haanel means by the individual mind. Then I'll teach you a pragmatic method for bringing your individual mind predictably in touch with the Universal Mind.

Manifestation is often considered an individual act of conscious willpower. We decide that we want to have something that we don't have or that perhaps doesn't even exist yet in our physical world. We choose to set our intent on acting to obtain this thing or situation or experience. We purposefully develop a strategy for how to manifest what we want and then go into action by using our intelligence and willpower to push ahead and do what must be done in order to achieve our goal.

When we perceive ourselves as isolated intelligent physical bodies driven by selfish egos, we limit our power of achievement to our biological potential, rather than our higher potential. There's nothing wrong with this, but indeed it does limit us considerably and inhibit the deeper feeling of fulfillment that we seek. Here's how Haanel says this:

> The fundamental principle of creative power is in the Universal, and therefore the idea of forcing an action by the power of the individual will is an inverted conception, which may appear to succeed for a while but is eventually doomed to failure—because it antagonizes the very power which it is seeking to use.

We have enough individual ego power to force a certain level of manifestation to happen. But Haanel continually insists that our personal will must be in harmony with the Greater Will if we are to not only grab what we want in life, but also come into possession of those things and situations and relationships that truly nurture deep satisfaction. And this higher path to fulfillment involves coordination of two quite different functions of the mind, so that our personal willpower and intellectual reasoning work together with the "higher" functions of the mind that are plugged into the Universal Mind and its infinite manifestation powers.

Reflecting the new psychological terminologies of his historic period, in which Sigmund Freud and Carl Jung were actively leading a revolution in human thinking, Haanel often used the terms "conscious" versus "subconscious," or "objective" versus "subjective," to differentiate two different vital functions of the human mind: our two "centers of our being," as he called them.

It is the coordination of these two centers of our being, and the understanding of their functions, which is the great secret of life. With this knowledge we can bring the objective and subjective minds into conscious cooperation and thus coordinate the finite and the infinite.

Our conscious mind is the perceptual observing mind of the senses, plus all the cognitive symbols and thoughts that emerge based on past experiences and rational reflection. We have an experience, respond to that experience, reflect upon it, categorize it, and perhaps change our ideas about life based on the experience. We also use past experience to fantasize and think up plans for the future—and decide how to act so as to manifest our creative projections.

The outward and changeable function has been termed the conscious mind, which deals with outward objects. Perceiving and operating through the five physical senses, the conscious mind deals with the impressions and objects of the outward life. It has the faculty of discrimination, carrying with it the responsibility of choice. It has the power of reasoning. It is the seat of the will.

Often people tend to think that this reasoning, willful, strategy-prone function of the mind is the primary driver of our manifestation powers. But for Haanel, the conscious mind comes into power only when it temporarily becomes quiet and surrenders to the other primary function of the mind, which he calls subjective, unconscious, intuitive, creative, and spiritual.

> We are related to the world within by the subconscious mind, which includes all subjective sensations such as joy, fear, love, emotion, respiration, imagination, insight, and wisdom. It is through the subconscious that we are connected with the Universal Mind and brought into relation with the infinite constructive forces of the universe.

This is a very strong statement from Haanel, and once again he's doing his best to employ words and concepts to speak of the ineffable dimensions of reality that lie beyond our senses, that transcend the conscious mind's rational vistas and limitations. And once again, I don't expect you to just nod your head and agree with these words. Rather, I hope to lead you through an experiential process that will let you find out for yourself what lies beyond these words.

Scientists remain mostly baffled by the phenomenon of intuition, by the creative flashes of insight and spiritual realization that all humans are prone to. Cognitive psychology has ascertained that the left side of the brain is associated with deductive conscious logic and reason, as well as perception and willful intent, and that the right side of the brain is mostly devoted to creativity, insight, and subjective feelings.

And at times, both sides seem to fire off together, in what some neurologists refer to as the "integrative function of the mind." But this is a mere label, aiming our attention toward a high-mind phenomenon that science cannot quite grasp. Why? Because right at the point where the conscious rational mind interacts with the unconscious intuitive mind, as we've seen, the traditional space-time material model of reality seems to expand into dimensions that science cannot as yet demonstrate.

So we have this universally shared understanding that our individual conscious minds do sometimes come into active contact with important but subtle realms of realization and empowerment, through the subconscious mind, and that if we properly manage our minds, through this interaction of personal and universal we can predictably tap into the manifestation power of our Creator.

> The subconscious mind perceives by intuition, and its processes are rapid. Those who trust the subconscious find that they have infinite resources at their command.

That said, what is the relationship between the conscious and the unconscious mind in the manifestation process? First we must learn, as stated before, how to quiet the chatter of the conscious mind long enough to tune into our unconscious needs and desires, and to link ourselves with the Universal Mind's wisdom and power. That accomplished, we can then use the conscious mind's special power to focus on our goals and to will our manifestation desires to happen step by step in our lives.

> When the conscious mind states to the subconscious mind specific things to be accomplished, forces are set in operation that lead to the result desired. Herein lies the power of the conscious mind: The subconscious can and will carry out such plans and ideas as may be suggested to it by the conscious mind.

Over and over, we're going to keep returning to this basic manifestation process, discovering step by step how to actually do what we're talking about. Let's pause a moment and reflect.

Do you agree with this basic understanding of who you are and how you can learn to manage your mind so as to achieve your higher goals?

Perhaps you might want to take a bit of time to put the book aside, and reflect upon your own feelings concerning your personal relationship with the Infinite Mind.

Does this discussion ring true for you? In your personal experience, are Haanel's lofty ideas just words on paper, or have you discovered in your own life that you are in fact more than just a physical brain and body?

Right now do you feel connected with an infinite Creative Source that brought this entire physical universe into existence? Or are you nothing more than an isolated bubble of awareness with no connection to a greater manifestation power?

Pause . . . and reflect.

QUIET YOUR MIND AND
TAP YOUR SOURCE

A key premise Haanel teaches is that you must learn how to regularly quiet the usual habitual thoughts in your mind, that stream of consciousness that chatters nonstop and occupies so much of your attention. Why stop this chatter? Because only in the midst of inner silence can you shift fully into the intuitive "unconscious" state of mind in which you connect with, listen to, and receive from the Universal Mind.

Stated succinctly:

> It is in the Silence that you will get into touch with the omnipotent power of the subconscious mind from which all power is evolved.

In all the world's meditative and contemplative traditions, this same basic notion is taught: that we must somehow quiet our minds and enter into the Silence if we want to tap into the infinite realms of consciousness that lie beyond the limited everyday realms of our senses and biological brains.

> Intuition usually comes in the Silence; great minds seek solitude frequently; it is here that all the larger problems of life are worked out. For this reason every businessman who can afford it has a private office, where he will not be disturbed; if you cannot afford a private office you can at least find somewhere where you can be alone a few minutes each day and enter into Silence, which will enable

you to develop that invincible power which you yearn to achieve.

One of the reasons I'm writing this book is because Haanel speaks so strongly about the requirement of regularly quieting the mind, but offers no concrete guidelines or methods for achieving this initial manifestation goal. He makes the following beginning statement, from which we will expand:

> The Silence is necessary, the senses must be stilled, the muscles relaxed, repose cultivated. When you come into possession of a sense of poise and power you will be ready to receive the information or inspiration or wisdom necessary for the development of your purpose.

Back in the late 1960s I was lucky enough to be at the right place at the right time to participate in seminal research exploring the underlying "quiet-mind" psychological process common to all the world's meditative traditions. New research has amplified these early discoveries. I'd like to share with you the formal quiet-mind process we've now developed, devoid of traditional theological and esoteric trappings, for quickly entering into the Silence.

Psychologically, most of us most of the time are caught up in nonstop thoughts and imaginings that pull our attention away from the present moment, into past and future fixations. We can continue with our mental ruminations and be aware of one present-moment sensory event at the same time.

But as soon as we focus our attention on two or more sensory events at the same time, all of our habitual thoughts temporarily stop.

It's that simple—and almost all meditative techniques from antiquity designed to quiet the mind's chatter have been based on this universal psychological fact.

Through combining old-time meditation techniques with current psychological insights, we've recently created a core method for quieting your mind and entering into the Silence whenever you so choose. This quiet mind is the primary foundation you will require in order to succeed in consciously creating the life that you desire.

STEP 2: QUIET YOUR MIND

As you learned in the previous chapter, the initial step (and the intent of the first Focus Phrase) in this method is always to pause and give yourself permission to feel good. Remember to say to yourself, "I choose to enjoy this moment."

The next step is also seemingly simple yet deeply profound: looking inward and actively turning your mind's focus of attention directly and with full concentration toward a core sensation that's happening all the time whether you're aware of it or not, the sensation of the air flowing in and out of your nose each new moment.

Even as you read these words, you can right now become aware of the air flowing in and out of your nose, not as an idea but as an actual sensation. Feel it!

Whenever you want to, you can use your thinking mind to direct your attention exactly where you want it by saying to yourself the following Focus Phrase:

"I feel the air flowing in and out of my nose."

Notice the careful selection of words here. Usually in a traditional breath meditation exercise you would be given the general instruction to watch your breathing, and then be left on your own. But what really is your breathing? This Focus Phrase is highly specific, aiming your attention not toward a general idea of breath awareness, but toward an actual feeling, a pure-sensation experience.

Right now, you can feel this sensation in your nose if you tune into it. Yes? You're pulling the atmosphere of the planet into your lungs through your nose, and then blowing that air out again into the atmosphere. This ongoing act is what keeps you alive, so tuning into your breath experience tunes you directly into your experience of being a living being on this planet; it's a wake-up process.

That's the power of successful affirmations: They aim your attention toward doing something that you can actually accomplish in the present moment.

As you experiment with saying this Focus Phrase to yourself, you'll discover that when you turn your mind's attention toward the experience of your breathing, you aim a spotlight directly onto the emerging present moment— you snap out of thoughts and imaginations of past and future, and re-enter the eternal here and now, where reality actually unfolds.

Because each emerging moment by definition has never happened before, you'll always have a new experience.

Now we're getting closer to the goal of passing through the quiet-mind portal into the Silence. The next essential step is to expand your awareness to include the sensations in your nose as you continue breathing, and also at the same time the inner movement sensations being generated lower in your chest and belly as you inhale and exhale.

As you expand your awareness in this natural process, your mind will naturally let go of busy everyday thoughts and concerns ("point fixation") as you focus on two or more sensations at the same time—which, as we saw, will almost instantly shift you into a more receptive, intuitive, creative mode of consciousness.

Just say to yourself on your next exhale:

"I also feel the movements in my chest and belly."

Go ahead and say this Focus Phrase to yourself and experience how the process of saying these words immediately aims your attention exactly where we want it to go, down and away from past and future thinking, toward quiet, organic, life-affirming present-moment experience.

Again, notice that the careful selection of words in the Focus Phrase continues to focus your attention specifically on physical sensations—in this case the host of movement sensations experienced in your muscles and skin as your torso expands and contracts during each new breathing cycle.

You are being challenged to continue experiencing the airflow sensations in your nose while you also expand your awareness to include a multitude of sensations in your chest and belly as you breathe.

This is a psychological judo move to help you transcend your usual thinking habits. You simply can't stay lost in past and future thoughts while also expanding your awareness to experience more than two distinct sensations at the same time.

You'll probably find that, at first, your attention will try to jump around like crazy from one sensation to the next, until later today, or tomorrow, or next week, you suddenly experience that primal desired shift in awareness from "point fixation" to "experiencing the whole at once."

Welcome to the Silence, wherein your connection with the Source can be experienced. This will benefit you greatly.

Note that when you're lost in thought, you're essentially "not here" in that you're not aware of your own physical presence in the here and now. In just a few breaths, once you get good at this quiet-mind process, you can bring yourself back to the present moment (which is where all manifestation actually happens) and experience your on-going participation in the unfolding of this new moment. This is so important because, as we'll see later, insight and empowerment from the Universal Mind flows into your personal consciousness only in the present moment.

So if you want to access inspiration, information, guidance, and power, you simply must regularly bring your focus of attention back to the present moment in your own body, so that you're present to receive that inflow.

Please don't be discouraged if, in your first few run-throughs with this Focus Phrase, your focus of attention does jump from one sensation to another, rather than expanding to experience the whole; this is to be expected, so be patient with yourself. The mental habit of chronic "thinking about" (deductive reasoning) rather than experiencing the whole at once (intuitive/integrative insight) is deeply ingrained. Only through repeatedly moving through this quiet-mind process will you begin to develop a new habit.

Once you get good at this shift into intuitive quiet-mind awareness, you'll find you can say these two breath-awareness Focus Phrases to yourself on two consecutive breaths, and almost instantly enter into the Silence.

There's a third Focus Phrase that rounds out this process. Once you've shifted into experiencing the air flowing in and out of your nose plus the movements in your chest and belly as you breathe, you'll find that your attention has expanded to include your head, your belly, your solar plexus, and your heart. Why not go the full distance, into being aware of your whole body at once here in this present moment?

"I'm aware of my whole body, here in this present moment."

Insight and empowerment from the Universal Mind or Creative Spirit flow into your body in the present moment. To maximize your reception of this inflow, it's wise to make sure you're "at home" to receive, and that's what this "whole body" Focus Phrase ensures, that you're fully present and conscious.

Say it. Do it.

To complete this quiet-mind section of the daily mani-festation process, there is one more very helpful Focus Phrase that will ensure your success with the process. Again the statement of intent is short and clear and powerful:

"My mind is quiet . . . I am now in the Silence."

Say these words to yourself as you exhale, and as you inhale experience your mind becoming fully quiet. It's that simple, and that profound!

You are now solidly into the learning process of memo-rizing and mastering the first part of Haanel's manifestation process, that of focusing your attention toward positive feel-ings and then turning inward to enter the Silence that links you with your higher manifestation powers. As you'll dis-cover in action, the "I choose to enjoy this moment" Focus Phrase will quite naturally encourage you to fully enjoy the breathing sensations that you tune into, so you immediately do feel better!

The next set of Focus Phrases that will consciously focus and activate your manifestation powers will be built solidly upon this joyful quiet-mind foundation.

Note that while moving through a manifestation session, it will be absolutely essential that you never let go of a height-ened ongoing awareness of your breathing. Even while you expand your awareness to include specific manifestation dimensions, you must continue to stay aware of the air flow-ing in and out of your nose and the movements in your chest and belly as you breathe—that's the key to success!

Whenever you lose breath awareness, it's essential to

immediately go back to the beginning and re-establish this breath focus.

Note also that Focus Phrases in general are designed to be "said" silently to yourself, not out loud. However, Focus Phrases have no real power if they're simply "thought"— you need to feel the subliminal movements in your tongue, throat, and lips, even though you don't audibly vocalize.

Say to yourself the statement of intent as you exhale . . . then as you inhale, right in the middle of your breath experience, be open to experience the impact of the words throughout your inner awareness. That's how to tap the power of Focus Phrases.

QUIET-MIND PROCESS

Entering the Silence

Here's the quiet mind process as a complete unit for you to memorize and master. In the next chapter we'll explore what to do after you successfully enter into the Silence.

"I choose to focus enjoyably inward."

"I feel the air flowing in and out of my nose."

"I also feel the movements in my chest and belly."

"I'm aware of my whole body, here in this present moment."

"My mind is quiet . . . I am now in the Silence."

ENTERING THE SILENCE

Practice Suggestions

All too often, we tend to approach manifestation as "no fun" work that we must force ourselves to do in order to achieve our goals. Yes, we must be diligent and persevere toward fulfilling our intent. But the spirit in which we approach manifestation needs to remain light, uplifting, enthusiastic, confident, and enjoyable.

Your challenge in the next days is to remember to remember, and to move through the Focus Phrases many times each day so that you internalize them, develop a new positive mental focusing habit, and master the fine art of waking up your own power to create the life you desire. Haanel is emphatic about the need to practice:

> Persistence will win, but persistence requires that you practice these exercises every day without fail.

What you'll probably discover as you begin practicing these first Focus Phrases is that (a) you have a hard time remembering to pause and move through the process, (b) you sometimes can't remember what the Focus Phrases are, and (c) even after saying the first Focus Phrase to yourself, your thinking mind will yank your attention away from the Focus Phrases and plunge your attention back into past and future mentation.

What to do?

1. **Write them down.** Take a few moments to physically write down the five Focus Phrases on paper or type them into a mobile device if you have one. The act of writing these statements of intent will help you to memorize them—and then you'll also have a copy of the Focus Phrases in hand to aid your memory when needed.

2. **Schedule them.** Decide to move through the quiet-mind process three times each morning, three times each afternoon, and once in the evening—or whatever schedule you prefer. What's important is to commit yourself to the learning process, so that you do this exercise often enough to get to the payoff and new mental habit. Commitment is key to manifestation success, so let's start here!

3. **Play the game.** With your list and schedule in hand, you're now ready to play the Entering the Silence game.

Entering the Silence Game

I'd like to teach you a way to turn the practice and memorization needed to master this process into a continually enjoyable experience. This game will highlight the fact that the very first Focus Phrases, in and of themselves, are remarkably powerful in transforming your moment-to-moment experience.

The goal of this game is to get through the list of five Focus Phrases in one sitting, without looking at your list as you move through the process.

To start, remember to remember to pause and take out your list of Focus Phrases if you need it and read through the list—then put the list away!

First, sit quietly for a few breaths to let the mental dust settle; then without effort, bring the first two words of the first Focus Phrase to mind, and say them to yourself:

"I choose . . ."

Now see if the next three words come to mind effortlessly, and if they do, say them to yourself:

". . . to focus enjoyably . . ."

Now your mind is focusing directly toward your root intent: to experience pleasure and serenity, fulfillment and happiness. And where specifically are you going to focus? Allow the last word to pop into your mind:

". . . inward."

Then, after saying these potent elicitor words, just relax a moment and experience the impact of this first Focus Phrase as you breathe, and perhaps say the Focus Phrase again to yourself until it fills your mind with clear intent.

Next, without looking at your list, and without mental effort, see if you remember the theme of the next Focus Phrase: breath awareness. All you need to do is to turn your attention to your nose, and see if the first two words of the second Focus Phrase come to mind. When they do, say these two words to yourself:

"I feel . . ."

This is a very powerful elicitor statement, which shifts your mind's attention from thinking mode to feeling mode. And now that you're tuned into feeling in your nose, see if the next two words come to mind. What do you feel?

". . . the air . . ."

And what is the air continually doing?

". . . flowing in and out of my nose."

Go ahead and take time to experience this breath sensation in your nose, for one or more breaths.

Finally, now that you have the general idea of how to approach each new Focus Phrase, you can continue with the next three on your list in this same manner. But whenever you need to look to your list, the rules of the game say that you must return to the beginning, and start over. Why? Because the quiet-mind experience needs to start at the beginning each time you move through it, for full impact.

The end of the game is when you do manage to make it to the final quiet-mind Focus Phrase. You can then just sit quietly in the Silence for as long as you choose, remaining aware of your breathing throughout. As Haanel puts it:

Go into the Silence, and know the Truth.

If you play by the rules and don't look at your list while saying the Focus Phrases to yourself, you will find that often, long before you get to the end of this game, your attention has wandered and dropped you back into everyday thoughts or imaginations. This is what makes this game fun: catching yourself drifting and mastering the focusing game of making it all the way to the end, into an immersive experience in Haanel's creative Silence.

Whenever you find that your attention has dropped away from the quiet-mind Focus Phrase experience and slipped into everyday plans, worries, and imaginations, your challenge is to return to the beginning and say to yourself again:

"I choose . . ."

And move through the process again, until you do make it to the end of the fifth Focus Phrase and enter into a unique new experience of inner silence. When you achieve this goal, you've won for the day!

Here's what's so interesting about this whole quiet-mind process: Most of us most of the time don't make it to the end of the game after we start playing it. The challenge seems so simple, and yet our thinking minds are so locked into the "thinking game" that we can't even move through five short sentences and breaths without drifting back into thought.

Playing this game will enable you to catch your mind in the act of slipping into relatively unconscious thought.

Often you won't notice that you've dropped out of the game halfway through until minutes or even hours later—and then a flash of awakening will occur. You'll realize that you're not choosing to enjoy the moment, and you'll begin the game at the beginning again, saying that most important Focus Phrase of all:

"I choose to focus enjoyably inward."

After you play this game for a few days, you'll notice that quite remarkable things will happen in your life. You'll find that you are indeed choosing to enjoy each new moment more often, and with greater success.

You are succeeding in changing a core mental habit in the direction of higher awareness and creative pleasure.

You'll find that as you get further and further into winning the game, you strengthen your mental ability to quickly shift into the Silence, and this will allow you to apply the manifestation Focus Phrases of later chapters more effectively.

The beauty of this game is that even when you don't win by getting to the end in one flow, you will win over and over again as you continue to return your attention to the beginning Focus Phrase and choose to enjoy, yet again, the emerging moment.

At some point, the Focus Phrase "I choose to focus enjoyably inward" will become a continual positive background thought in your mind, which in and of itself will bring a deep sense of fulfillment related to your happiness goal.

Here are the Focus Phrases all in one place, so you can copy them longhand onto paper, enter them into your mobile device, or photocopy them to memorize and master:

Entering the Silence

"I choose to focus enjoyably inward."
"I feel the air flowing in and out of my nose."
"I also feel the movements in my chest and belly."
"I'm aware of my whole body, here in this present moment."
"My mind is quiet . . . I am now in the Silence."

Once you practice this expanded version of the process for a while or so, you'll find that you can then shorten the Focus Phrases considerably.

As soon as you say, "I choose to focus enjoyably inward," your attention will naturally focus inward to your breathing experience, and this will naturally lead to a present-moment whole-body awareness, which naturally quiets your habitual thoughts, so that you move right from that Focus Phrase to the quiet-mind Focus Phrase.

That's your goal, and it will take some practice to attain it. Give yourself a couple of weeks before dropping the intermediate Focus Phrases.

CHAPTER 9

SHIFTING INTO RECEIVE MODE

Haanel strongly encourages us to enter into the Silence. But his guidance on what to do when we attain this inner quiet must be gleaned carefully from his writings, as he gives scant instruction at a practical level as to what to do right when we achieve a quiet mind. For many people who try various techniques based on his teachings, this step in accessing insight and higher guidance often presents a stumbling block that stops further progress.

> Silent thought concentration is the true method of reaching, awakening, and then expressing the wonderful potential power of the world within.

This may be true, but what is "silent thought concentration," and how do we achieve this? In this chapter I'd like to share with you both the psychological understanding and a pragmatic process that I've been exploring for many years, so that you will be able to not only enter into the Silence but achieve "silent thought concentration" each time you pause and move through a manifestation session.

First of all, let's do a quick review of why Haanel considers the quiet-mind phase so important. Here is a compression of his teachings on this point:

> Try to comprehend that Omnipotence itself is absolute silence. It is in the Silence that you get into touch with the omnipotent power of the subconscious mind from which all power is evolved.
>
> Intuition usually comes in the Silence. Great minds seek solitude; it is here that all the larger problems of life are worked out.
>
> Perception will come only in the Silence; this seems to be the condition required for all great purposes.
>
> Inspiration is from within. The Silence offers an ever available and almost unlimited opportunity for awakening the highest conception of Truth.
>
> The Silence is necessary in order to receive the information, inspiration, and wisdom necessary for the development of your purpose.

From this list, we can see that what we want to have happen when we enter the Silence is "to receive." If we are receptive, something will "come" to us—insight awakening, information, wisdom, inspiration, power, intuition, perception, greatness, solutions to problems, and communion with the Divine. What an amazing list of what we can receive—but only if we're open to receive!

For quite some time now, I've been exploring the very nature of "openness to receive," and have coined the term "receive mode" to indicate that there are three modes of consciousness that we can be in: broadcast mode, receive mode, and turned-off mode. I want to talk with you about these three modes of consciousness, because your entire success with this manifestation process depends on being able to shift into receive mode when you enter into the Silence.

As a beginning hint, note that Haanel makes the following statement:

> We have seen that every thought is received by the brain, which is the organ of the conscious mind.

He many times says that when we tune into the Universal Mind, we can "receive" inspired thoughts from this greater wisdom and intelligence. This is how we have a flash of creative insight that comes to us fully conceived beyond the bounds of logical deduction; this is how we experience "knowing" and spiritual realization.

There are indeed two sources of thought in the human mind: the biological ego's associative deductive rational thought process, and the intuitive reception of inspired ideas that emerge from an integration of the personal mind's creative function and nonpersonal spiritual inputs.

> When in silence you come into possession of a sense of poise and power, you will be ready to receive the infor-

mation, inspiration, or wisdom which may be necessary for the development of your purpose.

Haanel's "sense of poise" has fascinated me because "poise" is defined as "a state of equilibrium, a dignified, self-confident manner; self-possession and stability." To be poised means to hold a position where we're ready to act at any moment, but are presently calm and balanced and awaiting—alert but relaxed.

> To be in tune with eternal truth we must possess poise and harmony within. In order to receive intelligence the receiver must be in tune with the transmitter.

Here we have another hint about the quality of mind we want to nurture when we enter the Silence: We must have "poise and harmony within." When we quiet all our usual disruptive thoughts and focus on enjoying the present moment, we shift into a harmonious mood, as we learned in the previous chapters. But here we have a new thought: "In order to receive intelligence the receiver must be in tune with the transmitter."

Clearly, we must shift from being in broadcast mode, where we're the transmitter, into receive mode, where we're alert and receptive and focused directly toward the source of our inspiration and information.

How can you accomplish this goal, this shift into receive mode, each time you do a manifestation session? The answer is found once again in stating your intent as a very carefully worded Focus Phrase, so that your conscious mind turns its focus of attention exactly where needed: tuned in with the transmitter.

The best Focus Phrase we've developed to instantly provoke this shift into receive mode with attention fully aimed at the Source is this:

"I am open to receive guidance from my Source."

This is a perfect statement of intent. It's short, it generates a feeling of openness, and it aims your attention toward the inner wellspring of human inspiration and empowerment. You simply say the words to yourself and hold them in your mind and heart, and they will effortlessly resonate deep within your being and generate a unique inner experience.

Remember that Focus Phrases will have no power at all unless you continually remain aware of your breathing experience at the same time that you say the Focus Phrase to yourself.

You must "be here" as a physical presence if you're going to receive, and breath awareness is the indicator that you're here in the present moment, ready to receive.

Also, as we've seen, your mental chatter must stop in order for you to receive higher-order insights. When you're thinking habitual everyday ego-driven thoughts originating in your own brain, you are locked in broadcast mode—and you cannot be in broadcast mode and receive mode at the same time; that's one of the core laws of communication. Unfortunately most of us most of the time are busy thinking and therefore in broadcast mode, which means that most of the time, we simply aren't in receive mode—and therefore insights cannot reach us.

That's why regularly pausing for at least a few moments to move through the quiet-mind process can transform your life, because you're regularly shifting into receive mode, where the real gold is found in consciousness.

> The world within is the Universal Fountain of supply, and the world without is the outlet to the stream. Our ability to receive depends upon our recognition of this Universal Fountain, this Infinite Energy of which each individual is an outlet.

Haanel sees individual people as outlets for the divine flow of love and harmony, information and insight. All of life is a flow, and what is required of us is "our recognition of this Universal Fountain, this Infinite Energy." And to recognize something, we must turn our attention toward it and experience its reality. "Be still, and know that I am God."

First comes the act of silencing our mental chatter and shifting into receive mode. Then comes the remarkable human act of realizing what we're seeing before us. From this realization comes the knowing, and from the knowing comes the inflow of exactly what we need in our lives to live the good life attuned to God. As we quoted in the beginning, a single idea may be worth millions of dollars, and these ideas can come only to those who are receptive, who are prepared to receive them, and who are in a successful frame of mind.

Again we come to this notion of the frame of mind, the prevailing mood and attitude that you bring into the Silence. We've seen that "successful" for Haanel means being in a "happy and harmonious" state of mind. As you practice the quiet-mind part of this manifestation process, you'll find that the breath and whole-body awareness Focus Phrases will naturally help shift you into this positive frame of mind.

Then you say to yourself the specific receive mode Focus Phrase: "I am open to receive guidance from my Source." Stay aware of your breathing and whole-body presence, and relax into the Silence as you wait in a state of poise for the inflow of whatever information and empowerment might be available to you at that time. Here's another way Haanel explains this:

> The next step is to place yourself in position to receive this insight or power. As it is omnipresent, it must be within you. All power is from within.

Again we return to the notion that the insight, information, power, or guidance you seek is not coming from somewhere off in heaven or outside of you. Insight is a function of consciousness, which as we've seen operates outside the space-time continuum. You must aim your attention directly inward to your own center if you want to find the Universal Center. Your personal center and the Universal Center are one and the same—that's the whole point! This means that you are never separated from your Source, except to the extent that you fail to aim your attention inward and open up to receive.

> You must be receptive, and this receptivity is acquired just as physical strength is gained, by exercise.

Often we assume that being receptive is an innate quality, but here Haanel states clearly just the opposite—that "receptivity is acquired." I have found this to be entirely true. This means that the first time you do a manifestation session, you can't expect the angels to sing instantly to you in four-part harmony. You must exercise and develop your ability to receive, just as you would exercise to develop a capacity in sports.

Opening to receive is not just a lofty idea; it's a pragmatic process that you nurture and master. So your challenge ahead is to take time to move through a manifestation session quite often, perhaps three or four times a day, so that you develop your "receptivity muscle" and become strong in the art of receiving.

> From this process of self-contemplation comes inspiration, which is creative intelligence.

When you look inward toward your inner Source, you are indeed contemplating your own higher existence. And this inward-looking will prove a process of continual discovery, because you and the Universal Mind are one, which means that you yourself are infinite. That's giant notion. I challenge you to explore this concept through personal experience to discover if it is true for you.

As you open to receive while in the Silence, it's important to let go of expectations of your ego and to shift into more of a sensory of feeling mode of consciousness. Don't expect anything—just let yourself focus on feeling attuned to your infinite inner center of consciousness as you "touch the Universal Mind" with your own presence. Focus your attention not on the idea of your Creative Source, but on the actual feeling of being connected with this infinite presence that we call God or Divine Presence.

By whatever name, what's key is that you turn your attention directly inward to your own center, which is the connection point with the divine, and actually tune into experience the feeling of your connection.

You'll benefit here greatly by using the neutral word "Source" rather than "God" or any other religious term related to the ineffable Infinite Divine Creative Presence, because this neutral term sets you free to discover, through direct inner experience, what this Source truly is as an intimate inner feeling, not a traditional theological concept.

For Haanel, "feeling connected" is definitely key to success and deeper happiness, because our human feelings are the experiential passageway that energetically connects us with the Universal Mind. As we've seen, he identifies the subjective emotional realm of consciousness as our link with the Divine. Through this "feeling" link, transmissions from the Universal Mind flow in and are then processed by our personal minds and experienced as inspired thoughts, solutions, or realizations.

In this perspective, your challenge is to learn how to shift out of thinking mode into feeling mode more and more often. This is the manifestation-portal event.

As you shift from thinking to feeling, you pass through a portal into a new dimension. Here's a perhaps startling psychological fact: Linear deductive reasoning is actually a collapsed reality of only two dimensions. If you reflect a moment, you'll realize that there's no volume to analytical thought, no sense of depth at all. As cognitive scientists point out, our everyday thinking is a point-to-point linear mental process—it's a line through time.

Only when you temporarily quiet that habitual linear type of thinking do you pop once again into the volume of your senses and the experiential present moment, and regain the experience of real participation with the real world, which is where all manifestation occurs.

As you get good at quieting your mind and focusing inward in a receptive mood, you'll find that you often pop spontaneously into a truly expanded quality of consciousness, where there exists an infinity of dimensions. And this isn't just a way of talking; this can be a direct and utterly marvelous inner experience.

> Spirit is omnipresent, ever ready; all that is required is a proper recognition of its omnipotence and a willingness or desire to become the recipient of its beneficent effects.

Then you will find that the things you seek are seeking you.

I mentioned earlier the new vision and research of scientists such as Stephen Hawking who state that for the universe to function at all, there must be at least nine coexisting dimensions. They also postulate that every square inch of space throughout the universe is filled with matter and antimatter, and that the universe itself is a vast, intelligent, harmonious being in which everything is connected, beyond the space-time continuum, with everything else.

Haanel a hundred years ago seems to have had a direct vision of this expanded reality. He realized somehow that everything in the universe is connected with the Creative Source that brought this entire reality into being, and it's this direct, intimate, organic sense of connection that he encourages you to open up and plug into so that you "become the recipient of its beneficent effects" where "the things you seek are seeking you."

Let's end this chapter focusing on the pragmatics of all this.

STEP 3: OPEN TO RECEIVE

Let's move through what you've learned thus far: the three main Focus Phrases that take you beyond ideas directly into experiencing the receive mode state of consciousness. In the next chapter we'll explore what to do after you successfully enter into the Silence. (Please remember to move through the three breath/whole-body steps that quiet your thoughts to lead you into "I am now in the Silence," until this quiet-mind process becomes natural to you.)

1. *"I choose to focus enjoyably inward."*
2. *"My mind is quiet . . . I am now in the Silence."*
3. *"I am open to receive guidance from my Source."*

CHAPTER 10

CLARIFY YOUR CORE DESIRES

Most people assume that personal willpower and mental focusing generate the action leading toward manifestation. But as we've seen, Charles Haanel's writings, when read carefully, insist that thought alone can accomplish nothing new or creative. He says over and over that the driving power of manifestation is passion, emotion, desire—in sum, strong positive feeling.

In this chapter I want to teach you how to advance, while still in the Silence, into a sharp focus on experiencing your most important passion and desire at any moment. As you might guess, now that you've read this far into this book, at some point I'll introduce you to a special Focus Phrase that will generate the focus we aim for here.

In each manifestation session that you pause and move through, hopefully at least once a day, you will reach the point with this fourth Focus Phrase where you are able to look inward, observe your core passion at the moment, and decide through this process which driving intent to focus your power of attention upon during the session.

Often you'll find that the same passion and related goal returns over and over, for days or even weeks or months, until that goal and yearning is attained and fulfilled, but probably you'll find that you have more than one goal that you're advancing toward, step by step.

In traditional Buddhist, Hindu, and even Christian theologies, the very notion of desire carries a negative connotation. Most meditative and contemplative practices insist that desires of any kind are bad for the soul and must be repressed and put forcefully away if one is to attain spiritual awakening and fulfillment.

Haanel's system flies in the face of these beliefs, and it does so in a very specific way. He insists, as we began to explore earlier, that manifestation is driven by our feelings, our desires, and our yearnings, and that we will manifest nothing without bringing them to the fore. Again, here's the key quote:

A thought's vitality depends upon the feeling with which the thought is impregnated. If the thought is passionate and constructive, it will possess vitality; it will have life; it will grow, develop, expand; it will be creative; it will attract to itself everything necessary for its complete development.

Notice the word that he uses: "impregnated." That's a powerful way to state his meaning, because impregnation comes from the sexual act of creation, and it's the feeling that is the impregnator and the thought that is the receptive host. Wow.

And what are the "feeling" qualities that he specifically names for successful impregnation of a thought? Passionate and constructive.

"Passionate." What does that word convey to us? The dictionary defines passionate as "easily aroused; having, compelled by, ruled by, or expressing intense or vehement emotion or strong feeling."

Haanel asks you to focus inward, quiet your mind, look directly to your Source, open to receive higher guidance, and then tune into your most passionate yearning or desire at the moment.

Notice that the order here is crucial and psychologically astute. If you just suddenly try to identify your dominant passion, you're going to be looking with your everyday awareness, and who knows what you'll find.

Haanel requests that you first move through a serious meditative process, tune into your inner guide, and then (and only then) look to see what core passion you want to tap into and use to empower your manifestation process.

So many people, in their quest for successful manifestation of their dreams, fall flat right at this point. They might be driven by a host of conflicting desires fueled by the media, by past programming by their parents or peer group, by distorted ideas of what brings happiness in life. Very often, secondary or temporary hungers dominate their awareness, so that they almost never get a clear look at their deeper hungers, their higher passions, their true desires and needs.

For quite a number of years I've been looking closely at the whole phenomenon that we call "hunger" and "need" and "desire." Surely we all hunger for food to keep our physical bodies alive and well. We hunger for sexual intimacy and release. We crave stimulation when understimulated for too long, and yearn for peace and quite when over-stimulated for too long. We need a roof over our heads, a community to support us when we are in trouble, and regular bouts of frivolous play and entertainment.

Most animals share with us most of these needs. They're in fact programmed into our brains and drive us toward satisfactions of many different kinds. Usually we fixate on attaining secondary material expressions of our true desires—but often we remain unsatisfied deep down.

Haanel says it this way:

> If we think of some form of material wealth, we may secure it. By concentrated thought the required conditions will be brought about and the proper effort put forth, which will result in bringing about the circumstances necessary to realize our desires. But we often find that when we secure the things we thought we wanted, they do not have the effect we expected. That is, the satisfaction is only temporary, or possibly is the reverse of what we expected.

That's surely the universal experience of our advertisement-driven culture, in which we're actually led to believe that Coke's the thing, that a fancy car will solve all our problems, and that white teeth will answer all our romantic needs. Much of the shallow dimensions of the New Age movement were driven by what was called "spiritual materialism," in which people were led to believe that by grabbing onto high beliefs and esoteric practices, a deeper spiritual hunger could be satisfied.

In this chapter I want to challenge you to look more deeply toward the desires and passions you carry within you, so that you can clearly identify the underlying passion that drives you and focus specifically on satisfying that deeper itch, not the surface tingle.

There are without question a list of basic needs that all human beings share, and that we all need to focus on and satisfy, in order to be happy and harmonious in our lives. Here's the outline that Haanel offers:

> We cannot be happy unless we have health, strength, congenial friends, pleasant environment, and sufficient supply not only to take care of our necessities, but also to provide for those comforts and luxuries to which we are entitled.

Do you agree with his list? If so, when you look within to see what needs you have that require attention and manifestation, be sure to reflect on the following:

1. Are you physically healthy, or do you need to focus on healing and dietary and lifestyle changes?

2. Are you emotionally healthy, or does this need focused attention?

3. Are you strong, or feeling weak? Does this dimension of your life need attention?

4. Do you have deep friendships that nurture you? Do you feel adequately loved and appreciated? Or do you need to focus on bringing this congenial friends element to the fore?

5. Is your living and work environment harmonious and healthy, or are you stuck in an environment that grates on your nerves and erodes your sense of aesthetics and health?

6. Materially, do you have enough money and sources to obtain what you need so that you have good shelter, good food, and all the rest of the material possessions that you need?

7. Also, because we're here not only to survive but to thrive and enjoy life, are you making enough money, living in the proper community, and working at the proper job, so you can access the beyond-subsistence things you are entitled to?

This list can be shortened in your daily meditation to:

1. Health
2. Emotions
3. Power
4. Friendships

5. Environment
6. Survival
7. Pleasure

If you look deep within you and find one of these shouting for attention, definitely give it attention. Basic needs require regular attention to make sure you're keeping everything in balance. If you deny or ignore anything on this list, you're liable to get into compulsive behavior and avoidance patterns, such as drugs. Best to listen and respond with action.

But notice that Haanel lists these needs with the preface that we need to satisfy these needs in order to satisfy a deeper desire, in order to be happy. The driving intent is not to have a fancy house or flashy job; the intent is to fulfill temporary material needs in order to fullfill your deeper hunger, to experience enduring inner harmony and contentment. And usually, only when all of these needs are taken care of can you feel harmonious in your mind, your heart, and your relationships.

So do focus and manifest anything on that list of seven, so that you regularly experience the underlying emotion of happiness that comes with satisfying your human needs. But throughout, remember that you will need to focus on and sustain positive thoughts in order to manifest what you need in life. As Haanel says:

A happy thought cannot exist in an unhappy consciousness; therefore the consciousness must change.

So before you attempt to manifest something external that you hope will make you feel better inside, you're going to have to deal with any negative inner thoughts and feelings that are predictably manifesting the outer negatives in your life.

WHAT INNER FEELING
DO YOU HUNGER FOR?

As mentioned before, Haanel encourages us to not focus our manifestation energy on specific outward things that might be part of our desired happiness picture. Instead he suggests strongly that we look deep within, find the core positive yearning that's living under pressure in our hearts, and focus on manifesting that positive feeling, not as a future imagination, but as a present-moment experience inside us.

Please bear with me—this requires close attention to see adequately into the spiritual logic of this process. Yearning is a power under pressure. There is something that you hunger for, that you need, but that externally you don't have. However, that exact feeling inside you of yearning for something indicates that you already know this feeling, and want more of it in your life, yes?

Haanel insists, and I with him, that what we ultimately want is the feeling of being one with our Creator, of not feeling separated from God's love. Everything else is a secondary yearning, wouldn't you agree?

And here's the joke: If we can yearn for a feeling, that

means we already have a vague connection with that feeling. We're already plugged into happiness and harmony. But we've let the connection be mostly lost, in all our various negative attitudes and beliefs and judgments and all the rest. Our problem in feeling bad isn't external. The problem is that our internal condition is generating a negative outside world.

So we're back where we started a few pages ago—as Haanel put it earlier, "the consciousness must change" for the better if we want our external situation to change for the better. And how do we change our consciousness?

Once again, our ego minds cannot think us out of our ingrained attitudes and negative beliefs and emotions. Remember the adage, often attributed to Albert Einstein: "You can't solve a problem with the same kind of thinking that created the problem in the first place." Something new is needed, an inflow of fresh ideas, of more positive thoughts. And where do these come from?

From your Source. It's plain and simple, but so many intelligent people fail to get this very simple point. Inspiration is our godsend, as they say. Insight from our deeper source of wisdom is required to break us out of our mental habits and to impregnate our usual thoughts with higher realization and a better game plan.

And notice that that's exactly what we're doing here, and that's why I have suggested you first look inward, quiet your usual thoughts, enter the Silence, and open up to receive guidance from your Source before you look to your yearnings and see what the core yearning really is that you need to work to satisfy.

I suspect that there is a passionate pressure inside you right now—otherwise you wouldn't be motivated to read this book right now. If you can look directly inward and make contact with that passion, you will tap the power and energy that will then impregnate your thoughts with insight, wisdom, practical plans, and step-by-step procedures to begin to manifest not just a car or a house or a job, but an entire life that is an expression of your inner yearning.

The yearning ultimately comes from your Creator or Source, by whatever name. The yearning is to not only subsist and survive for a while on this planet; the yearning is to fulfill your purpose on this planet. People who have identified their purpose, tapped their deepest yearning, and welcomed Spirit into their hearts and minds to manifest their purpose are happy people.

Do you want to be one of these people?

If so, here's what you do.

As a regular daily habit, even hourly if you want to, you must remember to remember to pause, shift your attention to present-moment sensory experiences so that you temporarily quiet your regular thoughts, and enter into the Silence.

And as you breathe into that quiet-mind state of consciousness where Universal Mind can merge with your individual mind, say to yourself, "I am open to receive guidance from my Source."

And as you stay aware of your breathing, just see what

comes to you, as an experience, right in the middle of your breathing experience—that's where Spirit flows in!

At some point, when you're ready, you can use a special Focus Phrase that will gently awaken a realization inside you, of what you really desire deep down to bring into your life. Let the words of the Focus Phrase, in and of themselves, elicit a response and realization within you.

Simply say to yourself the following Focus Phrase:

"I know what I want."

Say the words, and at the same time continue to stay aware of your breathing experience in your nose, your chest, and your belly.

Most people most of the time do not know what they really need to be truly happy. You can begin to evolve into a person who does know what you want.

THE REAL SECRET

Most people, when they ask themselves what they want, think of a thing they want to possess and do something with. If you look inside and say, "I know what I want," and what you want is an ice cream bar, fine, don't belittle small desires—go get one!

But if you're this deep into this particular book, what you're looking for probably isn't a box of chocolate or any other temporary fix to push back your sense of frustration or incompleteness. You know you need something deeper than just another thing, or more of the things you already have. If you're in need of something, fine—this program will help you focus and manifest that thing. But there's a deeper dimension to satisfying your needs.

My experience in this regard (which runs parallel with Haanel's) is that what we really need to bring into our lives isn't a thing; it's a feeling, an inner experience.

If you say to yourself, "I need more . . ." and complete the sentence, what words come to mind?

Sometimes, you'll find your inner voice saying, "I need more money," and this will very possibly be a valid need—and this program will help you manifest that financial need.

Sometimes your voice might say, "I need more love," and this is definitely a serious yearning to respond to.

Perhaps you ask yourself what you truly desire, and your inner response (guided by the Universal Mind, which does know what you need) will say, "I need better health" or "I need to feel safe and free from all my worries."

But deeper down, always, what I'm hungering for is a shift in my feelings—I yearn to feel more of a core good feeling. That's the secret: What we truly yearn for, beyond things and situations, is the deeper positive feeling that these things and situations might bring us.

If you at first say to yourself that you need a better-paying job or a more fulfilling relationship, this is fine, but then look deeper. Look to see how you feel now in your heart, related to that need. And then look to see what feeling you hunger to feel inside you that a new job or relationship or whatever would hopefully bring you. Perceive the core yearning!

BASIC MANIFESTATION LOGIC

Let's take a closer look at Haanel's statement that began this chapter's discussion:

> A thought's vitality depends upon the feeling with which the thought is impregnated. If the thought is passionate and constructive, it will possess vitality; it will have life; it will grow, develop, expand; it will be creative; it will attract to itself everything necessary for its complete development.

You have the thought, "What I need is to lose ten pounds." Good, that's a thought that seems to represent a solid need or intent. But the thought on its own will accomplish nothing, because "a thought's vitality depends upon the feeling with which the thought is impregnated."

And where is that essential passionate and constructive feeling going to be found and tapped? That's the logic that you must return to over and over in this program. How do you access the feeling that will impregnate your thought and intent, so that your intent will grow, develop, expand, be creative, and attract everything necessary for its complete development?

You are, essentially, beyond all your thoughts and beliefs and ideas and judgments, a feeling deep inside your chest.

But to gain power; you must learn to focus regularly and steadily and positively on that core feeling, that dynamic yearning, and impregnate your manifestation thoughts with the passionate power of that feeling!

AGAIN, THE PROCESS

Here's what I often experience when I move through the manifestation process: I choose to look enjoyably inward, and I focus on my breathing to quiet my mind. This inner action of focusing in my chest area naturally brings me into deep encounter with the current feelings in my heart. I breathe into these feelings that are found right at the center of my heart experience, and then say to myself, "I am open to receive guidance from my Source," and tune into whatever new experience comes to me, from that deeper Source. And as I focus on that experience, I say to myself, "I know what I want."

Perhaps as I'm saying those words, I don't yet really know what I'm yearning for that day, but in the process of starting that "I know what I want," insight comes flowing into my mind from a deep source, and suddenly I do know!

That's what insight is all about. That's the "aha!" experience that is required right at this point. Perhaps in the first week or so of learning this process you won't have a flash of insight into your deeper needs. But trust me, at some point soon, you will. You'll make that vital inner "feeling" connection that carries the power to impregnate and activate your thoughts.

Again, I welcome you to move through the process yourself. As Haanel regularly said, it's essential to exercise the mental muscle in order to become strong in this process. Each time you pause and say these Focus Phrases to yourself, you're moving deeper into the Manifestation Process that will bring you what you desire.

Be sure to make your breath experience primary, and after you say each Focus Phrase, take time (one or more breaths) to open up and experience the resonance of the intent statement as it awakens deep feelings and insights within you, bringing your unconscious Universal Mind into full play.

1. *"I choose to focus enjoyably inward."*
2. *"My mind is quiet . . . I am now in the Silence."*
3. *"I am open to receive guidance from my Source."*
4. *"I know what I want."*

CHAPTER 11

TAP THE CREATIVE SOURCE

In many ways this chapter is the heart of this book. I want to talk deeper than I ever have before in print about what it means to feel connected with your Creative Source. And I want to complete the progression you've step by step been learning, to where you are indeed face to face with Universal Mind. I'll do my best to keep my psychologist's hat on for the duration of this ride, but it's going to push the limits of scientific discourse and then some for us to actually delve into the process of looking directly into the face of our Creator. Don't blink!

Consider this quote from Haanel:

By plainly stating to the subconscious mind certain specific things to be accomplished, forces are set in operation that lead to the result desired. Here is a source of power which places us in touch with Omnipotence. This is a deep principle well worth our most earnest study.

This is of course what Focus Phrases do: They plainly state to the unconscious mind specific things to be accomplished. I hope you're beginning to perceive that there's a multistep process taking place each time you state a Focus Phrase to yourself. First comes the remembrance of the Focus Phrase as a statement of intent. This comes the actual inner vocalization of the statement of intent. At this point, your unconscious mind receives the request of the conscious mind, and it responds immediately. Then comes the rising up of that response into consciousness, as a flash of insight, a realization, a special feeling, or a coherent thought.

When you say to yourself, "I feel the air flowing in and out of my nose," chances are you are *not* right at that moment in fact tuned into that sensory event. But as soon as you speak the intent to focus there, the unconscious mind responds and focuses your attention there. And after you speak your intent in the Focus Phrase, you immediately experience this shift in focus and become aware of the air flowing in and out of your nose.

Each Focus Phrase moves you through this process. On your exhale you say the statement of intent to yourself, and on your next inhale you experience the response of your deeper self to this statement of intent. The conscious ego speaks the words, the unconscious mind responds, and the conscious ego then experiences that response.

WHOM ARE YOU TALKING TO?

Let's be clear: In the act of speaking "to yourself" you are indeed speaking to your unconscious mind, to that vast realm of your being that exists just below or beyond your conscious awareness. The purpose of Focus Phrases in general is to stimulate this act of communication between the conscious and unconscious realms of the mind.

As already mentioned, Haanel firmly believes that your unconscious mind is your direct link with the Divine. And by speaking an intent to the unconscious mind, you are therein communicating your desire and intent to God.

That's pretty heavy stuff.

And that's exactly where true power to manifest comes from: your ability and intent to tap via your unconscious mind into Universal Mind's infinite power and intelligence, which then communicates back via the unconscious to your conscious ego mind, so that you can creatively imagine, visualize, and go into action to achieve a goal in your life.

Haanel saw human beings as infinite creatures with a conscious mind that has the power to aim its attention toward "the world within" in order to tap into an infinite intelligence and power, and then receive guidance from that infinite intelligence and power—and go into action to perform in the outside world and achieve the stated intent.

> The world within is the Universal Fountain of supply, and the world without is the outlet to the stream. Our ability to receive depends upon our recognition of this Universal

Fountain, this Infinite Energy of which each individual is an outlet.

Here we come to the ultimate challenge, that of tuning into the Universal Fountain, so that we can become an outlet to that source of supply. In order to manifest our desires, we need creative power, agreed? And where are we going to find that creative power? Let's review an important quote from Haanel in which he hits the nail on the head:

Creative power does not originate in the individual, but in the Universal, which is the source and foundation of all energy and substance; the individual is simply the channel for the distribution of this energy.

I want to keep returning to this basic notion until I'm sure it's fully understood and accepted in your own mind and heart: It's a myth to think that you as a separate ego body can accomplish anything new or creative at all. Yes, you can plug into the existing machine and habitually perform actions that generate results. But if you want to change your life for the better, you're going to have to do something creative, to bring into being a reality that did not exist before.

If you believe that you exist as an isolated bubble of awareness with no connection or dependence upon anything beyond or higher than yourself, of course this book will have no meaning, and you won't have read even this far into it without tossing it aside. So I assume you do experience in your life a greater reality than your ego bubble usually acknowledges. What we're doing here is learning how to regularly shift focus so as to look directly to your greater self; call it the Universal Mind or God or whatever other name you like.

I'm not a great fan of building abstract belief castles in the sky. I prefer to cut to the chase, and that's what we do with the next Focus Phrase in this manifestation process. If you want to access higher wisdom and empowerment and all the rest, what do you need? State that need clearly, as if it's already a done deal, and your unconscious mind will respond by doing what you request. Come on, let's admit it—we want to experience that core feeling of being connected with our Creative Source. Who wants to feel disconnected from their Source? Who wants to feel out of touch with their Creator?

You are seeking the power to change your life for the better. Say it. Do it.

"I feel connected with creative power."

Say these words to yourself, and let them reverberate throughout your being, aiming your mind's attention directly inward to establish a connection that you feel!

And what do you do now?

Please note carefully: You do nothing at all. You are in receive mode. You are open to receive whatever comes to you in this deep meditative state. That's what meditation is, after all: the entering into a quiet-mind quality of consciousness where you are tuned into your breathing first and foremost, because it will be right in the middle of your breathing that you will receive the inflow coming from the Universal into your individual mind.

Perhaps you stay in this meditative receptive mode of consciousness for one breath, for one minute, for one hour. It doesn't matter. Stay there a while, enjoy the bliss of being plugged into the Divine, and with your breathing as your medium of receptivity, allow new feelings, perhaps new thoughts, new whatever, to come flooding or seeping or flowing into your conscious mind.

"I feel connected with creative power."

RECEIVING THE VISION

Let's review again what we've explored thus far in this manifestation process, so that you can see the logic leading to the next step: (1) You've learned to use Focus Phrases to redirect your attention so as to quiet your mind and (2) open up to guidance from your higher Source; (3) through the influence of this guidance, you've tuned into the deeper yearnings and feelings in your heart so that you know what you really need right now; and (4) you've connected at the core feeling level with your creative source of power and inspiration.

Now what happens?

One way or another, now or sometime later, you will receive a flash of insight, a new idea, a vision of where you want to aim your attention so that you bring into being a new quality to your life.

In other words, your conscious mind has requested—even demanded—and then received a power-packed vision from the Universal Mind. You're inspired! Hold in mind what Haanel says about this:

> The unlimited creative power of the Universal Mind is within control of the conscious mind of the individual. We can have the inspiration of the omnipotent Universal Mind on demand at any time.

I hope that now you're beginning to see the fully interactive two-way dynamic of this manifestation process. You as an individual have the conscious power to ask for guidance, for insight, for the infinite wisdom of Universal Mind. And Universal Mind by its very nature responds and gives you the information, the power, the vision, and the will to carry out the actions step by step that will manifest the game plan.

Jesus said this so clearly: "Seek and it will be shown to you; ask and it will be given."

But most of us, in opening to receive a vision, expect to receive a vision of our outer physical world being transformed. We want to receive a game plan for manipulating the outer world in order to get what we want. Sometimes this might happen, and at certain stages of manifestation, particular outer-world details might come to us in this receive mode state.

But Haanel strongly advises not to anticipate this type of vision, because it's not going to be big enough to permeate and transform your world with a new experience. Instead, as we've seen already, he insists that we need to use our own conscious minds to manage our attention so that our inner world begins to change for the better. And when the inner changes, the outer naturally changes too. Here's how he puts it:

> The world without is a reflection of the world within. What appears without is what has been found within. Harmony in the world within will be reflected in the world without by harmonious conditions, agreeable surroundings, the best of everything. This inner harmony is the foundation of health and a necessary essential to all greatness, all power, all attainment, all achievement, and all success.

We are really cutting to the chase here, because we're considering the very nature of the vision we seek in order to be truly fulfilled in our lives. If our external world is "a reflection of the world within," then obviously we need to first change our world within if we want to change our outside world.

> The great fact is that the source of all life and all power is found within. This means that the insight, strength, and power to answer our needs will be found within.

Psychologists often point out rather despairingly that it's difficult to change a person's attitudes and inner mental habits, which in turn determine one's inner feelings and condition. Depressed people stay depressed, anxious people stay anxious, prejudiced people stay prejudiced, unhappy and disharmonious people stay that way. Such is life.

Not true, says Haanel. Not true, says John Selby. Not true, say many millions of people who have used their own conscious thoughts in order to positively change their inner lives and thus change their outer lives as well.

Right here is where I love Haanel the most, where he insists that we can rapidly improve our inner condition of harmony and clarity, power and compassion. All we need to do is to regularly move through the process of asking for and manifesting more harmony and love in our inner lives!

INNER HARMONY

When I work with a client in my therapy practice, one of the first things I like to do is to guide this person to the point of realizing what they really want: They want to feel better. That's the core driving desire and yearning that has brought them to see a therapist. They want more inner harmony and peace, they want more insight and love, and they want more trust and strength.

In sum, they want to feel more connected with the true infinite source of all those human feelings—and please note that they are feelings, not abstract ideals or material possessions.

People can do analytical therapy twice a week for twenty years and never really feel any better. They might understand why they have been conditioned to feel like they do, but the thinking mind cannot think itself into better feelings. It must do something ultimately humbling: It must ask for help.

That's what you're doing in this manifestation process: You're asking for help. Your ego mind and your personal conditioned mental and emotional reactions need something beyond themselves in order to let go of all the negativity and fear, the judgment and disharmony, and take the great leap into positive harmonious states of consciousness.

True, the old attitudes and programmings will always be there. Your saving grace is that you don't have to focus your attention in negative directions if you don't want to. In order to receive creative power and manifest your dream, you might need to change your core focusing habit—and without higher help, this can seem impossible to accomplish.

What you need is to tap into a higher vision so that you can actively hold your focus of attention in directions that keep you plugged into the Universal Mind's wisdom, compassion, and harmony. Hold in mind that you are seeking to gain creative power to manifest your deeper needs, and access to this creative power comes only when you choose to manifest a brighter and more positive experience inside your own heart.

> We can come into harmonious relationship with the Universal, and when we have accomplished this we may ask anything to which we are entitled, and the way will be clear.

Here we see again Haanel's nonstop insistence on the need to accomplish the inner work and transformation before you can accomplish the outer manifestations. Once inner harmony with the Universal has been accomplished, the outer material fulfillment is relatively easy.

I've seen this happen often in my professional life. A person suffering from inner disharmony, confusion, anxiety, and depression will almost always manifest that kind of negative outer life as well. Social workers struggle so hard, for instance, to help people change their outer lives, but usually fail unless an inner transformation comes first.

But almost like a miracle, some seemingly charmed people are suddenly able to transform their outer lives in harmonious ways. Why? Because they have found inner harmony; they have opened up to their Creator (not through submission, but through clear positive intent) and asked for the guidance and vision needed to become aligned with the Universal Harmony that is now flooding into their lives because they asked for it.

I assume that you desire fairly rapid positive change in your life. I intend to give you the tools to accomplish this. Once again, take time to reflect on the Focus Phrase you've learned in this chapter, upon the statement of intent that will step by step over the next weeks bring you into full realization of what you really desire to manifest in your life.

1. *"I choose to focus enjoyably inward."*
2. *"My mind is quiet . . . I am now in the Silence."*
3. *"I am open to receive guidance from my Source."*
4. *"I know what I want."*
5. *"I feel connected with creative power."*

CHAPTER 12

MANIFEST YOUR
HIGHER PURPOSE

In the last chapters, you've focused your attention further and further inward, to the point where you find yourself focusing directly upon the Creative Source—the infinite, intelligent, compassionate power that manifested this entire world and universe. That's quite an amazing thing to do, to humbly and courageously see your Creator eye to eye.

I hope you understand that this inward turning to enter the Divine Presence isn't something you just do once and are done with it. This process is a lifelong path to follow, in which every day you return to this inner focus on the Universal and tune into whatever insights and guidance and power you are naturally ready to receive to further your life. And each time you look within, you will open yourself to receive a new experience, because time marches on, and it's always a new moment.

At the end of this book, we'll offer a number of ways in which you can in the next weeks train your mind to move through the first part of the Manifestation Process. We are now ready in our discussion to move on to the final step, in which you once again turn your mind's attention outward and allow Spirit to guide your thinking mind toward manifesting a new vision that you go into action to achieve.

In essence, what you've done in the first part of the process is to shift from your everyday pragmatic conscious mode of consciousness into the equal and opposite function of the mind, the unconscious intuitive spiritual mode of awareness. Now it's time to bring your deeper insights back into conscious focus, so that your thinking mind can merge with your deeper being and generate action to manifest your desire. Remember earlier, when I quoted Haanel as saying:

> It is the coordination of these two centers of our being (conscious and unconscious) which is the great secret of life. With this knowledge we can bring the objective and subjective minds into conscious cooperation and thus coordinate the finite and the infinite.

That's your challenge now: how to do this, how to bring the infinite inspiration and creativity of the Universal Mind down into your individual thoughts and vision. Notice that Haanel talks about "conscious cooperation" between the finite and the infinite. There is to be no ego struggle for dominance here, nor any overpowering of the Divine—it must be a team deal, and it's going to play itself out as a conscious experience.

Here's more specific instruction to help us from Haanel's writings:

> When you come into possession of a sense of poise and power you will be ready to receive the information or inspiration or wisdom necessary for the development of your purpose.

Hopefully you're in progress already in learning how to "come into possession of a sense of poise and power." The key words in this quote for us now relate to the three inputs that you can receive from the Divine: information, inspiration, and wisdom.

Those are what you want to bring back from your immersion in the presence of Universal Mind during your meditations. And you do bring them back with you. It's so important to begin to fully accept the fact that your inspired thoughts do come from this deeper source beyond your personal bubble of awareness.

> Every thought is received by the brain, which is the organ of the conscious mind. Spirit is omnipresent, ever ready; all that is required is a willingness or desire to become the recipient of its beneficent effects.

So a primary desire within you must be this desire to receive wisdom, information, and inspiration into your brain as a conscious thought or vision or realization or whatever. Do you truly hunger for an inflow from the Universal Mind into your personal mind? And if you do, how can you optimize the communication from the Infinite to your conscious awareness?

Let's dig into this deeply, because once again we've hit a step in this manifestation process where so many people stumble and fall. And again, let's look to the master for insight into this question of how and where do we receive inputs from beyond:

> We are related to the world within by the subconscious mind. The solar plexus is the organ of this mind. It is through the subconscious that we are connected with the Universal Mind and brought into relation with the infinite constructive forces of the universe.

This statement is true as you open up to make contact. It's also equally true as you consciously open up to bring the Infinite into finite expression in your mind. You have spent time way out beyond your mortal limitations, using your unconscious presence as your link with the Universal Mind. Now you must actively bring the desired wisdom and information and inspiration into your body, literally, and thus to your brain and into conscious thought.

The trick isn't to fixate your attention on your brain. Haanel insists that you focus instead elsewhere in your body, a particular location that functions as the receiver for the incoming broadcast from Universal Mind. I quickly mentioned this step in the introduction. Let me show you a key quote again because it will make much more sense here than it did earlier in this book:

The solar plexus is the point at which the part meets with the whole, where the Infinite becomes finite, Universal becomes individualized, Invisible becomes visible. It's the point at which life appears, and there is no limit to the amount of life you can generate from this solar center.

That's a rather strong statement. And you will find this statement to be one of the most important in this book, because most people are simply looking in the wrong place, in their desire to receive insight from God to help them in their lives. They look to their hearts usually, but that's not quite where the inflow happens.

So what is the big deal about the solar plexus? It's a key chakra location in ancient Hindu tradition, and it's the center of power in the body and in the subtle astral system according to Yoga masters. We noted earlier that what you need in order to manifest is power. And the solar plexus does seem to be the center of power in the body.

The solar plexus is also the epicenter of your breath reflex. The diaphragm muscle is right in the middle of the solar plexus, and, as you have seen, deep breath awareness is the key link that shifts you from mundane thought into the Silence, where you receive insight and empowerment.

Already, in practicing the breath-awareness meditation learned earlier in this book, you've been learning to focus your attention directly toward the solar plexus, so this isn't a new experience for you; it's just being used in a different step of the manifestation process.

Before you say the next Focus Phrase to yourself, the

crucial act is always to first make sure you're still aware of your breathing experience. Otherwise, you're simply not going to be plugged in, and nothing's going to happen in terms of receiving manifestation power and vision.

I hope you are staying aware of your breathing while reading this book, page by page. You can of course do everything in your life while also staying aware of your ongoing breath experience, and you'll do what you're doing with more inspiration and power. For instance, right now I'm writing these words while staying aware of my breath experience. That's my constant discipline for writing anything, because it allows Spirit to be right here writing this with me.

You can have Spirit right here with you right now as you read these words, not as an idea, but as an actual presence, a presence found . . . where?

Right in the middle of your breath experience.

Right at the center of your solar plexus.

Right . . . now.

CREATIVE AND INSPIRED THOUGHT

Each time in this manifestation process when you say to yourself the fifth Focus Phrase, "I feel connected with creative power," you are plugging in to receive. And in order to receive, please note that you need to shift your attention directly to the region of your solar plexus, located deep within the center of your torso, just below your heart.

Your mind is quiet. You're focused on what you deeply

desire. You've temporarily surrendered your personal ego thoughts and opened up to receive inspired thoughts. Now, all you do is breathe into whatever comes to you as you remain focused on your solar plexus and your breathing, which are one and the same. And in this state of expanded awareness, you let Spirit come flowing into you and also radiate out through you into the world.

Infinite Life flows through you; is you.

Its doorways are the faculties of your consciousness.

To keep open these doors is the secret of power.

With your doors open, right here in this process is the moment when, as you keep your everyday mind quiet, you begin to experience the infusion of new ideas rising up from your solar plexus, into your heart, then into your throat and tongue, and into your thinking mind. You might hear your inner voice of wisdom speaking to you. You might see a vision of what you want to accomplish. You might flash with a realization of your higher purpose. You might move into a flow of inspired thoughts that come to you and become yours.

What's important is keeping the mind quiet so that Spirit can speak. And please hold in mind that insights often don't come right away. Sometimes you'll finish a session and nothing at all seemed to come to you, but then, as you're driving to work, or as you take a shower, or go for a walk, or begin to slip into sleep, suddenly, pow! You receive the full complete vision.

I hope you can now see why doing this short manifestation process often, at least once a day, is crucial to fulfillment. You must lead your horse to water, even though you can't make him drink. You must regularly bring your mind into the presence of Creative Power, even though you can't make inspiration happen on demand. You must become temporarily passive, receptive, silent, humble, and open, and, with your focus on your solar plexus and your breathing, let Spirit do what it wants.

Your ego self is temporarily surrendering to your higher infinite self. There's going to be plenty of time when the thinking, conscious mind is going to take the lead, as we'll see in the next chapter. But the conscious mind first requires the inflow and cooperation of the unconscious mind and its infinite spiritual link in order to gain the creative power and vision to act.

FINALLY, TIME TO MANIFEST

What's so special about Charles Haanel, as we've just seen, is that before he sends you into action to manifest what you need to fulfill your life, he requires that you first stop and move through the deep inner process described thus far in this book, so that you're charged with the power you need to truly change your life. Like my grandfather used to say,

"Don't go hunting without first loading your gun." Don't try to manipulate the world with your personal ego power. Instead, choose to participate in the world with the infinite guidance and empowerment of natural law and spiritual help.

So often, people chase from one thing to another, getting this, then getting that. With their focus on short-term goals, they fail to establish the long-term vision that will lead them to lasting satisfaction. Each day, I am encouraging you to look inward to reaffirm your true purpose, your spiritually imbued vision, which will lead you step by step through all the various manifestations that create the full life you desire.

But how do you know what to do, right now, each new moment? How do you go from the perfect vision to the details of advancing your life as you so desire?

At this point, we come full circle. I began this book by asking you to learn how to quiet your thinking mind so that you can enter into the Silence and receive a vision based on your heart's deeper passion. Now I'm saying it's time once more to fire up the brain and get your mind in gear again. Remember: It's always a coordinated action of conscious and unconscious, between mind and spirit, that generates significant change.

If we find wisdom in the world within, we shall have the understanding to discern the marvelous possibilities that are latent in this world within, and we shall be given the power to make these possibilities manifest in the world without.

As you use this book's manifestation process to tap into the "wisdom in the world within" and are therein "given the power to make these possibilities manifest in the world without," you reach the point each day where you are ready to apply your personal will to express the Universal Will:

> As we become conscious of the wisdom in the world within, we mentally take possession of this wisdom, and by taking mental possession we come into actual possession of the power and wisdom necessary to bring into manifestation the essentials necessary for our most complete and harmonious development.

The key action here is caught in the words "become conscious of the wisdom in the world within." That's the "aha!" moment in which you experience flashes of insight, which in turn stimulate your thinking mind to begin to make plans that will lead to changes in your life that you desire.

But remember that your thoughts need to remain impregnated with the passion that underlies your vision. If you lose touch with the passion, you'll lose your power to manifest in positive directions. That's why it's so important each day to move through the manifestation process and again say to yourself, "I know what I want," and experience the core yearning that is empowering your mind's planning and actions.

Every day, go into the Silence and ask your higher self what you need to focus on and manifest. Find out where your passion lies in the present moment, and bring this insight and power back in through your solar plexus and thus up into your thinking mind, where it will "take possession" of the inspired vision and transform it into action.

INSPIRED MIND

Your mind naturally becomes active when it's inspired by a great idea. That's what passion does: It powers the mind. And with a direct link being kept open between the subconscious and the Creative Source, the thinking mind will be inspired with ideas of what to do each new moment to evolve your deeper dream into reality.

Many people make the mistake of thinking that the ego mind can generate all the steps along the path to fulfillment. This does not seem to be the case. The conscious mind is limited to its sensory inputs, to past experience, and to future projections based on past experience. Its creativity is limited to its personal knowledge.

But an inspired mind draws from the Universal Mind's infinite knowledge of what's possible, and therefore it can guide an individual person in directions the ego mind would never venture toward. That's why trusting Spirit for guidance each new day leads to greater fulfillment than letting the ego mind direct the show.

Your finite mind cannot inform the Infinite. You are simply to say what you desire, not how you are to obtain it.

When you clarify that deep down what you desire is a brighter, more loving, happier inner feeling, then the Infinite will guide your thoughts step by step each day in directions that help you feel that heightened sense of positive life and love.

This is the giant difference between the ego mind trying to manipulate the world selfishly to satisfy its lower-level needs and passions, and the coordinated mind choosing to participate in God's creation so as to create a truly more harmonious and happy world. Once you see the difference, you'll regularly choose the latter, because the payoff is vastly greater for all.

So I challenge you, each new day, to tune deeply into the Source. Listen to your inner voice. Bring wisdom and vision into your mind through your solar plexus. And then enjoy the rush as your thoughts begin to play with the vision and to imagine new game plans for actively improving the world and your role in the world.

CREATIVE CONSCIOUS THOUGHT

Once your mind has generated a vision of your ultimate aim and purpose, be it for a large or small aspect of your life, it's time to apply your inspired vision to the outer world. And the first step in this outward movement of creation is to inform your unconscious mind of your vision, so that all aspects of your personal being are working together to create the world you desire.

You have brought your vision into your conscious mind through your solar plexus and subconscious awareness. You have taken the inspired vision and consciously created ideas and imaginations of your intended goal. You have a perfect vision of what you want to do, and now you must broadcast this vision out into the world, so that by the Law of Attraction you will bring to you everything you need to manifest your vision.

How do you clarify to your subconscious mind and to the world around you what your vision is? Again, Haanel surprises us out of our habitual assumptions by stating that the conscious mind must now broadcast its intent out to the world, through the solar plexus.

> The solar plexus is omnipotent because it is the point of contact with all life and all intelligence. It can therefore accomplish whatever it is directed to accomplish—and herein lies the power of the conscious mind; the subconscious can and will carry out such plans and ideas as may be suggested to it by the conscious mind.

Do you know that wonderful creative feeling when you're in the flow, when everything is going right in your life, when your whole being seems to be participating in perfect harmony with the outside world? That's the feeling that comes when your conscious mind successfully broadcasts to your unconscious mind and to the world outside how you want to work harmoniously in a win-win world to create a new vision that came to you from God.

That's the same feeling of passion that you tapped into when deep in communion with your Creator. Now your passion is manifesting in the world. And that's why it's vital to regularly pause and regain your oneness with your higher desire to manifest an inspired vision in the world.

Once your thinking mind becomes impregnated with spiritual power and vision, that same thinking mind that was once perhaps fixated on negative attitudes and disharmonious thoughts becomes transformed. In its limited, conditioned, fear-based state, the thinking mind can be highly destructive and a master of self-sabotage. But in its awakened state, your thinking mind becomes the champion leader of a new vision. People will follow this leader, come together to fulfill the dream, and create a sense of community that lets Spirit fill everyone's hearts.

That's beautiful vision—and it's what most of us want to participate in. When more and more of us learn to manage our minds so that we regularly tap into spiritual insight and guidance, that's the kind of world we can have.

> Conscious thought, then, is master of the solar plexus, from which the life and energy of the entire body flows. The quality of the thought which we entertain determines the quality of the thought which we radiate, which consequently will determine the nature of the experience which will result.

Which is to say, let's manage our thoughts and infuse them with Spirit, so that the quality of our thoughts broadcasts a positive vision.

LET YOUR LIGHT SHINE

We'll speak more of this theme in later chapters. It's now time to end the chapter by sharing with you a Focus Phrase designed to bring your focus directly to the perfect vision that has come to you in your manifestation process. Haanel insists that rather than fixating overmuch on the details of your vision (which will emerge step by step as you go about your day), continue to hold in your mind your perfect vision. Imagine the completed dream, hold this perfect goal strongly and with passion in your heart, and broadcast this perfect vision (which is more a feeling than a concept) out into the world through your solar plexus.

Here's the Focus Phrase that stimulates this process:

"My vision is right now perfect and complete."

Hold this thought in your conscious mind, speak it and broadcast it, and your unconscious mind will believe it, take it in, and act on it.

And with every new breath, breathe your vision out into the world! I love how Haanel says this:

It is evident, therefore, that all we have to do is to let our light shine; the more energy we can radiate, the more rapidly shall we be enabled to transmute undesirable conditions into sources of pleasure and profit.

I can guarantee you that if you regularly say this Focus Phrase to yourself, if you hold your perfect spiritually imbued vision in mind and let this passionate light shine in the world, you will effortlessly begin to manifest this inspired vision in the world.

Are you managing to read these pages while staying aware of your breathing at the same time?

Let's pause again so that you can tune fully into your breathing experience and move through the evolving manifestation process that you're learning by heart step by step:

1. *"I choose to focus enjoyably inward."*
2. *"My mind is quiet . . . I am now in the Silence."*
3. *"I am open to receive guidance from my Source."*
4. *"I know what I want."*
5. *"I feel connected with creative power."*
6. *"My vision is right now perfect and complete."*

Part Three

ACHIEVE GENUINE
FULFILLMENT

CHAPTER 13

APPLY THE DAILY
ATTRACTION PROCESS

Long before you read this book and considered consciously applying a daily manifestation process to boost your sense of success and fulfillment, you were already manifesting the world you live in. When you were a baby and you felt hungry, your body responded with the cry reflex, which brought your mother or father or other caregiver to you to satisfy your need. The act of manifestation is the core process through which you have survived every day of your life.

Now, as an adult, it's important to acknowledge that you're already fairly good at manifesting what you need. One way or another, you get up and manifest the money you need to pay for food and housing and other things. You work to manifest and maintain loving relationships. Same with good health and all the rest. Everything you see around you is caught up in your own manifestation powers.

How does this work? It's really very simple. You feel a need within you. You visualize what you imagine you require in order to satisfy that need or desire. Then—and here's the key of this chapter—you focus your attention concertedly in the direction that you imagine will supply the fulfillment of your need . . . right?

If you seek abundance of whatever kind—material, emotional, spiritual—you move through the process of attracting to you whatever you want. Haanel says this succinctly:

> Abundance will not come to you out of the sky; neither will it drop into your lap. But a conscious realization of the Law of Attraction, plus the intention to bring it into operation, plus the will to carry out this purpose, will bring about the materialization of your desire.

If you are out of work and need money, you will feel this need acutely at some point. This inner emotional pressure will stimulate ideas about how to make money, and then you will act on this idea by going out into the world to manifest what you need.

It's the same with relationships. If you're lonely and hungry for love, you'll experience an intense yearning, which will stimulate a vision of the ideal relationship you want, which in turn will generate pragmatic ideas of what you need to do. Then you'll act on those ideas and begin to attract to you the person you hunger for. I've written extensively about this particular application of the attraction meditation process in *Let Love Find You*, and the principle and the process are the same here.

What we're doing in this book is raising into clear

pragmatic consciousness all of the steps needed to truly satisfy your desires. Perhaps your ego mind conjures up an ideal sexual mate and you find that ego ideal, but the relationship remains unfulfilling. In this manifestation process, you will know that there are deeper steps to be made if you're to manifest a lasting relationship that meets your core desires.

Haanel's approach to all this is fundamental because, as we've seen, he challenges you to tap deeper than your personal ego so that you are guided not just by your individual life experience and programming but by a universal perspective on your needs. I've walked you through this process of quieting your ego mind, looking inward to your Source, tapping insight and guidance from the Infinite Mind, and then bringing this insight and creative power back into your personal consciousness, where it will stimulate your imagination and thoughts.

That's the masterful approach to manifestation, and it leads us to a primary question: What is imagination, and how can you put your imagination to work in your conscious mind, so that you have a clear ideal vision of what you want to attract into your life?

TAPPING THE POWER OF IMAGINATION

We've seen that for high-level, long-term results, your personal imagination must be stimulated by your inner passion and inspired by the guidance and wisdom of Universal Mind if you're to generate an ideal vision that will propel your life forward to satisfy your desire. Imagination is that infinite meeting point between individual and Infinite. Ideas just pop into your head out of the blue—that's imagination. Here's what Haanel says:

> Imagination is the light by which we can penetrate new worlds of thought and experience. Imagination is a plastic power, molding the things of sense into new forms and ideals. Imagination is the constructive form of thought which must precede every constructive form of action.

Note that imagination is a "power" that takes your present reality and generates something new from your available resources at hand. This is creative power! In order to manifest something new, you must construct in your imagination the ideal image or thought and then proceed with constructive action.

Over and over, Haanel insists that you must focus your attention diligently not toward the details of your vision, but toward the ideal vision itself, the imagination in your mind's eye. And you are to focus in the present moment upon your vision as if it were already complete—that's so important!

> We are first to believe that our desire has already been fulfilled. Its accomplishment will then follow. This is a concise direction for making use of the creative power of thought—by impressing on the universal subjective mind the particular thing which we desire as an already existing fact.

You must experience your imagined ideal vision as perfect in your own mind, and believe that it is in the process of manifesting in the outer world. Hold true to your dream, as they say.

If you desire to visualize and manifest a different environment, the process is to hold your ideal in mind until your vision has been made real. Give no thought to persons, places, or things; these have no place in the absolute. The environment you desire will contain everything necessary; the right persons and the right things will come at the right time and in the right place. Natural laws work in a perfectly natural and harmonious manner; everything seems to "just happen."

But to work within and activate these natural laws of attraction, you must discipline your mind to focus on your vision constantly for as long as it takes for the outer world to respond to your inner dream. This means that you must focus your mind's attention over time upon your ideal intent, until you attract to your life the material expression of what you are imagining.

In order to cultivate the imagination it must be exercised. Constructive imagination means mental labor, by some considered to be the hardest kind of labor, but it yields the greatest returns. All the great things in life have come to men and women who had the capacity to think, to imagine, and to make their dreams come true.

The practical reason that I keep insisting that you develop a daily or even hourly manifestation practice is because imagination "must be exercised." It takes concentration over time to make your dreams come true. But please don't think that I'm asking you to do something that is drudgery. Just the opposite: I'm asking you first to get in touch with your core driving desire, which you already at emotional levels strongly yearn to focus upon, then to use that passion to motivate and animate your "mental labor" so that labor is a pleasure.

> Concentration is much misunderstood; there seems to be an idea of effort or activity associated with it, when just the contrary is necessary. In true concentration you should be so interested in your thought, so engrossed in your subject as to be conscious of nothing else. Such concentration leads to intuitive perception and immediate insight into the nature of the object concentrated upon.

If you spend most of your time worrying about what you don't have, if you let your attention drift all over the place rather than holding it where it will serve you best, if you let your thoughts fixate on negative attitudes and emotions, then chances are high that you will not succeed with your vision.

Your primary personal power, as mentioned before, is your power of attention. You get what you focus on. My hope is that this book and set of online support systems will help you to manage your power of attention more effectively, so that you focus more often on what you want and less often on what you don't have or don't want. And what positive incentive will we be using to spur this focused attention?

The incentive of attention is interest. The greater the interest, the greater the attention; the greater the attention, the greater the action. So begin by paying attention. Before long you will have aroused interest. This interest will attract more attention, and this attention will produce more interest, and so on. This practice will enable you to cultivate the power of attention.

THE ATTENTION MAGNET

Charles Haanel insists that everything you need is already present around you—you're simply not focused on it, and thus not attracting it (through your power of attention) to become part of your life. Hopefully this book and process will help you focus and thus attract what you hunger for. Haanel points out over and over that nine-tenths of the work in satisfying your needs is done in your own mind, not in the outside world.

And indeed this is true—once you get clear in your head what you truly need to be happy, these external environments tend to appear almost miraculously. But it's no miracle; you've simply applied a deeper logic to the manifestation process. Rather than our ego presence going out and trying to grab what you think you need, your higher presence attracts what you need to you.

Let's take a closer look at this whole notion of attraction. Haanel says this about the inner dynamic of the process:

> In manifestation, your predominant thought or mental attitude is the magnet. The Law of Attraction states that "like attracts like." Consequently your mental attitudes will invariably attract such conditions as correspond to their nature. If you wish a change in conditions, all that's necessary is changing your thought; this will in turn change your mental attitude, which will in turn change your personality, which will in turn change the persons, things, conditions, and experiences that you meet in life.

And so we return to the most resonant notion that Haanel brings to our discussion: If we focus our desired vision not on outer manifestations but on the manifestations of a more positive, brighter, and more loving inner world, then the outer world will naturally respond positively, because indeed like does attract like.

The Law of Attraction will certainly and unerringly bring to you the conditions, environment, and experiences in life corresponding with your habitual, characteristic, predominant mental attitude. It's not what you think once in a while but your predominant mental attitude that counts.

So what is your inner dream? If you hunger for a new person in your life, what is the inner change that you hope that person will bring to your heart's experience? Go into the Silence and let your higher wisdom answer that question for you, not as a philosophical ideal, but as a feeling ideal. How do you really want to feel inside your own skin? Tap into that core positive emotion as an ideal vision and focus on manifesting that feeling inside you. Then that feeling will attract like people and situations that will express and nurture that feeling.

> Create the mental image; make it clear, distinct, perfect; hold it firmly in your mind and heart. The ways and means will develop; supply will follow the demand; you will be led to do the right thing at the right time and in the right way.

By focusing on manifesting an inner emotional experience rather than an outer material environment that stimulates an inner experience, you're again cutting to the chase rather than getting lost in details. You're clarifying that you want most material things because of how they will make you feel. And you're choosing to focus on first manifesting the feeling inside your own being, and then letting the Law of Attraction naturally bring you the outer expression of your inner feeling.

LOVE IS STILL THE ANSWER

I mentioned in the beginning that Charles Haanel made a gigantic leap in his understanding of the power of attraction in the universe when he directly equated the Law of Attraction with the power of love:

> The principle which gives thought the dynamic power to correlate with its object and therefore master every adverse human experience is the Law of Attraction, which is another name for love. There is no getting away from the Law of Love. It is the feeling that imparts vitality to thought. Feeling is desire, and desire is love. Thought impregnated with love becomes invincible. It is the combination of thoughts and love which forms the irresistible force called the Law of Attraction.

What a quote! Haanel has given us the master key to the manifestation of fulfillment in our lives. Science has been busy for the last hundred years since Einstein proving that the universe operates on basic laws of attraction that hold everything from subatomic particles to galaxies together. Haanel is simply applying the outer laws to our inner lives. Love is the power of attraction that brings us what we need to be whole.

Haanel often uses the words "resonance" or "harmony" in place of "love," but they're the same thing, and deep down we feel good when we resonate in harmony with our own selves and with others.

And what determines if we are harmonious and focused on positive loving feelings or disharmonious and caught up in judgmental, fearful, antagonistic, or other negative feelings?

The key is to be aware of and utilize the Law of Attraction every day and as often as possible. Your mental attitude is the most important factor for generating happiness and abundance.

As we saw earlier, we can spend years in therapy and never really change our attitudes, unless at some point we simply make the choice to stop focusing on negative thoughts and beliefs and attitudes and judgments, and choose instead to take charge of our own minds and focus our attention toward a loving vision of who we are.

We are what we focus on. We evolve in the direction that we focus our attention on. We have the power to shift our focus of attention at will. The choice is always before us. The challenge is to remember to make the shift away from fear-based thoughts and imaginings toward love-empowered thoughts and imaginings.

Let me review what we've already learned from Haanel concerning the process for creating more fulfilling and loving inner environments in our own minds and hearts—a process that is also the basis of effective cognitive therapy and successful meditation programs. He says it simply. If you want to change your inner life:

> . . . hold in mind the condition desired; affirm it as an already existing fact. This indicates the value of a powerful affirmation. By constant repetition it becomes a part of you. You are actually changing yourself; you are making yourself what you want to be.

Over the next few weeks, as you regularly enter into the Silence and open up to insights into the quality of inner feeling you desire deep down to be happy and fulfilled, you'll begin to generate a powerful ideal feeling imbued with the attracting power of love. You'll come to know with great gusto what you really want. You'll feel connected with your creative power to manifest this inner atmosphere and environment based on love rather than fear. Your inner vision of your ideal emotional condition will become perfect and complete.

And you will be ready for our final Focus Phrase, which will evolve your entire personality and inner sense of emotional well-being in the positive direction you are choosing and focusing on. Here's the seventh and final Focus Phrase of this manifestation process:

"Each new moment is manifesting my dream."

INTENT AS A PHYSICAL POWER

For thousands of years, human beings in all cultures around the world have developed religions in which human thought can directly impact the material world. The power of mind over matter became generally debunked as traditional Newtonian science gained influence over people's beliefs. But recently, more and more scientific studies have demonstrated that focused thought can indeed impact the outer material world. A hundred years ago Charles Haanel certainly believed this to be true and based his entire manifestation process on that belief: Thought has power to impact the material world.

The underlying principles of subatomic physics state very clearly that the entire universe is one great resonant entity in which each tiny energetic particle in the universe is connected and influenced by every other particle. Indeed each particle is constantly moving back and forth from form to energy and interacting with the summation of energy fields surrounding it. The whole universe seems to consist of energetic bundles and waves that cannot be defined except in resonant participation with all other energetic bundles.

But how do human thought, desire, intent, and focus fit into this new scientific understanding of life? Traditional Greek philosophy dictated that thought is not a material phenomenon at all, and that consciousness operates in a different dimension than do material things. However, new theories in physics now insist that for the universe to work, there are indeed more than three dimensions at play—at least seven at last count.

Consciousness does seem to function both within the space-time continuum and also in other dimensions, thus our ability to tap into the Source that, by definition, as the Creator of the universe, operates beyond its physical manifestation. And the Haanel vision makes perfect sense in this expanded sense of the interplay of the material world and the more subtle dimensions that must underlie three-dimensional functioning.

Perhaps the most important research that demonstrates

how your inner thoughts have the power to affect the physical world around you is the Princeton Engineering Anomalies Research (PEAR) of the last thirty years, now completed but still just beginning to impress our minds with its discoveries. You can visit the official Princeton website at www .princeton.edu/~pear to read more deeply into this important set of studies conducted by the Princeton Engineering Department, but here's the gist of the research.

Many hundreds of subjects were asked to sit for half an hour and focus their power of intent directly at a random number generator to see if they could will the machine to generate more ones than zeros. The scientists doing the study wanted to prove Einstein wrong in his statement that "the intent of the experimenter influences the outcome of the experiment."

To make a fascinating long story very short, the statistical data showed that the random number generator did in fact skew its performance in the direction the subjects willed it to skew. After more than ten years of trying to refute the data, the scientists had to admit that indeed the human mind somehow can muster a force as yet unidentified and change the performance of a very physical and trustworthy machine beyond any chance effects.

This was a massive discovery. They then did studies that for the first time proved that ESP is scientifically valid. One human being can focus on a particular shape or number, aim this mental image toward another person in another room, and influence that person's choice of shapes or numbers. Again, the power of focused thought and intent was demonstrated to influence the outside world, in this case another person's mental activity.

The head of PEAR, a conservative aeronautical engineer whom I knew personally when I was at Princeton, then expanded his study with the random number generator to see what happened when more than one person participated in a test study. The results were jolting and proved Haanel's assertion that love is a physical force in the universe.

When two unrelated people focused their attention at the random number generator, the effect was doubled. But get this: When two people in a love relationship participated together, the effect was tripled. They had more power to influence the outside world than two people who were not emotionally related.

I relate these facts because with this and related research now formally completed in the scientific community, each of us must now realize that we are indeed impacting the world around us with our focused intentful thoughts. When we think negative thoughts about a person and aim these thoughts with passion at that person, we're actually assaulting that person physically. Thus the need for a new sense of responsibility for how we employ our thoughts.

Furthermore, from Haanel's perspective, when you generate an ideal image in your mind and concertedly broadcast that ideal mental image outward, you are indeed impacting the outer world with your focused intent, and the outer world will respond predictably. This is a clear, demonstrated scientific model for how the manifestation process actively brings you what you purposefully intend to receive.

If you have been faithful to your ideal, you will hear the call when circumstances are ready to materialize your plans, and results will correspond in the exact ratio of your fidelity to your ideal. The ideal steadily held is what predetermines and attracts the necessary conditions for its fulfillment.

So each day, pause to generate and reinforce your ideal, and broadcast it outward. Nurture the inner feeling you desire, and the world around you will begin to respond, not just as a foggy fantasy of manifestation power, but as a scientifically proven process in which you attract to you what you truly desire.

AFFIRM YOUR INNER NEED

Let's finish this chapter by returning to the core affirmation that Haanel taught, because it will help you to focus on the inner attitudes and conditions that will then empower the outer environment that nurtures your inner reality. Here is the quote you read before; now you will understand its power more fully:

> The affirmation "I am whole, perfect, strong, powerful, loving, harmonious and happy" will bring about harmonious conditions. The reason for this is because the affirmation is in strict accordance with the Truth, and when Truth appears every form of error or discord must necessarily disappear.

If you regularly hold that basic affirmation in your mind, with those seven inner qualities that together generate the core positive feeling we call happiness, then you will actively step by step shift your focus of attention away from the negative, fear-based thoughts that pull you down to the positive, inspired thoughts that will attract everything you need in the outside world to resonate with your new inner experience.

Finally, here's Haanel's formula in a nutshell:

Earnest desire will bring about confident expectation, which in turn will be reinforced by firm demand. These three cannot fail to bring about attainment, because the earnest desire is the feeling, the confident expectation is the thought, and the firm demand is the will. Feeling gives vitality to thought and the will holds thought steadily until the law of Growth brings the vision into manifestation.

So be it.

YOUR DAILY MANIFESTATION PRACTICE

Now that we've reached the end of the formal training part of this book, my challenge to you is that each new day, at least once, you spend three minutes or more doing the seven-step manifestation process that you've learned from this discussion.

I also encourage you to return to earlier chapters at some

point and reread the explanation of each of the seven Focus Phrases, so that you begin to internalize the deeper aspects of each statement of intent. The Focus Phrases are portals that direct your attention toward vast realms of inner experience—and like I said before, each time you say one of them, you'll have a new experience.

If you have an amazing experience when saying a Focus Phrase, be sure *not* to try to repeat that experience the next time, because you never will. Time moves on, each moment is unique, and it's the newness of the experience that carries the insight and power and creativity you're seeking in this program.

Each day you will have particular needs and desires that are prominent in your mind. Most of these needs and desires will be of the temporary kind: financial, interpersonal, health-related, and so forth. It's fine to focus on temporary material or emotional needs and to use this manifestation process to move you in the direction of getting what you want. But hold in mind that temporary needs and hungers reflect a deeper yearning for a shift in the overall quality and focus of your life, so tap your deeper Source for insight, inspiration, and creative power.

Most people tend to focus on external things and situations they want to manifest in their lives. But as we've seen, it's the internal attitudes and feelings that really need attention and advancement. So when you do the daily manifestation practice, be sure to give time and attention to quieting negative thoughts and reactions, and to nurturing positive feelings and attitudes, because that's the change that transforms your life.

As a training adjunct that can make all the difference in truly succeeding with this program, we offer free online audio and video guidance through the manifestation process, so that you don't have to make overmuch effort to remember and move through the process. This multimedia support ensures that, wherever you are, you can pause and gain access to guidance and support, plus stay up to date on new developments in this program and the ever growing *Tapping the Source* community. Just pause and go online, any time of the day or night, to enjoy streaming audio and video guidance. You can also download the video files to your computer and put them into your mobile phone to play on the go while commuting or at work. You can also burn a DVD version of the guided manifestation videos to play on your home entertainment system.

We've made this free online support and reinforcement system as effortless as possible so that your focus can remain more on the new experiences that come to you each time you move through the process rather than on discipline and memorization issues.

And so, here's the core method. Be sure that you master and include the three-step breath-awareness process in item 2 so that throughout you remain aware of your breathing, which, as we've seen, is the "awareness medium" that guidance, insight, creativity, and manifestation function within:

1. *"I choose to focus enjoyably inward."*
2. *"My mind is quiet . . . I am now in the Silence."*
3. *"I am open to receive guidance from my Source."*
4. *"I know what I want."*
5. *"I feel connected with creative power."*
6. *"My vision is right now perfect and complete."*
7. *"Each new moment is manifesting my dream."*

CHAPTER 14

DISCOVER THE SECRET
OF GIVING

Experts in science, economics, and ethics all agree—
no one operates as an isolated entity in this world.
Regardless of our needs, we satisfy them as we
interact with other people. And the spiritual adage of the
ages remains as relevant now as it was in the past: In order
to receive, we must also give.

Haanel was vehement about the inclusion of active and
eager giving at the heart of the manifestation process. Here's
how he states this:

> We make money by making friends, and we enlarge our
> circle of friends by making money for them, by helping
> them, by being of service to them. The first law of success
> is service.

Often in the pursuit of selfish acquisitions and triumphs,
people lose touch with the underlying reality that in order to
receive, we must serve. Every job on this planet is one of

service, from the president, executive, and general on down to the ditch digger, dishwasher, and janitor. We all get up in the morning and do something that benefits other people and receive income or other things in exchange for our service.

Haanel points out in the quote that friendship is the core positive ingredient in our financial endeavors. Superficially competition might seem to be the order of the day in business. But in reality, most of us spend most of our time at work engaged in cooperative relationships. We might compete with another company, but we cooperate inside our company for the common good and shared success. And ultimately our entire world economy is one large organism that survives and thrives through cooperation and friendship, not through negative attitudes and hostility.

Perhaps I can best summarize Haanel in this manner: harmony, friendship, love, and happiness are the key ingredients in anyone's success. We make money (or any other article of exchange) by helping our friends make money, by serving them.

> You can make a money magnet of yourself, but to do so you must first consider how you can make money for other people. Your greatest success will come as you are enabled to assist others. What benefits one must benefit all.

What truly makes you feel good? Unless your heart is seriously contracted, you'll probably admit that you feel good in your heart when you're helping someone. Greedy grabbing from other people just doesn't feel as good as friendly giving, does it? Of course you need to receive. But if you consider the act of receiving, you'll realize that someone else is giving what you need to you—that's key!

And of course the logic under the surface observation of giving and receiving is that we're continually giving and continually receiving, but very often, if we don't give first, and give willingly and happily, the flow through which we receive gets stifled and cut off, and we experience shortage and failure.

A generous thought is filled with strength and vitality. A selfish thought contains the germs of dissolution; it will disintegrate and pass away. Our greatest success will come as we recognize that it is just as essential to give as to get.

With this quote we're again back to the notion that giving isn't just a physical outer act. Giving springs from generous thoughts, and generous thoughts, being imbued with love and harmony, give us strength and vitality. Thus if we focus on giving with a generous thought behind the act of giving, we create the positive inner attitude that is essential to manifesting what we ourselves want to receive.

So as you do your daily manifestation process, please include in your focus not just what you want to receive, but also what you have and want to give. If what you're truly seeking deep down is a brighter, happier feeling inside your own heart, hold in mind that your vision will need to include not just the things and experiences you want, but also what you are going to give in exchange for what you receive.

You will get only what you will give; those who try to get without giving always find the Law of Compensation relentlessly bringing about an exact equilibrium.

AVOIDING EXTREMES

I've noticed that all too often people swing from the extreme of grabbing all they can to trying to kill off their personal quest for what they need themselves and focusing entirely on trying to be giving. The truth is that there must be a harmonious balance between giving and receiving. They can't really be separated, or the vitality of human exchange is lost.

> Self-denial is not success. We cannot give unless we get; we cannot be helpful unless we are strong. If we wish to be of service to others we must have power—but to get it we must give it; we must be of service.

The basic laws of science clearly state that nothing is lost nor gained in the universe. Rather, there is a constant flow of particles and energy circulating, but not ultimately becoming less nor greater. For an economic system to work, money must flow through all hands. Money is powerful when in circulation, which means when it is being given and received over and over.

It's the same in a successful relationship. Both parties in the relationship must regularly give their love and attention, and both parties must be open to regularly receive. The vitality of relationship depends directly upon the flow happening between two people.

So observe carefully over the next weeks and months, when you pause to move through the manifestation process, whether you are generating visions and intent and imaginations that are purely selfish, or if you're building into your ideal vision the constant act of sharing, of helping and serving those around you. Take time to contemplate your current attitudes about giving and serving, and in the act of contemplation, while plugged into your higher self, you'll begin to wake up to your full potential for generosity.

Again, let's look at what Haanel says:

> A generous thought is filled with strength and vitality. A selfish thought contains the germs of dissolution; it will disintegrate and pass away.

Rather than fixating upon just yourself in your vision, begin to expand your vision to include other people. To succeed with your plans, include others. Your plan requires participation with other people to succeed. So consciously begin to expand your vision bubble to include what you are going to give to other people in exchange for what you're going to receive.

Generous thoughts can exist only in the mind of a person who feels that there is plenty for all. You must perceive yourself as someone who has enough so you can give some away—so that in the act of giving, you stimulate the inward flow of what you want.

At the heart of all this is the notion that the Law of Attraction functions within the higher power of love. When you are feeling selfish and greedy, there is no love in your heart at that moment. In this state of mind you are sabotaging your own success, because you will have no power to attract what you need. This might sound simplistic, but in reality it is a profound insight that Haanel is laying out for us to reflect and act upon.

> We will get exactly what we give, but we shall have to give it first. It will then return to us manyfold.

Many times Haanel states that we must first give in order to receive. This is important. So many people plunge into doing a manifestation method fixated only on their need to get something. Their passion seems to focus only on the need to change their lives in directions they think will satisfy them. But they directly violate core principles of manifestation right at the start, and so fail in their efforts.

Often when people start to realize they must give in order to receive, they give without generosity or love, and of course they don't end up getting what they want. Furthermore, people tend to think that all they have to give are things, but the reality is that what they really have to give are positive, loving thoughts that in turn generate positive feelings in the other person.

There are a great many gifts we can give to other people, just by radiating our positive presence outward in their direction. As we saw in the last chapter, our thoughts do radiate outward and impact other people's inner lives, as well as the physical world.

With this scientific proof in mind regarding what you have to "give to the world," you can begin to circulate positive thoughts and feelings as a primary "thing you give" in exchange for what you receive. As usual, Haanel says it best:

> Giving is a mental process, because thoughts are causes and conditions are effects. Therefore in giving thoughts of courage, inspiration, health, or help of any kind you are setting positive causes in motion which will in turn bring about their positive effect.

Each moment of your day, as thoughts run through your mind, you're impacting the world. If you want to manifest your vision, you must begin to be more aware of all those thoughts that you're broadcasting, otherwise you're directly thwarting your success.

Please take time over the next weeks to reflect upon this primal aspect of success in life. Every moment, as thoughts move through your mind, you are determining your fate. And you do have the power to quiet negative thoughts when you get caught up in them.

Remember earlier chapters in which we talked about quieting the mind. All you need to do when you're caught up in negative thoughts is to turn your attention to the air flowing in and out of your nose, and expand your awareness to include the movements in your chest and belly as you breathe, and all thoughts will temporarily stop.

Once you've quieted your thoughts, it's time to go ahead and tune into your inner voice, tap your higher passion and vision, and then bring that vision in through your solar plexus and up into your mind. Lo and behold, you'll find yourself with brighter thoughts springing to mind, thoughts that carry positive feelings and intent that will positively impact those around you.

> The quality of the thought which you entertain determines the quality of the thought which you radiate, which consequently will determine the nature of the experience which will result.

It's not just the thought itself; it's the quality of that thought that matters. And by quality Haanel means the emotional charge accompanying the thought. Almost all thoughts pack an emotional charge, which stimulates glandular and muscular experiences throughout your body. And it's that whole-body charge that radiates out and impacts the world.

So giving implies monitoring the quality of your thoughts and taking responsibility for quieting negative, fear-based thoughts and nurturing positive, love-focused thoughts. Your ego can't force or manipulate the feeling of generosity into your thoughts. But if you regularly pause and tap into your Source, you access infinite loving intelligence and power. That's what this is all about: receiving love from God and giving it to the world.

CHAPTER 15

ACHIEVE ENDURING ABUNDANCE

The opposite of abundance is scarcity, which is a dreaded word that makes people feel immediately anxious and stressed. When there isn't enough to go around, naturally we panic. And, truth be told, most people seem to chase after abundance because deep down they're afraid of and running away from scarcity, because, when taken to the extreme, scarcity ends up in starvation and death—the ultimate fear.

When we let fear be what drives us, we tend to generate fairly miserable lives because, as we've seen in this book, we tend to manifest what we focus on. If we're focusing on worries and negative images of the future, we're going to create situations that reflect our negative focus.

So the first step toward creating enduring abundance in our lives is to consciously examine any existing fear-based attitudes and images that we might be holding chronically in our minds, and then go into action to shift our focus from fearful to hopeful images and actions.

Haanel had much to say about fear and how fearful thoughts and images erode our capacity to mobilize the powers of positive manifestation that lead to abundance. For instance, reflect a moment on this quote:

> The one archenemy which must be absolutely destroyed is fear. Fear hides the sun and causes a perpetual gloom; it must be eliminated; it must be expelled. When fear is eliminated, your light will shine, the clouds will disperse, and you will have found the source of power, energy, and life.

Of course, fear is so dominant in most people's minds and lives that it seems like wishful thinking to talk about eliminating and expelling fear. How on earth could we achieve this massive psychological transformation? This question has been a primary quest in my own work as a psychologist, and I am pleased to say that within the world-view that Haanel offers, there is the power and guidance required to put aside fear-based thoughts in exchange for positive, hopeful thoughts.

The only solution to feeling chronically anxious, from both a spiritual and a cognitive therapy perspective, is to choose not to focus on images that generate the fear response. Instead, we do have the power to hold our focus on positive thoughts and images. This does not mean that we hide our heads in the sand and go into denial of the dangers life inevitably throws our way. It simply means that we focus on positive solutions to the danger rather than fixating on horrid worst-case scenarios. Haanel describes this cognitive-shifting dynamic in the following words:

> Physically, two things cannot exist in the same place at the same time. The same is true in the mental and emotional world. Therefore the remedy to feeling timid, vacillating, anxious, and harassed by negative thoughts is to substitute thoughts of courage, power, self-reliance, and confidence for those of fear, lack, and limitation.

This might sound simplistic, but Haanel's hundred-year-old logic is exactly the same logic that cognitive psychologists have recently developed and acted on. We do have the power to focus on what we want to in our own minds. If we learn to employ that power, we can put aside the negative thoughts and images that generate an emotional fear response. We can "substitute thoughts of courage, power, self-reliance, and confidence for those of fear, lack, and limitation."

> When you realize that you are one with the Infinite Power, and that you can consciously overcome any adverse condition by the power of your thought, you will have nothing to fear; fear will be destroyed and you will come into possession of your birthright.

Again notice that realization is always key in Haanel's formula for improving your life. And this realization is not an intellectual process in his understanding—it's a deeper spiritual process that comes to you when you pause, quiet your mind, and enter into the Silence.

Haanel suggests developing particular affirmations, or Focus Phrases as we're calling them here, that will accurately point your mind's deeper attention toward a specific intent you want to activate, in this case the intent of shifting your attention away from tense, fear-based thoughts toward peaceful, harmonious, positive thoughts. In my therapy practice I often teach the following Focus Phrase for this situation:

"I put aside all my worried thoughts,
and feel confident and peaceful."

As mentioned before, when you create Focus Phrases for a specific intent, make sure you put into words exactly the action you want to accomplish in your mind. This is what successful mind management is all about. Here's how Haanel talks about this process:

The way to fight darkness is with light; the way to fight cold is with heat; the way to overcome evil is with good. To achieve what you require, make use of the appropriate affirmation. Take it into the Silence with you, until it sinks into your subconscious.

If every time you think about abundance you feel anxiety about not having enough, then you'll want to seriously delve into the power of this specific application of the manifestation process I've been teaching you. Most people are chronically caught up in worried thoughts and fear-based images of the future—don't feel you're alone in this. Just choose right now to begin actively refocusing your attention away from anxious thoughts.

> If you wish to eliminate fear, concentrate on courage. If you wish to eliminate lack, concentrate on abundance. If you wish to eliminate disease, concentrate on health.

INNER AFFLUENCE

Notice what happens in your mind reflexively when you think about affluence and how your life would change if you became truly affluent, if you had more than enough to sustain long-term happiness and confidence. Does your mind immediately imagine a big house, plenty of money in the bank and stocks in your name, protection from any and all dangers that might threaten you physically, and so on and so forth?

I suspect you know by now that building up outer wealth is no guarantee of long-term affluence, because there are many variables in life beyond material goods that determine whether you're truly affluent. I don't mean to preach an obvious observation. But so often we tend to overlook the obvious in our pursuit of a better life.

Especially in America we have been sold on the false assumption that money can buy us pretty much everything we need. But of course it can't, so when you enter into your daily meditation to activate the Law of Attraction and bring to you what you need to be happy, it's wise to consciously hold in mind what you truly yearn for in life.

We've seen that our outer world tends to end up looking pretty much like our inner world, especially emotionally. If we're caught up in hostile, fearful, negative emotions day in and day out, we tend to attract those like emotions and breed more anxiety and disharmony. So perhaps the big change in our lives is not the usual material affluence, but something far more trustworthy and lasting: inner affluence.

Affluence within is found to be the secret of attraction for affluence without.

And what does "affluence within" really mean? It means holding thoughts and images and emotions and visions within our hearts and minds that plug us into the Infinite Fountain of affluence—that's where genuine well-being is found.

Our permanent well-being will be best conserved by a conscious cooperation with the continuous forward movement of the Great Whole.

I love Haanel's choice of words: "conscious cooperation with the continuous forward movement of the Great Whole." The whole world is unfolding according to a long-term natural plan.

The ancient Chinese called this the Tao, or the Way, or the Flow. By whatever name, there is a natural unfolding taking place in the world, and you are a participant in this natural unfolding. If you focus on "conscious cooperation" with the forward movement of the Great Whole, you predictably will attain and conserve a quality of permanent well-being in your life.

From my understanding, the only way to consciously cooperate with the Universal Mind's unfolding is to regularly pause and focus inward to tap guidance from the Creator. That's why the establishment of a daily practice, as we're exploring in this book, seems to be the only logical path to walk if you want to walk the path of abundance.

BECOMING GENUINELY WEALTHY

Affluence means wealth. It means having plenty, so that you are not wanting. It means being plugged into the flow of goods and resources so that you're regularly refreshing your abundance even as you use it up. I know people living utterly simple material lives who seem radiant with well-being and happiness.

> Material wealth should never be desired as an end, but simply as a means of accomplishing an end. Success is contingent upon a higher ideal than the mere accumulation of riches, and he who aspires to such success must formulate an ideal for which he is willing to strive.

Let's once again make a list of what most humans need in order to feel a sense of well-being in all aspects of their lives. Each time you pause and move into meditation on manifesting what you yearn for, make sure you're covering all these bases.

Material Abundance

> Money is of no value except to bring about the conditions you desire. These conditions are necessarily harmonious.

It's no fun to run out of rent money or cash to go buy the groceries. Let's not fool ourselves; money counts! On the other hand, a lot of money brings a lot of responsibility; you must pay attention to your money or you lose it, and you can easily fall victim to worrying about your money rather than enjoying it. So keep this desire for cash and possessions in perspective with the other three equal needs.

Relationship Abundance

> Whatever you desire for yourself, affirm it for others, and it will help you both. You reap what you sow. If you send out thoughts of love and health, they return to you like bread cast upon the waters.

People who are friends to others find that they indeed have friends. Radiate love and happiness to those you encounter, and this love and happiness will be radiated back to you. True relationship abundance is both deep and wide. Ideally you have a deep resonance with family, and you and your intimate partner have broad goodwill toward those with whom you work, play, and interact on a daily basis. The Beatles had it right: All you need is love, and truly the love you give will come back to you many times over.

Health Abundance

Every cell in your body is intelligent and will respond to your direction. The cells are all creators and will create the exact pattern which you give them. Therefore, when perfect images are placed before the subjective, the creative energies will build a perfect body.

Everybody knows that, except for medical interventions, money can't buy back your health, and a great deal of health depends on nonmaterial variables such as the amount of stress in your life, the impact of negative thoughts and emotions on your health, and the underlying spiritual soundness of your beliefs and aspirations. Using the manifestation process to generate health abundance can be a vital aspect of this program. We'll talk more about this in the next chapter.

Spiritual Abundance

If you see only the incomplete, the imperfect, the relative, the limited, these conditions will manifest in your life; but if you train your mind to see and realize the spiritual ego, the "I" which is forever perfect, complete, and harmonious, then wholesome and healthful conditions will be manifested.

One of my main reasons in deciding to write this book and highlight the teachings of Charles Haanel is that he brought such a remarkable spiritual depth to the whole notion of manifesting one's dreams in life.

Highest happiness is attained through your understanding of and conscious cooperation with natural laws.

Haanel brought God and nature, Spirit and science, together. For him there was no separation of our individual consciousness and Universal Mind. Whereas so many later writers fixated on Haanel's Law of Attraction and affirmation process as a get-rich-quick trick, Haanel continually returned in his writings to the essential requirement of first becoming attuned to God's will, and then manifesting a personal vision in harmony and resonance with God's will.

In this spirit, I strongly encourage you to approach your daily manifestation process as an opportunity to regularly look inward directly to your Source, so that you can fill your heart with spiritual inspiration and guidance as you go into action to fulfill your individual needs and desires.

CONTINUALLY IN RELATIONSHIP

As we've seen, wealth and well-being can't really be separated from your interaction and cooperation with other people. Wealth is a flow, not an accumulation. And as Haanel points out repeatedly, generosity is the truly satisfying path to affluence, not indulgence in selfish greed.

Furthermore, love is the core passion that motivates the power of thought. As Haanel said:

> It is love which imparts vitality to thought and thus enables thought to germinate. The Law of Attraction is the Law of Love; they are one and the same.

How do the Law of Attraction and the manifestation process operate in finding and sustaining a deep love relationship? In earlier books such as *Finding Each Other, Sex and Spirit*, and *Let Love Find You*, I've written extensively on the psychological dynamics of using the principles and practices outlined in this present book to attract a perfect sexual mate and long-term life partner. The same principles apply to attracting a new business partner or even tennis partner. First you must move through the process that brings you into deep contact with your yearning and desire. You must ask for guidance and help in manifesting a person who meets your need. And then daily you must return your focus to that desire and intent, and broadcast your intent outward.

As we saw in the PEAR studies, you have the mental power to contact and impact people around you with your thoughts and feelings. There are lots of people in the world who are also looking for someone like you, people you naturally will be in harmony with when you come together. In *Finding Each Other* and *Let Love Find You* I told my own story of discovering a meditation that very clearly brought my wife and I together twenty-five years ago. It was like a true miracle, and the basic process I'm teaching you in this book is the process that brought us together.

Life is without question greater than we can even imagine. What Haanel encourages us to do is to cooperate with the infinite mystery in which our lives unfold. Wealth and well-being, pleasure and fulfillment are our birthright. If we let the power of love guide us in our manifestations, there is without question plenty for all.

Let's let Haanel end this chapter with his predictably clear and potent words:

> Thoughts of courage, power, confidence, and hope all produce a corresponding state. All we have to do is let our light shine; the more energy we can radiate, the more rapidly shall we be enabled to transmute undesirable conditions into sources of pleasure and profit.

CHAPTER 16

HEAL YOURSELF AT
CORE LEVELS

Health and wellness are issues for most of us, and material abundance can mean absolutely nothing when we're seriously sick. Therefore focusing on and manifesting long-term health must be a vital aspect of this program. How can you maximize wellness each and every day, and also regain your health if you lose it? This chapter is dedicated to exploring the answer to this question by showing how to modify the daily manifestation session into a regular wellness-amplification process.

We'll talk about what to do when facing a current health problem, how to help others in this regard, and how to regularly act to maintain your optimum health. We're also going to take a clear Haanelian look at how to manifest and move through the last phase of one's mortal presence in optimum spirit and health, while also surrendering to the inevitable full cycle of life on earth.

It's now well proven that the thoughts you chronically

hold in your mind generate parallel emotional and physio-logical conditions in your body that either support good health or undermine it. You've perhaps read or seen news reports on how stress, anxiety, depression, or anger, when continued over time, progressively reduce your immune system's ability to maintain optimum health.

Long before medical evidence was compiled regarding the influence of thoughts and emotions on physical health, Haanel identified the root cause of emotionally generated disease:

> When one's thought has been filled with envy, hatred, jealousy, criticism, or any of the other thousand and one forms of discord, certain vibrations have been set in motion that, if kept up, result in discord, in harmony and disease.

There are of course genetic and environmental factors also involved in disease, but the psychosomatic dimension is the factor that you can act upon and have immediate power to alter. Haanel stated his core wellness procedure thus:

> When your thought becomes uplifted, progressive, con-structive, courageous, noble, kind, or in any other way desirable, you set in motion vibrations which bring about mental, moral, and physical health.

So again we see that positive mind management is the key to emotion management, which is the long-term key to good health. When you are caught up too long in anxious or hostile thoughts about the future or perhaps guilt and grief about the past, you have the power to immediately redirect your attention away from negative, stress-generating memories, fantasies, and images and refocus in more positive present-moment directions, as we've seen already.

When you pause to move through a daily manifestation session, you are actively making this shift into a better emotional state, plus you can identify your desire for optimum health and then tap health-related insight and guidance from your Source so that your conscious mind can begin to visualize your ideal health condition.

Remember, however, that Haanel advises you to keep your ideal visualization within the realm of realistic scientific possibility. Many people make the manifestation mistake of imagining their bodies transformed into an unrealistic health state that violates all natural law. Haanel insists that the ideal image and condition resonate in harmony with your natural potential—otherwise you're violating the very Intelligence of the universe that will empower your movement toward optimum physical health.

The only real power which you can have is the power to adjust yourself to divine and unchangeable principles. You cannot change the Infinite, but you can come into an understanding of natural laws and adjust your thought faculties with the Universal Thought. Your ability to cooperate with this Omnipotence will indicate the degree of success with which you meet.

If you are seeking success in recovering from a disease, Haanel insists that you must adjust yourself to the principles within which the universe operates, which include biological principles. Because biological principles include a remarkable capacity for healing the body, you do have the power to "adjust your thought faculties" and cooperate with your natural healing power.

Within the Haanel vision, you carry the ability to make remarkable recovery from illness. But you must tap your passion for recovery and draw on the Universal Mind's deeper healing power steadily over time if you're going to activate your recovery potential. And you must construct a mental image of the perfect health you seek to regain:

> Construct mental images that are scientifically true. Subject every idea to analysis and accept nothing which is not scientifically valid. When you do this you will attempt nothing but what you know you can carry out, and success will crown your efforts.

CELLULAR INTELLIGENCE

As biochemistry affirms, right now there are billions of specialized cells in your body that have no great conscious overview of your body as a whole, yet they are functioning in perfect harmony and resonance and coordination with all the other cells in your body in order to keep you alive and healthy. This natural cellular intelligence and cooperation is one of the truly amazing phenomena of life in the universe.

Every cell in your body is intelligent and will respond to your direction. The cells are all creators and will create the exact pattern which you give them. Therefore, when perfect images are placed before the subjective, the creative energies will build a perfect body.

We've been exploring in this book how you can create an ideal image of whatever you want. Broadcast this desired image from your conscious mind down through your solar plexus, and plug your driving intent into the infinite unconscious Spiritual Intelligence that includes each cell in our body. Hold the ideal in your mind with passion and hope and love, and the healing process is maintained in motion.

Let's listen to Haanel's discussion on cellular intelligence and metaphysical healing:

All your cells are moving for a common purpose, and each one is not only a living organism but also has sufficient intelligence to enable it to perform its necessary duties. It is also endowed with sufficient intelligence to conserve energies and perpetuate its own life. This is the scientific explanation for metaphysical healing, and it will enable anyone to understand the principle upon which this remarkable phenomenon rests.

Again remember that Haanel does not expect you, nor advise you, to try to visualize the specific step-by-step healing process that your cells are going to move through to help you regain optimum health. Rather, he insists that you turn your focus with passion to the ideal image in your mind that you want to manifest as a physical reality in the outer material world.

> Your expectation determines everything. If you expect nothing, you shall have nothing; if you demand much, you shall receive the greater portion. The world is harsh only as you fail to assert yourself.

And how do you assert yourself? Through pausing for just a few minutes, many times a day, to move through the manifestation process and reaffirm your intent and your specific ideal image as your dominant thought activity in your conscious mind.

You want to believe utterly in your perfect inner reality and broadcast this perfection out to your cellular presence, so that beyond your conscious awareness the infinite unconscious power of the universe can be working to heal you. And if you are currently healthy, regularly tap into your desire to stay healthy and broadcast this desire and inner faith and harmony to your cellular level of being:

> Inner harmony is the foundation of health. The knowledge of your ability to consciously radiate health, strength, and harmony will bring you into a realization that there is nothing to fear, because you are in touch with Infinite Strength.

FEAR ITSELF

I've recently been working with hospices to bring the power of Focus Phrases to people in the last phase of life on this planet. From a therapist's perspective, the vast majority of our population is in serious denial about their own impending death. Rather than holding the full biological scope of birth, life, and death in mind as the complete progression of human experience, we tend to fight against rather than surrender to the natural path of life.

My professional observation is that trying to run away from one's own ultimate demise generates chronic anxiety. We know deep down that we're going to die, yet we try to fool ourselves into thinking we're going to live forever. In the process, we fail to develop a relationship with our own death and make death an enemy rather than our final friend who completes our human journey.

Hospice is a wonderful service because it offers people help in making peace with their own coming death, and helps to make the dying experience low on fear and high on acceptance and surrender. As long as a person is fighting death, this struggle keeps the soul in a very negative reactionary condition and the emotions thrashing around in the ultimate ego fear: that of the biologically grounded brain and personality ceasing to exist.

It is important for all of us, regardless of age or health, to learn to come to peace with the cycle of life and death. I hope you'll consider how the manifestation process can be used to help you come into touch with your infinite self through connecting with your Source regularly. This is of course what meditation is all about, and why meditation can ease fears of death so dramatically. When the ego regularly experiences communion with the Divine, it matures, lets go of its fantasy of eternality, and opens up to whatever comes beyond death.

The key is to be realistic in your intent. I don't mean to deny any religious belief about life after death, only to point out that we really don't know what's going to happen, so it's best to accept the biological truth that your body is going to cease to exist, whatever might happen at deeper spiritual levels. By preparing the ego (which is indeed a biochemical brain function of the body) for its ultimate demise, a great deal of core anxiety can be relieved, which in turn will improve your overall physical health dramatically.

You can begin to develop your ideal image of how you want to experience the last days of your life. You can manifest whatever kind of final-days experience you desire, as long as your desire and ideal image are in harmony with the laws of nature. Again, let's return to what Haanel says in this regard:

> Construct mental images that are scientifically true. Subject every idea to analysis and accept nothing which is not scientifically valid. When you do this you will attempt nothing but what you know you can carry out, and success will crown your efforts.

In sum, chronic fear-based thoughts and images erode your health. When analyzed carefully, it seems clear psychologically that the core fear that underlies all other fears is the fear of your own death, of your inevitable mortal demise. If you begin to nurture a realistic positive image of your own final days, you can defuse a great deal of your anxiety, which will directly boost your well-being. Please reflect upon this logic and use the manifestation process to regularly advance your positive relationship with your coming death. You can't avoid it, but you surely can make the process vastly more acceptable and spiritually valuable.

HELPING OTHERS HEAL

A great many people, especially those who are parents, tend to worry chronically about the health and well-being of other people. What's really going on here? Does it help to worry about someone else, or does it actively push them in the direction of the worry? Furthermore, can positive focusing on another person help them heal?

We saw with the PEAR studies that our thoughts and projected intent, when aimed at another person, definitely impact that person at material and thought levels. (I encourage you again to visit the site that explains this research if it's new to you, because this will help you with the scientific analysis that Haanel was just talking about: You can indeed include thought power as part of your ideal image and intent.)

If you worry about someone's health and well-being, you're broadcasting that negative, fear-based image out at that person, and from my understanding, it will actually push that person in the feared direction. So there is even responsibility to consider here: You are impacting the world with your negative thoughts. Once you realize this, you'll have the desire to stop doing this.

Instead, you can tap your passion to help someone you love to attain better help by moving through the manifestation process to where you're holding an ideal image of this person's healthy body in your mind and projecting this out to the universe to respond to. One of my colleagues, Larry Dossey, M.D., has written several books that offer a review of the scientific proof that prayer, when used in this basic formula, does provoke significant improvement in healing. But, curiously, it was found that the more specific your prayer, the less effective the prayer was. Just generally praying for a positive health condition was most effective, as Haanel would predict.

> If you desire to help someone, the correct method is not to think specifically of the person whom you wish to help; the intention to help them is entirely sufficient, as this puts you in mental touch with the person. Then drive out of your own mind any belief of lack, limitation, disease, danger, difficulty, or whatever the trouble might be. As soon as you have succeeded in doing this, the result will have been accomplished, and the person will be free.

What's essential in this process of helping someone heal is your preparation: pausing, quieting your mind, entering into the Silence, focusing on your passion to help the person heal, and then holding the ideal image of health for that person in your mind—regularly, over and over again.

In fact, as with other dimensions of manifestation, you

will learn to take your ideal image and passion with you after the session, so that all day long your mind is holding the ideal image and broadcasting this ideal outward.

But hold in mind that this broadcast happens only when you maintain a core focus of attention down in your breathing, in your solar plexus. That's where your passion that will empower your visualization is found. Breath is the vehicle that moves your vision into manifestation. Then, with every new breath, you will be radiating health toward your sick friend.

> Every time you breathe, you breathe life, love, and spirit.
> This "breath of life" is the essence of the "I am." It is pure
> "Being" or Universal Substance. Your conscious unity with
> it enables you to localize it, and thus exercise the powers
> of this creative energy.

WELLNESS AND HEALING FOCUS PHRASES

In addition to moving often through the manifestation process to aim healing power wherever needed, there are specific Focus Phrases that you can hold in mind all day to help you move in the direction of less fear of dying and more focus on wellness and healing.

For instance, if you find that you are indeed caught up in chronic worries or denial about your own coming demise, you can say to yourself often:

"I surrender to my own coming death."

If you are currently sick and want to boost your healing potential, you can say to yourself:

"I am becoming more healthy with each new breath."

If you know someone who needs to heal, you can say:

"I am sending healing energy to my friend."

And if you want to communicate to your own cells your intent and desire to remain optimally healthy, say often to yourself:

"I am manifesting perfect health."

And once again, as a brief refresher, here's the full daily manifestation process that you're currently learning by heart. Be sure to also use the online guidance for mastering this process.

1. "I choose to focus enjoyably inward."
2. "My mind is quiet . . . I am now in the Silence."
3. "I am open to receive guidance from my Source."
4. "I know what I want."
5. "I feel connected with creative power."
6. "My vision is right now perfect and complete."
7. "Each new moment is manifesting my dream."

CHAPTER 17

RADIATING SPIRITUAL INTENT

We've seen that becoming engaged in the act of
manifestation makes sense only when we currently possess an emotive charge, a yearning,
or a need that's under pressure inside us and that we long to
satisfy. Take away the need, the frustration with present circumstances, and the pressure for change, and human beings
tend to ease up and do nothing at all. We shift from doing
to being.

But, curiously, most of us seem to possess a lifelong longing to feel more connected with a higher spiritual presence,
which we often call God. Haanel refined our deistic terminology in the following way:

> People have generally used the word "God" to indicate
> this universal, creative principle, but the word "God" does
> not convey quite the right meaning. Most people under-
> stand this word to mean something outside of themselves
> while exactly the contrary is the fact. God is our very life.

The minute the Spirit leaves the body, we are as nothing. Therefore, Spirit is really all there is of us.

Haanel preferred to talk about Universal Mind, Infinite Creator, Creative Spirit, or the Divine, rather than using the traditional religious term "God." But by whatever name, as we've seen, the foundation of Haanel's entire manifestation process is based not only on the existence of an Infinite Creator who continues to actively permeate the universe, but also upon our communing directly with this Creator on a regular basis.

Writing a hundred years ago, Haanel was infected with the radical new writings and theories and worldviews of scientists such as Albert Einstein. He also seems to have been familiar with early English translations of ancient Eastern texts such as the *Tao Te Ching* and the *I Ching*. In later years he wrote in-depth books on yoga and Hindu meditation. So it was natural for him to use terms and philosophical concepts that reflected a break away from traditional Christian understandings and a tight integration of meditative and scientific notions of reality.

The Universal Mind is the totality of all mind which is in existence. Spirit is Mind, because spirit is intelligent. The words are, therefore, synonymous.

Haanel placed individual consciousness on a par with Universal Mind. He experienced his own personal consciousness as a unified extension of the Creative Consciousness that manifested the universe itself, and therefore he saw human beings as tiny expressions of God, capable of actually demanding manifestation power from the Creator and receiving what they demanded. This reflects the Taoist and Hindu view of our relationship with the Creator quite closely.

> Mind is not individual. It is omnipresent. It exists everywhere. In other words, there is no place where it is not. It is, therefore, Universal.

What Haanel offers us is a pragmatic process for regularly accessing the Universal Mind and bringing its infinite creative power directly into our own minds, from where individual and universal operate in resonance to manifest the new.

We saw before that Haanel speaks often in words similar to those of Jesus when he gave the ultimately powerful challenge: "Be ye therefore perfect, even as your Father in Heaven is perfect." This perfect state of spiritual being is available to human beings upon request, and it's that perfect state that we are encouraged to focus on and envision in any part of our life that we want to improve.

> If you see only the incomplete, the imperfect, the relative, the limited, these conditions will manifest in your life; but if you train your mind to see and realize the spiritual ego, the "I" which is forever perfect, complete, and

harmonious, then wholesome and healthful conditions will be manifested.

In my understanding of Haanel's teachings, you cannot tap into the manifestation powers that he's describing as your birthright unless and until you discipline your mind to temporarily stop focusing outward and focus inward toward the very center of your spiritual being. This is the meditative process through which you come into the presence of the Infinite Divine and through which your mind merges with the Universal Mind so that you are one and the same at that moment.

The method for removing the cause of problems is to go into the Silence, and know the Truth. And because all mind is one mind, you can do this for yourself or anyone else. If you have learned to form mental images of the conditions desired, this will be the easiest and quickest way to secure results.

Again we have a parallel quote to one that Jesus is said to have spoken: "Know the Truth, and the Truth will set you free." The key term here is "know." As in Eastern traditions and science itself, just believing in something doesn't get the job done. What is required is actual experience, in which we move beyond believing to knowing that something is true.

That's what Haanel challenges you to do each time you pause and move through the manifestation process: to "go into the Silence, and know the Truth." And it is in this communion with the Universal Mind that you come to know if your passion or desire is truly what you need deep down:

> No matter what the difficulty is, no matter where it is, no matter who is affected, you have nothing to do but to convince yourself of the truth which you desire to see manifested.

I can't overemphasize the fact that the foundation of this manifestation program lies in regularly moving into the Silence and communing with Truth, with the wisdom of the Greater Intelligence. And again let me state clearly that you cannot enter into the Silence unless and until you practice sufficiently so you can quiet your usual mental chatter. This is accomplished through focusing on two or more breathing sensations at the same time.

COOPERATING WITH NATURAL LAWS

What happens when you quiet your mind, assume an inner meditative pose, and enter into the Silence? This is the most spiritual question one can ask, and of course words will not be able to grasp an experience that lies beyond words. But it is fair to say that when you quiet your individual mind and shift into receive mode, you will be able to directly experience insights that let you know the Truth. In the Silence, God can speak to you. You merge with the God-head and thus know what God knows. This might sound like nonconformity from a theological perspective, but it's the mystic experience that lies as the foundation to all theology.

Haanel perceived the universe and its natural laws as the material expression of an infinite creation that we participate in when we merge our biological awareness with spiritual consciousness. Natural laws run the universe at both material and nonmaterial levels. And our lives must resonate in accordance with these natural laws if we're to express and also to advance God's creation through our personal lives.

> Your highest happiness will be best attained through your understanding of and conscious cooperation with natural laws.

At the heart of Haanel's spiritual vision, there is both the core process of surrendering to God's natural laws and the process of coming into full conscious possession of your own vast powers.

As mentioned earlier, Haanel puts forth a fairly startling and from my experience entirely correct vision when he insists that the conscious individual mind is connected with the Universal Mind through our emotions and the unconscious dimensions of our personal consciousness.

> It is through the subconscious that we are connected with the Universal Mind and brought into relation with the infinite constructive forces of the universe. It is the coordination of these two centers of our being which is the

great secret of life. With this knowledge we can bring the objective and subjective minds into conscious cooperation and thus coordinate the finite and the infinite.

And once again, I quietly state the obvious: Only when you regularly move into the Silence do you gain the infinite spiritual perspective that enables you to successfully coordinate individual and universal in your own inner experience.

When you regularly turn inward and recharge your individual spiritual batteries by plugging into the Infinite Energy Supply, you not only empower and enlighten your own life, you also broadcast this spiritual radiance outward into the world around you, touching every heart.

YOUR DAILY PRACTICE

And so we come to the essential question of this book. I've shared with you a process through which you can manifest anything in your life that resonates with your deeper needs. You now know the basic theory as well as practice for this process. The book is coming to an end quite soon. When you close this book, are you going to discipline your mind's focus of attention to where you regularly take perhaps five or ten minutes a day to activate your higher creative potential and incorporate a daily manifestation program in your routine?

I am giving you cognitive tools that you can use to improve your life. Watch yourself the next few weeks, and be conscious of what you do or do not do. From that self-observation will come all you need to choose your course of action or inaction.

The manifestation process can be moved through in just a few minutes. You can do a short version of the process several times a day, which is highly recommended. You can also devote perhaps fifteen to twenty minutes or more once a day to move through a more in-depth manifestation meditation. This in-depth meditation can become your core spiritual practice if you find that you are longing for this depth of communion with the Divine.

REINFORCEMENT AND SUPPORT

This book comes with its own support website (www.tap pingdaily.com), where you can receive free audio and video guidance through the core daily manifestation process. Letting me guide you through the process via media inputs is not cheating in terms of discipline; it's a valuable extension of this written guidance you have in hand, in a format that has been found ideal for training a new cognitive process. By not only reading but hearing the guidance, you can let go of self-discipline and shift into total experiential mode. This has proven of great value.

You will reach a point after a few weeks of working with this book and the online training programs where suddenly you realize you've internalized the seven-step manifestation process. That's what we're aiming for in the training.

Because each moment is new by definition, you'll always have a new experience each time you go through the process. The process is a portal leading you into infinite experience. Move through the portal into ever-expanding experience.

1. *"I choose to focus enjoyably inward."*
2. *"My mind is quiet . . . I am now in the Silence."*
3. *"I am open to receive guidance from my Source."*
4. *"I know what I want."*
5. *"I feel connected with creative power."*
6. *"My vision is right now perfect and complete."*
7. *"Each new moment is manifesting my dream."*

Part Four

PRACTICE MAKES PERFECT

CHAPTER 18

FINAL WORDS FROM
CHARLES HAANEL

We never reach a point in our lives where we don't need to continue manifesting the world we need in each new moment. It's an ongoing daily process. Even if you reach the point spiritually where you have few material desires or emotional yearnings and feel satisfied deep down, you'll still want to return to the Silence for insight and wisdom, as well as the power to broadcast positive healing vibes out into the world as your ongoing gift and contribution. So, one more time: Be sure to make the process of tapping into your manifestation Source a new essential habit in your daily routine.

I've now come to the end of what I want to say in this book, and I feel the desire to end this discussion by offering you a final immersion in pure Haanel wisdom. I might mention that I have taken the editorial liberty throughout this book of slightly modifying Haanel's quotes so that they read smoothly, are in the same tense as the manuscript, and communicate just one thought per paragraph. I initially went through the entire document and selected what seemed to be the best 20 percent of his writings for this book. Then I did minimal line editing so that the quotes read easily without any outdated terminology. In this way, I translated his hundred-year-old quotes into our current wording and punctuation.

And now, in the same spirit that I've been offering psychological and spiritual commentary upon Haanel's seminal paragraphs throughout this book, it's now your turn to read what we consider some core direct quotes from Haanel and experience your own insights and reflections. Some of the following quotes are ones you've already read that beg further reflection; others will be new to you.

First, be sure to take a minute or so to pause and enter into the Silence. Then, as you stay tuned into your breath experience (which connects you with deeper insight), read a quote and be open to whatever inner flashes of realization emerge effortlessly from your Source after reading that quote. Listen to your own inner voice, and enjoy!

If you wish to express abundance in your life, you can afford to think abundance only, and as words are thoughts taking form, you must be especially careful to use nothing but constructive and harmonious language, which, when finally crystallized into objective forms, will prove to your advantage.

Whatever you desire for yourself, affirm it for others, and it will help you both. You reap what you sow. If you send out thoughts of love and health, they return to you like bread cast upon the waters.

Always concentrate on the ideal as an already existing fact; this is the germ cell, the life principle which goes forth and sets in motion those causes which guide, direct, and bring about the necessary relation, which eventually manifest in form.

Thought constantly, eternally is taking form, is forever seeking expression. If your thought is weak, critical, destructive, and negative generally, it will manifest in your body as fear, worry, and nervousness; in your finances as lack and limitation; and in discordant conditions in your environment. If your thought is powerful, constructive, and positive, this will be plainly evident in the state of your health, your business, and your environment.

Concentrate only upon the things you desire. Thought is creative. When you meet with success, gain, or any other desirable condition, you will naturally concentrate upon the effects of these things and thereby create more, which leads to even more.

Abundance will not come to you out of the sky; neither will it drop into your lap. You must focus on the Law of Attraction and the intention to bring this law into operation.

The affirmation "I am whole, perfect, strong, powerful, loving, harmonious, and happy" will bring about harmonious conditions. The reason for this is because the affirmation is in strict accordance with the Truth, and when Truth appears every form of error or discord must necessarily disappear.

Successful people hold in their minds the ideal of the condition they wish to realize. They constantly bring to mind the next step necessary to manifest their ideal. Thoughts are the materials with which they build, and the imagination is their mental workshop.

Imagination is the matrix in which all great things are fashioned. An ideal steadily held is what predetermines and attracts the necessary conditions for its fulfillment. Mind is the ever-moving force with which you secure the persons and circumstance necessary to build your success structure.

Through a powerful statement of intent, hold in mind the condition desired; affirm it as an already existing fact. This indicates the value of a powerful affirmation. By constant repetition it becomes a part of you. You are actually changing yourself; you are making yourself what you want to be.

Make a mental image of physical perfection; hold it in the mind until it is absorbed by your consciousness. If the desire is one which requires determination, ability, talent, courage, power, or any other spiritual power, these are necessary essentials for your picture. Build them in. They are the vital part of the picture; they are the feeling which combines with thought and creates the irresistible magnetic power which draws the things you require to you.

When the conscious mind is certain that a thought is true, that thought is sent to the subjective mind to be made into flesh, to be brought forth into the world as reality. Impress on the universal subjective mind the particular thing which you desire as an already existing fact. Believe that your desire has already been fulfilled; its accomplishment will then follow.

If you wish harmonious conditions in your life, you must develop a harmonious mental attitude. And in order to possess vitality your inner thought must be impregnated with love. Love is a product of the emotions; therefore, let your emotions be controlled and guided by intellect and reason.

The first form which thought will find is language, or words. This determines the importance of words; they are the first manifestation of thought. Thought may lead to action of any kind, but whatever the action, it is simply the thought attempting to express itself in visible form.

Insight enables you to plan properly and to turn your thought and attention in the right direction, instead of into channels which will yield no possible return.

The most commonly accepted definition of wealth is that it consists of all useful and agreeable things which possess exchange value. It is this exchange value which is the predominant characteristic of wealth.

The power to create depends entirely upon spiritual power. Therefore the successful businessperson is more often than not an idealist ever-striving for higher and higher standards.

You have the power to form your own mental images, regardless of the thoughts of others, regardless of exterior conditions and environments. By exercising this mental power and freedom you can control your own destiny, body, mind, and soul.

In the last analysis, thinking is the one great cause in life. To control thought is to control circumstances, conditions, environment, and destiny.

If you desire to visualize and manifest a different environment, the process is to hold your ideal in mind until your vision has been made real. Give no thought to persons, places, or things; these have no place in the absolute. The environment you desire will contain everything necessary; the right persons and the right things will come at the right time and in the right place.

What you visualize already exists in the spiritual world; this visualization is a substantial token of what will one day appear in the objective world, if you remain actively faithful to your ideal.

Imaginative visualization forms impressions on the mind, and these impressions in turn form concepts and ideals.

They in turn are the plans from which your vision turns into material form.

There is but one sense, the sense of feeling. All other senses are modifications of this one sense. Feeling is the foun-tainhead of power. This is why you must put feeling into your thought if you wish results. Thought and feeling are the irresistible combination.

Construct mental images that are scientifically true. Sub-ject every idea to analysis and accept nothing which is not scientifically valid. When you do this you will attempt nothing but what you know you can carry out, and success will crown your efforts.

If you desire material possessions of any kind, your chief concern should be to acquire the mental attitude which will lead to the result desired. This mental attitude is generated by a realization of your spiritual nature, and your unity with the Universal Mind which is the substance of all things.

Become so interested in thinking about what you desire, so engrossed in your subject that you are conscious of nothing else. Such concentration leads to intuitive percep-tion and immediate insight into the nature of the object concentrated upon.

Concentration does not mean mere thinking of thoughts, but the transmutation of these thoughts into practical values. Fundamentally the subconscious is omnipotent; there is no limit to the things that can be done when it is given the power to act.

Your degree of success is determined by the nature of your desire. If the nature of your desire is in harmony with natural law or the Universal Mind, it will gradually emancipate the mind and give you invincible courage.

You will get only what you give; those who try to get without giving always find the Law of Compensation relentlessly bringing about an exact equilibrium.

Cultures are continually making progress in the methods which they use to come into communication with the Universal Mind and its infinite possibilities.

Begin by paying attention. Before long you will have aroused interest. This interest will attract more attention, and this attention will produce more interest, and so on. This practice will enable you to cultivate the power of attention.

You must "be" before you can "do," and you can "do" only to the extent to which you "are," and so what you do will necessarily coincide with what you "are"—and what you are depends upon what you "think."

Large ideas have a tendency to eliminate all smaller ideas so that it is well to hold ideas large enough to counteract and destroy all small or undesirable tendencies. This is one of the secrets of success: Think big thoughts. The creative energies of mind find no more difficulty in handling large situations than small ones.

If you wish a change in conditions, all that's necessary is changing your thought; this will in turn change your mental attitude, which will in turn change your personality, which will in turn change the persons, things, conditions, and experiences that you meet in life.

And once again, here are your Focus Phrases:

1. *"I choose to focus enjoyably inward."*
2. *"My mind is quiet . . . I am now in the Silence."*
3. *"I am open to receive guidance from my Source."*
4. *"I know what I want."*
5. *"I feel connected with creative power."*
6. *"My vision is right now perfect and complete."*
7. *"Each new moment is manifesting my dream."*

AFTERWORD

So here you are. You've come to the end of this amazing book. I consider this an amazing book because it is so simple and yet so profound. True happiness is about so much more than material abundance. In working with and speaking to hundreds of thousands of people throughout my life, I know that what has given me most joy is not the acclaim and material comforts I have generated for myself and my family, but the inspiration and sense of hope and purpose that I have given to others. It has been a true blessing to be able to help lift others up, and I feel honored to have been asked to write the afterword for *Tapping the Source*, for it too is a work that is dedicated to helping others and sharing the practical secrets of how to make this a better world.

Many books contain uplifting stories and good practical advice. What is so special about *Tapping the Source* is that you now have an easy-to-follow series of Focus Phrases that you can use five to ten minutes a day for the rest of your life. Think of it as stretches you would do before doing physical activity to be sure that your body is ready for action. These are mental stretches, if you will, that will ensure that you stay focused on what matters and not allow the distractions of the outer world to bruise or injure your mental and emotional body. Haanel was one of the first great Western thinkers to clearly see that your emotional and mental body was as important as your physical body. *Tapping the Source* has taken this wisdom to the next level. Use this book daily. Share it with friends.

Two of my favorite quotes from Charles Haanel's *Master Key System* are "Concentrate only upon the things you desire" and "You reap what you sow. Send out thoughts of love." The focus phrases in *Tapping the Source* will allow you to increase your ability to concentrate upon the things you desire and send out thoughts of love. I guarantee you that you will start to see a difference in your life just from doing these simple mental stretches five minutes a day. And when you do, you will be amazed by what you create for yourself and those you love.

With my fondest wishes
for your success and happiness,
Jack Canfield

ACKNOWLEDGMENTS

John Selby would like to acknowledge his wife and film partner, Birgitta Steiner, for her spiritual inspiration, creative insight, and ongoing support while writing this book and producing the related Manifesting Your Core Desires video training programs.

William Gladstone and Richard Greninger would like to acknowledge their families, including Gayle Newhouse and Carol Ryckoff, who have supported them throughout the writing of this book. Thanks also to Sterling editor Kate Zimmermann and editorial director Michael Fragnito, as well as Marcus Leaver, president of Sterling Publishing.

In addition the authors would like to acknowledge personal communications from the following authors, friends, and associates, all of whose communications have enhanced both the book and the accompanying feature film *Tapping the Source*:

Patricia Aburdene, Marc Allen, Dennis Andres, Aunty Angeline, José Argüelles, Bani Ashtiani, Janet Attwood,

Collette Baron-Reid, Marty Birrittella, Rinaldo Brutoco, Connie Buffalo, Jack Canfield, Sam and Kate Cawthorn, Deepak Chopra, Richard Cohen, Michelle Cohen, DC Cordova, Barbara De Angelis, Chip Duncan, Hale Dwoskin, Crystal Dwyer, Jesse Dylan, Ehekateotl, Kamran Elahian, Arielle Ford, Linda Francis, Michael Gosney, Martin Gray, Jean Houston, Alexis Kaplan, Constance Kellough, Linda Kennedy, Harrison Klein, Sharmen Lane, Loral Langemeier, Ervin Laszlo, Barbara Marx Hubbard, Fred Matser, Sarah McLean, Drunvalo Melchizedek, Andrea Metcalf, Kristen Moeller, Sue Morter, Peggy O'Neill, Grandma Aggie Pilgrim, Debra Poneman, Sri Sri Ravi Shankar, Greg Reid, Gary Renard, Sonia Ricotti, Lucinda Ruh, Masami Saionji, Gerard Senehi, Marci Shimoff, Mark Sisson, Marilyn Tam, Eckhart Tolle, Alexis Traynor-Kaplan, Mark Victor Hansen, Victor Villasenor, Neale Donald Walsch, Marcia Wieder, John Woods, Gary Zukav

ADDITIONAL RESOURCES AND ONLINE PROGRAMS

ONLINE TRAINING, INSPIRATION, AND REINFORCEMENT

Most people tend to finish a book . . . and then forget to do the exercises even if they value them. For enjoyable effortless help in developing a long-term manifestation practice, please go to our TappingDaily.com website regularly. Enjoy our ever-expanding audio and video guidance and inspiration, plus chat rooms and forums where you can share with each other your experience with this program, while also accessing new short videos and written insights by the authors. From daily Haanel quotes to online seminars and special Source events, this TappingDaily.com site is your home for mastering the Daily Manifestation Process and participating in our *Tapping the Source* community. We will also be posting information about events on www.tap pingthesourcebook.com, so visit both sites.

ADVANCED COACHING AND DVD PROGRAMS

Also at TappingDaily.com you can learn about one-on-one coaching to help you manifest your specific dreams, as well as additional inspirational and training video programs available as DVDs, cell phone reminders, and computer downloads.

LIVE SEMINARS AND CONFERENCES

The authors offer special regional *Tapping the Source* seminars and conferences, which will be posted and described on www.TappingDaily.com. Tune in regularly to find out when there's a *Tapping the Source* event near you!

www.TappingDaily.com
and
www.tappingthesourcebook.com

READING GROUP QUESTIONS

This book is ideal for small groups to read and discuss in depth. The final pages of this book include a helpful guide for stimulating group exploration of this book's themes and manifestation methods. Here are twenty-four focus questions to reflect upon after reading this book:

1. A basic premise of the book is that there exists a Creator of the universe who permeates everyday consciousness and whose power and guidance can be "tapped into" at will by any of us. Do you agree with this?

2. The book's manifestation technique is based on the merger of psychological and spiritual understandings of human consciousness, where our personal bubble of awareness is able to connect with Universal Mind through entering the Silence and receiving insight and empowerment via the unconscious mind. How do you feel about this possibility?

3. Charles Haanel prefers not to talk about God, but rather to use other terms such as "Universal Mind," "the Divine," "Creative Source," and so forth. Do

you agree with the spiritual premises of this book, or do they violate some of your religious beliefs?

4. The book mentions the PEAR studies, which seem to prove that the human brain does have the power to broadcast its intent and impact on the actual physical world. Did you examine the online evidence of this research? How do you feel about the implications of this study?

5. John Selby claims to have integrated cognitive science with spiritual meditative practice in developing the manifestation process taught in this book. Do you feel he succeeded in this merger of science and spirit? Or are the two so different that they cannot be integrated?

6. This book leans in the direction of deeper spiritual dimensions of manifestation and human happiness, rather than focusing primarily on the attainment of material wealth. Are you comfortable with this focus on spiritual dimensions of manifestation as being compatible with the practical attainment of material desires? Why or why not?

7. Much of the book focuses on teaching a daily meditation practice that touches the depths of both material and spiritual needs and desires. Did you feel the book adequately taught you the manifestation process? Have you been practicing this method daily? What have been your experiences with this process?

8. The first part of the process is supposed to help you quiet all the thoughts running through your mind so

that you can enter into the Silence. When you focus on your breathing and present-moment experience by using the Focus Phrases, do your thoughts become quiet? What do you think of the whole notion of quieting your mind so that you can listen to your inner voice of wisdom and guidance?

9. Charles Haanel insists that your success in manifesting your dreams must be driven not just by thoughts of what you want, but also by your deeper passions and yearnings, by your positive emotions. Do you agree with this? How well have you been able to identify what your core passions and yearnings are?

10. The author talks about "shifting into receive mode" during a manifestation session so that you can receive insight, guidance, wisdom, and power to help you manifest your dreams. What do you think of this process? Can you do it yet?

11. Charles Haanel says, "What you and I desire, what everyone is seeking, is happiness and harmony." He urges you to aim toward manifesting these two qualities of consciousness in your life, rather than focusing on material things that you desire. Do you agree with this, or is he being too simplistic?

12. In general, were you satisfied with the book's focus on deeper spiritual aspects of fulfillment in life? After reading the book, are you clear about what you personally need to make you happy? Is happiness really what you want, or are you focused on something else?

13. This book insists that you must pay attention to your

thoughts at all times and take responsibility for focusing your thoughts in positive directions if you want to manifest a satisfying life situation. Is it true in your experience that your thoughts always precede your actions? Do you feel you can take charge of your thoughts, rather than letting them run wild?

14. The Law of Attraction plays an important role in this book's manifestation process. Science has proven the physical Law of Attraction in atoms and so forth, but do you believe there is a mental and spiritual Law of Attraction as well? If so, do you feel you understand how to work with this Law of Attraction in your own life?

15. Another premise of this book is that there is "enough for all" and that abundance is something everyone in the world can experience. Is this just wishful thinking? If everyone in the world practiced this book's manifestation process regularly, would everyone be able to get what they truly need to be happy in life?

16. Charles Haanel and the authors of *Tapping the Source* have been called heretical because they see human beings as expressions of the Universal Mind, which means they're putting humans and God on an equal footing, with humans as material manifestations of the Infinite Creator. Do you agree with the authors? Are you actually able to tap into and channel God's power and wisdom into your personal mind?

17. Charles Haanel often stated that he was averse to all religion, and that his manifestation methods were

based on science and spiritual insight, not traditional religious beliefs. But much of what he taught—for instance, focusing on giving rather than receiving, and making love the ultimate true power—sounds like the teachings of Jesus. Was he just using new words to express traditional beliefs, or did he bring a genuinely new vision of spiritual life into being?

18. The use of Focus Phrases seems to be the driving force of this manifestation process. Did the book adequately teach you what Focus Phrases are and how to use them? Do you find them powerful and effective? Is it true that just by thinking a statement of intent to yourself you can generate movement toward what you want to manifest? Have you yet memorized the seven Focus Phrases that make up this book's method? What do you think of holding these Focus Phrases in your mind throughout the day?

19. Charles Haanel goes against the usual meditation grain when he insists that the solar plexus is the center of the human body and the point where Spirit flows in. Usually we think it's the heart or the mind, not the solar plexus. The book teaches that breathing is the core factor in awareness and manifestation, and that the solar plexus, which drives our breathing, must therefore be the key to manifestation. Do you agree with this? When you practice the manifestation process, can you focus down to your solar plexus? What do you experience?

20. The book talks about the necessity of changing your

mental attitudes if you are to change your life for the better. Do you agree with this? Do you feel you can use the methods in this book to change your mental attitudes?

21. Power is also talked about, but with a particular Haanel twist that is different from the way most self-help and spiritual books treat it. Charles Haanel teaches that you must first go into the Silence and bring your personal intent into resonance and harmony with the laws of nature and Universal Mind's wisdom if you are to receive higher power beyond your ego's manipulations. Does this make sense to you? Do you want to do this in your life?

22. The book says that if you stay in conscious contact with your higher primary yearnings, each moment will manifest what you need in order to advance step by step toward your higher goal. Do you like this "higher vision" focus? Is it effective for you in also manifesting practical material abundance as well?

23. The book challenges you to use the free online training programs daily and to develop a strong daily habit of pausing to go into the Silence and tap your higher manifestation powers. Do you think you will discipline yourself enough to make this manifestation process a lifelong daily habit?

24. You can have the identity of a seeker and move on now to find more books that might hold the answers you're looking for, or you can see yourself as a tracker,

and settle in with this manifestation method as your fulfilling process. Which do you think you will choose?

For further exploration of the questions, themes, and programs in this book, please visit www.TappingDaily.com.

THE
MASTER
KEY
SYSTEM

JEREMY P. TARCHER / PENGUIN
a member of Penguin Group (USA)
New York

THE
MASTER
KEY
SYSTEM

CHARLES F. HAANEL

CONTENTS

Foreword   *255*

PART ONE   *263*

PART TWO   *273*

PART THREE   *283*

PART FOUR   *292*

PART FIVE   *301*

PART SIX   *310*

PART SEVEN   *319*

PART EIGHT   *329*

PART NINE   *339*

PART TEN   *349*

PART ELEVEN   *358*

PART TWELVE   *368*

PART THIRTEEN   377

PART FOURTEEN   386

PART FIFTEEN   395

PART SIXTEEN   404

PART SEVENTEEN   414

PART EIGHTEEN   424

PART NINETEEN   432

PART TWENTY   440

PART TWENTY-ONE   449

PART TWENTY-TWO   458

PART TWENTY-THREE   467

PART TWENTY-FOUR   476

About the Author   487

FOREWORD

Some men seem to attract success, power, wealth, attainment, with very little conscious effort; others conquer with great difficulty; still others fail altogether to reach their ambitions, desires and ideals. Why is this so? Why should some men realize their ambitions easily, others with difficulty, and still others not at all? The cause cannot be physical, else the most perfect men, physically, would be the most successful. The difference, therefore, must be mental—must be in the mind; hence mind must be the creative force, must constitute the sole difference between men. It is mind, therefore, which overcomes environment and every other obstacle in the path of men.

When the creative power of thought is fully understood, its effect will be seen to be marvelous. But such results cannot be secured without proper application, diligence, and concentration. The student will find that the laws governing in the mental and spiritual world are as fixed and infallible as in the material world. To secure the desired results, then, it is necessary to know the law and to comply with it. A proper compliance with the law will be found to produce the desired result with invariable exactitude. The student who learns that power comes from within, that he is weak only because he has depended on help from outside, and who unhesitatingly throws himself on his own thought, instantly rights himself, stands erect, assumes a dominant attitude, and works miracles.

It is evident, therefore, that he who fails to fully investigate and take advantage of the wonderful progress which is being made in this last and greatest science will soon be as far behind as the man who would refuse to acknowledge and accept the benefits which have accrued to mankind through an understanding of the laws of electricity.

Of course, mind creates negative conditions just as readily as favorable conditions, and when we consciously or unconsciously visualize every kind of lack, limitation and discord, we create these conditions; this is what many are unconsciously doing all the time.

This law as well as every other law is no respecter of persons, but is in constant operation and is relentlessly bringing to each individual exactly what he has created; in other words, "Whatsoever a man soweth that shall he also reap."

Abundance, therefore, depends upon a recognition of the laws of Abundance, and the fact that Mind is not only the creator, but the only creator of all there is. Certainly nothing can be created, before we know that it can be created and then make the proper effort. There is no more Electricity in the world today than there was fifty years ago, but until someone recognized the law by which it could be made of service, we received no benefit; now that the law is understood, practically the whole world is lit by it. So with the Law of Abundance; it is only those who recognize the law and place themselves in harmony with it who share in its benefits.

The scientific spirit now dominates every field of effort, relations of cause and effect are no longer ignored.

The discovery of a region of law marked an epoch in human progress. It eliminated the element of uncertainty and caprice in men's lives, and substituted law, reason and certitude.

Men now understand that for every result there is an adequate and definite cause, so that when a given result is desired, they seek the condition by which alone this result may be attained.

The basis upon which all law rests was discovered by inductive reasoning which consists of comparing a number of separate instances with one another until the common factor which gives rise to them all is seen.

It is this method of study to which the civilized nations owe the greater part of their prosperity and the more valuable part of their knowledge; it has lengthened life, it has mitigated pain, it has spanned rivers, it has brightened the night with the splendor of day, extended the range of vision, accelerated motion, annihilated distance, facilitated intercourse, and enabled men to descend into the sea, and into the air. What wonder then that men soon endeavored to extend the blessings of this system of study to their method of thinking, so that when it became plainly evident that certain results followed a particular method of thinking it only remained to classify these results.

This method is scientific, and it is the only method by which we shall be permitted retain that degree of liberty and freedom which we have been accustomed to look upon as an inalienable right, because a people is safe at home and in the world only if national preparedness means such things as growing surplus of health, accumulated efficiency in public and private business of whatever sort, continuous advance in the science and art of acting together, and the increasingly dominant endeavor to make all of these and all other aspects of national development center and revolve about ascending life, single and collective, for which science, art and ethics furnish guidance and controlling motives.

The Master Key is based on absolute scientific truth and will unfold the possibilities that lie dormant in the individual, and teach how they may be brought into powerful action, to increase the person's effective capacity, bringing added energy, discernment, vigor and mental elasticity. The student who gains an understanding of the mental laws which are unfolded will come into the possession of an ability to secure results hitherto undreamed of, and which has rewards hardly to be expressed in words.

It explains the correct use of both the receptive and active elements of the mental nature, and instructs the student in the recognition of opportunity; it strengthens the will and reasoning powers, and teaches the cultivation and best uses of imagination, desire, the emotions and the intuitional faculty. It gives initiative, tenacity of purpose, wisdom of choice, intelligent sympathy and a thorough enjoyment of life on its higher planes.

The Master Key teaches the use of Mind Power, true Mind Power, not any of the substitutes and perversions; it has nothing to do with Hypnotism, Magic or any of the more or less fascinating deceptions by which many are led to think that something can be had for nothing.

The Master Key cultivates and develops the understanding which will enable you to control the body and thereby the health. It improves and strengthens the Memory. It develops Insight, the kind of Insight which is so rare, the kind which is the distinguishing characteristic of every successful business man, the kind which enables men to see the possibilities as well as the difficulties in every situation, the kind which enables men to discern opportunity close at hand, for thousands fail to see opportunities almost within their grasp while they are industriously working with situations which under no possibility can be made to realize any substantial return.

The Master Key develops Mental Power, which means that others instinctively recognize that you are a person of force, of character—that they want to do what you want them to do; it means that you attract men and things to you; that you are what some people call "lucky," that "things" come your way, that you have come into an understanding of the fundamental laws of nature, and have put yourself in harmony with them; that you are in tune with Infinite;

that you understand the Law of Attraction, the natural laws of growth, and the psychological laws on which all advantages in the social and business world rest.

Mental Power is creative power, it gives you the ability to create for yourself; it does not mean the ability to take something away from someone else. Nature never does things that way. Nature makes two blades of grass grow where one grew before, and Mind Power enables men to do the same thing.

The Master Key develops insight and sagacity, increased independence, the ability and disposition to be helpful. It destroys distrust, depression, fear, melancholia, and every form of lack, limitation and weakness, including pain and disease; it awakens buried talents, supplies initiative, force, energy, vitality—it awakens an appreciation of the beautiful in Art, Literature, and Science.

It has changed the lives of thousands of men and women, by substituting definite principles for uncertain and hazy methods— and principles for the foundation upon which every system of efficiency must rest.

Elbert Gary, the chairman of the United States Steel Corporation, said, "The services of advisors, instructors, efficiency experts in successful management are indispensable to most business enterprises of magnitude, but I deem the recognition and adoption of right principles to be of vastly more importance."

The Master Key teaches right principles, and suggests methods for making a practical application of the principles; in that it differs from every other course of study. It teaches that the only possible value which can attach to any principle is in its application. Many read books, take home study courses, attend lectures all their lives without ever making any progress in demonstrating the value of the principles involved. The Master Key suggests methods by which the value of the principles taught may be demonstrated and put in actual practice in the daily experience.

There is a change in the thought of the world. This change is silently transpiring in our midst, and is more important than any which the world has undergone since the downfall of Paganism.

The present revolution in the opinions of all classes of men, the highest and most cultured of men as well as those of the laboring class, stands unparalleled in the history of the world.

Science has of late made such vast discoveries, has revealed such an infinity of resources, has unveiled such enormous possibilities and such unsuspected forces, that scientific men more and more hesitate to affirm certain theories as established and indubitable or to deny certain other theories as absurd or impossible, and so a new civilization is being born; customs, creeds, and cruelty are passing; vision, faith and service are taking their place. The fetters of tradition are being melted off from humanity, and as the dross of materialism is being consumed, thought is being liberated and truth is rising full-orbed before an astonished multitude.

The whole world is on the eve of a new consciousness, a new power and a new consciousness, a new power and a new realization of the resources within the self. The last century saw the most magnificent material progress in history. The present century will produce the greatest progress in mental and spiritual power.

Physical science has resolved matter into molecules, molecules into atoms, atoms into energy, and it has remained for Sir Ambrose Fleming, in an address before the Royal Institution, to resolve this energy into mind. He says: "In its ultimate essence, energy may be incomprehensible by us except as an exhibition of the direct operation of that which we call Mind or Will."

Let us see what are the most powerful forces in nature. In the mineral world everything is solid and fixed. In the animal and vegetable kingdom it is in a state of flux, forever changing, always being created and re-created. In the atmosphere we find heat, light and energy. Each realm becomes finer and more spiritual as we pass from the visible to the invisible, from the coarse to the fine, from the low potentiality to high potentiality. When we reach the invisible we find energy in its purest and most volatile state.

And as the most powerful forces of nature are the invisible forces, so we find that the most powerful forces of man are his invisible forces, his spiritual force, and the only way in which the spiritual force can manifest itself is through the process of thinking. Thinking is the only activity which the spirit possesses, and thought is the only product of thinking.

Addition and subtraction are therefore spiritual transactions; reasoning is a spiritual process; ideas are spiritual conceptions; questions are spiritual searchlights and logic, argument and philosophy is spiritual machinery.

Every thought brings into action certain physical tissue, parts of the brain, nerve or muscle. This produces an actual physical change in the construction of the tissue. Therefore it is only necessary to have a certain number of thoughts on a given subject in order to bring about a complete change in the physical organization of a man.

This is the process by which failure is changed to success. Thoughts of courage, power, inspiration, harmony, are substituted for thoughts of failure, despair, lack, limitation and discord, and as these thoughts take root, the physical tissue is changed and the individual sees life in a new light, old things have actually passed away, all things have become new, he is born again, this time born of the spirit, life has a new meaning for him, he is reconstructed and is filled with joy, confidence, hope, energy. He sees opportunities for success to which he was heretofore blind. He recognizes possibilities which before had no meaning for him. The thoughts of success with which he has been impregnated are radiated to those around him, and they in turn help him onward and upward; he attracts to him new and successful associates, and this in turn changes his environment; so that by this simple exercise of thought, a man changes not only himself, but his environment, circumstances and conditions.

You will see, you must see, that we are at the dawn of a new day;

that the possibilities are so wonderful, so fascinating, so limitless as to be almost bewildering. A century ago any man with a Gatling Gun could have annihilated a whole army equipped with the implements of warfare then in use. So it is at present. Any man with a knowledge of the possibilities contained in the Master Key has an inconceivable advantage over the multitude.

PART ONE

It is my privilege to enclose herewith Part One of the Master Key System. Would you bring into your life more power? Get the power consciousness. More health? Get the health consciousness. More happiness? Get the happiness consciousness. Live the spirit of these things until they become yours by right. It will then become impossible to keep them from you. The things of the world are fluid to a power within man by which he rules them.

You need not acquire this power. You already have it. But you want to understand it; you want to use it; you want to control it; you want to impregnate yourself with it, so that you can go forward and carry the world before you.

Day by day as you go on and on, as you gain momentum, as your inspiration deepens, as your plans crystallize, as you gain understanding, you will come to realize that this world is no dead pile of stones and timber, but that it is a living thing! It is made up of the beating hearts of humanity. It is a thing of life and beauty.

It is evident that it requires understanding to work with material of this description, but those who come into this understanding, are inspired by a new light, a new force, they gain confidence and greater power each day, they *realize their hopes and their dreams come true, life has a deeper, fuller, clearer meaning than before.*

And, now, Part One.

1. That much gathers more is true on every plane of existence and that loss leads to greater loss is equally true.

2. Mind is creative, and conditions, environment and all experiences in life are the result of our habitual or predominant mental attitude.

3. The attitude of mind necessarily depends upon what we think. Therefore, the secret of all power, all achievement and all possession depends upon our method of thinking.

4. This is true because we must "be" before we can "do," and we can "do" only to the extent which we "are," and what we "are" depends upon what we "think."

5. We cannot express powers that we do not possess. The only way by which we may secure possession of power is to become conscious of power, and we can never become conscious of power until we learn that all power is from within.

6. There is a world within—a world of thought and feeling and power; of light and life and beauty and, although invisible, its forces are mighty.

7. The world within is governed by mind. When we discover this world we shall find the solution for every problem, the cause for every effect; and since the world within is subject to our control, all laws of power and possession are also within our control.

8. The world without is a reflection of the world within. What appears without is what has been found within. In the world within may be found infinite Wisdom, infinite Power, infinite Supply of all that is necessary, waiting for unfoldment, development and expression. If we recognize these potentialities in the world within they will take form in the world without.

9. Harmony in the world within will be reflected in the world without by harmonious conditions, agreeable surroundings, the best of everything. It is the foundation of health and a necessary essential to all greatness, all power, all attainment, all achievement and all success.

10. Harmony in the world within means the ability to control our thoughts, and to determine for ourselves how any experience is to affect us.

11. Harmony in the world within results in optimism and affluence; affluence within results in affluence without.

12. The world without reflects the circumstances and the conditions of the consciousness within.

13. If we find wisdom in the world within, we shall have the understanding to discern the marvelous possibilities that are latent in this world within, and we shall be given the power to make these possibilities manifest in the world without.

14. As we become conscious of the wisdom in the world within, we mentally take possession of this wisdom, and by taking mental possession we come into actual possession of the power and wisdom necessary to bring into manifestation the essentials necessary for our most complete and harmonious development.

15. The world within is the practical world in which the men and women of power generate courage, hope, enthusiasm, confidence, trust and faith, by which they are given the fine intelligence to see the vision and the practical skill to make the vision real.

16. Life is an unfoldment, not accretion. What comes to us in the world without is what we already possess in the world within.

17. All possession is based on consciousness. All gain is the result of an accumulative consciousness. All loss is the result of a scattering consciousness.

18. Mental efficiency is contingent upon harmony; discord means confusion; therefore, he who would acquire power must be in harmony with natural law.

19. We are related to the world without by the objective mind. The brain is the organ of this mind and the cerebro-spinal system of nerves puts us in conscious communication with every part of the body. This system of nerves responds to every sensation of light, heat, odor, sound and taste.

20. When this mind thinks correctly, when it understands the truth, when the thoughts sent through the cerebro-spinal nervous system to the body are constructive, these sensations are pleasant, harmonious.

21. The result is that we build strength, vitality and all constructive forces into our body, but it is through this same objective mind that all distress, sickness, lack, limitation and every form of discord and inharmony is admitted to our lives. It is therefore through the objective mind, by wrong thinking, that we are related to all destructive forces.

22. We are related to the world within by the subconscious mind. The solar plexus is the organ of this mind; the sympathetic system of nerves presides over all subjective sensations, such as joy, fear, love, emotion, respiration, imagination and all other subconscious phenomena. It is through the subconscious that we are connected with the Universal Mind and brought into relation with the infinite constructive forces of the Universe.

23. It is the coordination of these two centers of our being, and the understanding of their functions, which is the great secret of life. With this knowledge we can bring the objective and subjective minds into conscious cooperation and thus coordinate the finite and the Infinite. Our future is entirely within our own control. It is not at the mercy of any capricious or uncertain external power.

24. All agree that there is but one Principle or Consciousness pervading the entire Universe, occupying all space, and being essentially the same in kind at every point of its presence. It is all powerful, all wisdom and always present. All thoughts and things are within Itself. It is all in all.

25. There is but one consciousness in the universe able to think; and when it thinks, its thoughts become objective things to it. As this Consciousness is omnipresent, it must be present within every individual; each individual must be a manifestation of that Omnipotent, Omniscient and Omnipresent Consciousness.

26. As there is only one Consciousness in the Universe that is able to think it necessarily follows that your consciousness is identical with the Universal Consciousness, or, in other words, all mind is one mind. There is no dodging this conclusion.

27. The consciousness that focuses in your brain cells is the same consciousness which focuses in the brain cells of every other individual. Each individual is but the individualization of the Universal, the Cosmic Mind.

28. The Universal Mind is static or potential energy; it simply is; it can manifest itself only through the individual, and the individual can manifest himself only through the Universal. They are one.

29. The ability of the individual to think is his ability to act on the Universal and bring it into manifestation. Human consciousness consists only in the ability of man to think. Mind in itself is believed to be a subtle form of static energy, from which arises the activities called "thought," which is the dynamic phase of mind. Mind is static energy, thought is dynamic energy—the two phases of the same thing. Thought is therefore the vibratory force formed by converting static mind into dynamic mind.

30. As the sum of all attributes are contained in the Universal Mind, which is Omnipotent, Omniscient and Omnipresent, these attributes must be present at all times in their potential form in every individual. Therefore, when the individual thinks, the thought is compelled by its nature to embody itself in an objectivity or condition which will correspond with its origin.

31. Every thought therefore is a cause and every condition an effect; for this reason it is absolutely essential that you control your thoughts so as to bring forth only desirable conditions.

32. All power is from within, and is absolutely under your control; it comes through exact knowledge and by the voluntary exercises of exact principles.

33. It should be plain that when you acquire a thorough understanding of this law, and are able to control your thought processes, you can apply it to any condition; in other words, you will have come into conscious cooperation with Omnipotent law which is the fundamental basis of all things.

34. The Universal Mind is the life principle of every atom which is in existence; every atom is continually striving to manifest more life; all are intelligent, and all are seeking to carry out the purpose for which they were created.

35. A majority of mankind lives in the world without; few have found the world within, and yet it is the world within that makes the world without; it is therefore creative and everything which you find in your world without has been created by you in the world within.

36. This system will bring you into a realization of power which will be yours when you understand this relation between the world without and the world within. The world within is the cause, the world without the effect; to change the effect you must change the cause.

37. You will at once see that this is a radically new and different idea; most men try to change effects by working with effects. They fail to see that this is simply changing one form of distress for another. To remove discord, we must remove the cause, and this cause can be found only in the world within.

38. All growth is from within. This is evident in all nature. Every plant, every animal, every human is a living testimony to this great law, and the error of the ages is in looking for strength or power from without.

39. The world within is the Universal fountain of supply, and the world without is the outlet to the stream. Our ability to receive depends upon our recognition of this Universal Fountain, this Infinite Energy of which each individual is an outlet, and so is one with every other individual.

40. Recognition is a mental process, mental action is therefore the interaction of the individual upon the Universal Mind, and as the Universal Mind is the intelligence which pervades all space and animates all living things, this mental action and reaction is the law of causation, but the principle of causation does not obtain in the individual but in the Universal Mind. It is not an objective faculty but a subjective process, and the results are seen in an infinite variety of conditions and experiences.

41. In order to express life there must be mind; nothing can exist without mind. Everything which exists is some manifestation of this one basic substance from which and by which all things have been created and are continually being re-created.

42. We live in a fathomless sea of plastic mind substance. This substance is ever alive and active. It is sensitive to the highest degree. It takes form according to the mental demand. Thought forms the mold or matrix from which the substance expresses.

43. Remember that it is in the application alone that the value consists, and that a practical understanding of this law will substitute abundance for poverty, wisdom for ignorance, harmony for discord and freedom for tyranny, and certainly there can be no greater blessing than these from a material and social standpoint.

44. Now make the application: Select a room where you can be alone and undisturbed; sit erect, comfortably, but do not lounge;

let your thoughts roam where they will but be perfectly still for from fifteen minutes to half an hour; continue this for three or four days or for a week until you secure full control of your physical being.

45. Many will find this extremely difficult; others will conquer with ease, but it is absolutely essential to secure complete control of the body before you are ready to progress. Next week you will receive instructions for the next step; in the meantime you must have mastered this one.

PART ONE:
STUDY QUESTIONS WITH ANSWERS

1. What is the world without in its relation to the world within?
   The world without is a reflection of the world within.

2. Upon what does all possession depend?
   All possession is based on consciousness.

3. How is the individual related to the objective world?
   The individual is related to the objective world by the objective mind; the brain is the organ of this mind.

4. How is he related to the Universal Mind?
   He is related to the Universal Mind by the subconscious mind; the Solar Plexus is the organ of this mind.

5. What is the Universal Mind?
   Universal Mind is the life principle of every atom which is in existence.

6. How can the individual act on the Universal?

   The ability of the individual to think is his ability to act upon the Universal and bring it into manifestation.

7. What is the result of this action and interaction?

   The result of this action and interaction is cause and effect; every thought is a cause and every condition an effect.

8. How are harmonious and desirable conditions secured?

   Harmonious and desirable conditions are obtained by right thinking.

9. What is the cause of all discord, inharmony, lack and limitation?

   Discord, inharmony, lack and limitation are the result of wrong thinking.

10. What is the source of all power?

    The source of all power is the world within, the Universal Fountain of Supply, the Infinite Energy of which each individual is an outlet.

PART TWO

Our difficulties are largely due to confused ideas and ignorance of our true interests. The great task is to discover the laws of nature to which we are to adjust ourselves. Clear thinking and moral insight are, therefore, of incalculable value. All processes, even those of thought, rest on solid foundations.

The keener the sensibilities, the more acute the judgment, the more delicate the taste, the more refined the moral feelings, the more subtle the intelligence, the loftier the aspiration—the purer and more intense are the gratifications which existence yields. Hence it is that the study of the best that has been thought in the world gives supreme pleasure.

The powers, uses and possibilities of the mind under the new interpretations are incomparably more wonderful than the most extravagant accomplishment, or even dreams of material progress.

Thought is energy. Active thought is active energy; concentrated thought is a concentrated energy. Thought concentrated on a definite purpose becomes power. This is the power which is being used by those who do not believe in the virtue of poverty, or the beauty of self-denial. They perceive that this is the talk of weaklings.

The ability to receive and manifest this power depends upon the ability to recognize the Infinite Energy ever dwelling in man, constantly creating and *re-creating his body and mind, and ready at any moment to be made manifest through him in any needful manner. In exact proportion to the recognition of this truth will be the manifestation in the outer life of the individual.*

Part Two explains the method by which this is accomplished.

1. The operations of the mind are produced by two parallel modes of activity, the one conscious, and the other subconscious. Professor Davidson says: "He who thinks to illuminate the whole range of mental action by the light of his own consciousness is not unlike the one who should go about to illuminate the universe with a rushlight."

2. The subconscious' logical processes are carried on with a certainty and regularity which would be impossible if there existed the possibility of error. Our mind is so designed that it prepares for us the most important foundations of cognition, whilst we have not the slightest apprehension of the modus operandi.

3. The subconscious soul, like a benevolent stranger, works and makes provision for our benefit, pouring only the mature fruit into our lap; thus ultimate analysis of thought processes shows that the subconscious is the theater of the most important mental phenomena.

4. It is through the subconscious that Shakespeare must have perceived, without effort, great truths which are hidden from the conscious mind of the student; that Phidias fashioned marble and bronze; that Raphael painted Madonnas and Beethoven composed symphonies.

5. Ease and perfection depend entirely upon the degree in which we cease to depend upon the consciousness; playing the piano, skating, operating the typewriter, the skilled trades, depend for their perfect execution on the process of the subconscious mind. The marvel of playing a brilliant piece on the piano, while at the same time conducting a vigorous conversation, shows the greatness of our subconscious powers.

6. We are all aware how dependent we are upon the subconscious, and the greater, the nobler, the more brilliant our thoughts are, the more it is obvious to ourselves that the origin lies beyond our ken. We find ourselves endowed with tact, instinct, sense of the beautiful in art, music, etc., of whose origin or dwelling place we are wholly unconscious.

7. The value of the subconscious is enormous; it inspires us; it warns us; it furnishes us with names, facts and scenes from the storehouse of memory. It directs our thoughts, tastes, and accomplishes tasks so intricate that no conscious mind, even if it had the power, has the capacity for.

8. We can walk at will; we can raise the arm whenever we choose to do so; we can give our attention through eye or ear to any subject at pleasure. On the other hand, we cannot stop our heartbeats nor the circulation of the blood, nor the growth of stature, nor the formation of nerve and muscle tissue, nor the building of the bones, nor many other important vital processes.

9. If we compare these two sets of action, the one decreed by the will of the moment, and the other proceeding in majestic, rhythmic course, subject to no vascillation, but constant at every moment, we stand in awe of the latter, and ask to have the mystery explained. We see at once that these are the vital processes of our physical life, and we cannot avoid the inference that these all-important functions are designedly withdrawn from the domain of our outward will with its variations and transitions, and placed under the direction of a permanent and dependable power within us.

10. Of these two powers, the outward and changeable has been termed the "Conscious Mind," or the "Objective Mind" (dealing with outward objects). The interior power is called the "Subconscious Mind," or the "Subjective Mind," and besides its work on the mental plane it controls the regular functions which make physical life possible.

11. It is necessary to have a clear understanding of their respective functions on the mental plane, as well as of certain other basic principles. Perceiving and operating through the five physical senses, the conscious mind deals with the impressions and objects of the outward life.

12. It has the faculty of discrimination, carrying with it the responsibility of choice. It has the power of reasoning—whether inductive, deductive, analytical or syllogistic—and this power may be developed to a high degree. It is the seat of the will with all the energies that flow therefrom.

13. Not only can it impress other minds, but it can direct the subconscious mind. In this way the conscious mind becomes the responsible ruler and guardian of the subconscious mind. It is this high function which can completely reverse conditions in your life.

14. It is often true that conditions of fear, worry, poverty, disease, inharmony and evils of all kinds dominate us by reason of false suggestions accepted by the unguarded subconscious mind. All this the trained conscious mind can entirely prevent by its vigilant protective action. It may properly be called "the watchman at the gate" of the great subconscious domain.

15. One writer has expressed the chief distinction between the two phases of mind thus: "Conscious mind is reasoning will.

Subconscious mind is instinctive desire, the result of past reasoning will."

16. The subconscious mind draws just and accurate inferences from premises furnished from outside sources. Where the premise is true, the subconscious mind reaches a faultless conclusion, but, where the premise or suggestion is an error, the whole structure falls. The subconscious mind does not engage in the process of proving. It relies upon the conscious mind, "the watchman at the gate," to guard it from mistaken impressions.

17. Receiving any suggestions as true, the subconscious mind at once proceeds to act thereon in the whole domain of its tremendous field of work. The conscious mind can suggest either truth or error. If the latter, it is at the cost of wide-reaching peril to the whole being.

18. The conscious mind ought to be on duty during every waking hour. When the "watchman" is "off guard," or when its calm judgment is suspended, under a variety of circumstances, then the subconscious mind is unguarded and left open to suggestion from all sources. During the wild excitement of panic, or during the height of anger, or the impulses of the irresponsible mob, or at any other time of unrestrained passion, the conditions are most dangerous. The subconscious mind is then open to the suggestion of fear, hatred, selfishness, greed, self-depreciation and other negative forces, derived from surrounding persons or circumstances. The result is usually unwholesome in the extreme, with effects that may endure to distress it for a long time. Hence, the great importance of guarding the subconscious mind from false impressions.

19. The subconscious mind perceives by intuition. Hence, its processes are rapid. It does not wait for the slow methods of conscious reasoning. In fact, it cannot employ them.

20. The subconscious mind never sleeps, never rests, any more than does your heart, or your blood. It has been found that by plainly stating to the subconscious mind certain specific things to be accomplished, forces are set in operation that lead to the result desired. Here, then, is a source of power which places us in touch with Omnipotence. Here in is a deep principle which is well worth our most earnest study.

21. The operation of this law is interesting. Those who put it into operation find that when they go out to meet the person with whom they anticipate a difficult interview, something has been there before them and dissolved the supposed differences; everything is changed; all is harmonious; they find that when some difficult business problem presents itself they can afford to make delay and something suggests the proper solution; everything is properly arranged; in fact, those who have learned to trust the subconscious find that they have infinite resources at their command.

22. The subconscious mind is the seat of our principles and our aspirations. It is the fount of our artistic and altruistic ideals. These instincts can only be overthrown by an elaborate and gradual process of undermining the innate principles.

23. The subconscious mind cannot argue controversially. Hence, if it has accepted wrong suggestions, the sure method of overcoming them is by the use of a strong countersuggestion, frequently repeated, which the mind must accept, thus eventually forming new and healthy habits of thought and life, for the subconscious mind is the seat of Habit. That which we do over and over becomes mechanical; it is no longer an act of judgment, but has worn its deep grooves in the subconscious mind. This is favorable for us if the habit be wholesome and right. If it be harmful, and wrong, the remedy is to recognize the omnipotence of the subconscious mind and suggest present actual freedom. The subconscious being creative and one with our divine source will at once create the freedom suggested.

24. To sum up: The normal functions of the subconscious on the physical side have to do with the regular and vital processes, with the preservation of life and the restoration of health; with the care of offspring, which includes an instinctive desire to preserve all life and improve conditions generally.

25. On the mental side, it is the storehouse of memory; it harbors the wonderful thought messengers, who work, unhampered by time or space; it is the fountain of the practical initiative and constructive forces of life: It is the seat of habit.

26. On the spiritual side, it is the source of ideals, of aspiration, of the imagination, and is the channel through which we recognize our Divine Source, and in proportion as we recognize this divinity do we come into an understanding of the source of power.

27. Someone may ask: "How can the subconscious change conditions?" The reply is, because the subconscious is a part of the Universal Mind and a part must be the same in kind and quality as the whole; the only difference is one of degree. The whole, as we know, is creative, in fact, it is the only creator there is, consequently, we find that mind is creative, and as thought is the only activity which the mind possesses, thought must necessarily be creative also.

28. But we shall find that there is a vast difference between simply thinking, and directing our thought consciously, systematically and constructively; when we do this we place our mind in harmony with the Universal Mind, we come in tune with the Infinite, we set

in operation the mightiest force in existence, the creative power of the Universal Mind. This, as everything else, is governed by natural law, and this law is the "Law of Attraction," which is that Mind is creative, and will automatically correlate with its object and bring it into manifestation.

29. Last week I gave you an exercise for the purpose of securing control of the physical body; if you have accomplished this you are ready to advance. This time you will begin to control your thought. Always take the same room, the same chair, and the same position, if possible. In some cases it is not convenient to take the same room, in this case simply make the best use of such conditions as may be available. Now be perfectly still as before, but inhibit all thought; this will give you control over all thoughts of care, worry and fear, and will enable you to entertain only the kind of thoughts you desire. Continue this exercise until you gain complete mastery.

30. You will not be able to do this for more than a few moments at a time, but the exercise is valuable, because it will be a very practical demonstration of the great number of thoughts which are constantly trying to gain access to your mental world.

31. Next week you will receive instructions for an exercise which may be a little more interesting, but it is necessary that you master this one first.

> *Cause and effect is as absolute and undeviating in the hidden realm of thought as in the world of visible and material things. Mind is the master weaver, both of the interior garment of character and the outer garment of circumstance.*
>
> —JAMES ALLEN

PART TWO:
STUDY QUESTIONS WITH ANSWERS

11. What are the two modes of mental activity?
    Conscious and subconscious.

12. Upon what do ease and perfection depend?
    Ease and perfection depend entirely upon the degree in which we cease to depend upon the conscious mind.

13. What is the value of the subconscious?
    It is enormous; it guides us, warns us, it controls the vital processes and is the seat of memory.

14. What are some of the functions of the conscious mind?
    It has the faculty of discrimination; it has the power of reasoning; it is the seat of the will and may impress the subconscious.

15. How has the distinction between the conscious and subconscious been expressed?
    "Conscious mind is reasoning will. Subconscious mind is instinctive desire, the result of past reasoning will."

16. What method is necessary in order to impress the subconscious?
    Mentally state what is wanted.

17. What will be the result?
    If the desire is in harmony with the forward movement of the great Whole, forces will be set in motion which will bring about the result.

18. What is the result of the operation of this law?

    Our environment reflects conditions corresponding to the predominant mental attitude which we entertain.

19. What name has been given to this law?

    The Law of Attraction.

20. How is the law stated?

    Thought is a creative energy, and will automatically correlate with its object and bring it into manifestation.

PART THREE

You have found that the individual may act on the Universal, and that the result of this action and interaction is cause and effect. Thought, therefore, is the cause, and the experiences with which you meet in life are the effect.

Eliminate, therefore, any possible tendency to complain of conditions as they have been, or as they are, because it rests with you to change them and make them what you would like them to be.

Direct your effort to a realization of the mental resources, always at your command, from which all real and lasting power comes.

Persist in this practice until you come to a realization of the fact that there can be no failure in the accomplishment of any proper object in life if you but understand your power and persist in your object, because the mind-forces are ever ready to lend themselves to a purposeful will, in the effort to crystallize thought and desire into actions, events and conditions.

Whereas in the beginning each function of life and each action is the result of conscious thought, the habitual actions become automatic and the thought that controls them passes into the realm of the subconscious; yet it is just as intelligent as before. It is necessary that it become automatic, or subconscious, in order that the self-conscious mind may attend to other things. The new actions will, however, in their turn, become habitual, then *automatic, then subconscious in order that the mind again may be freed from this detail and advanced to still other activities.*

When you realize this, you will have found a source of power which will enable you to take care of any situation in life which may develop.

1. The necessary interaction of the conscious and subconscious mind requires a similar interaction between the corresponding systems of nerves. Judge Troward indicates the very beautiful method in which this interaction is effected. He says: The cerebro-spinal system is the organ of the conscious mind and the sympathetic is the organ of the subconscious. The cerebro-spinal is the channel through which we receive conscious perception from the physical senses and exercise control over the movements of the body. This system of nerves has its center in the brain.

2. The Sympathetic System has its center in a ganglionic mass at the back of the stomach known as the Solar Plexus, and is the channel of that mental action which unconsciously supports the vital functions of the body.

3. The connection between the two systems is made by the vagus nerve which passes out of the cerebral region as a portion of the voluntary system to the thorax, sending out branches to the heart and lungs, and finally passing through the diaphragm, it loses its outer coating and becomes identified with the nerves of the Sympathetic System, so forming a connecting link between the two and making man physically a "single entity."

4. We have seen that every thought is received by the brain, which is the organ of the conscious; it is here subjected to our power of reasoning. When the objective mind has been satisfied that the thought is true it is sent to the Solar Plexus, or the brain of the subjective mind, to be made into our flesh, to be brought forth into the world as reality. It is then no longer susceptible to any argument whatever. The subconscious mind cannot argue; it only acts. It accepts the conclusions of the objective mind as final.

5. The Solar Plexus has been likened to the sum of the body, because it is a central point of distribution for the energy which the body is constantly generating. This energy is very real energy, and this sun is a very real sun, and the energy is being distributed by very real nerves to all parts of the body, and is thrown off in an atmosphere which envelops the body.

6. If this radiation is sufficiently strong the person is called magnetic; he is said to be filled with personal magnetism. Such a person may wield an immense power for good. His presence alone will often bring comfort to the troubled minds with which he comes in contact.

7. When the Solar Plexus is in active operation and is radiating life, energy and vitality to every part of the body, and to everyone whom he meets, the sensations are pleasant, the body is filled with health and all with whom he comes in contact experience a pleasant sensation.

8. If there is any interruption of this radiation the sensations are unpleasant, the flow of life and energy to some part of the body is stopped, and this is the cause of every ill to the human race, physical, mental or environmental.

9. Physical because the sun of the body is no longer generating sufficient energy to vitalize some part of the body; mental because the conscious mind is dependent upon the subconscious mind for the vitality necessary to support its thought, and environmental, because the connection between the subconscious mind and the Universal mind, is being interrupted.

10. The Solar Plexus is the point at which the part meets with the whole, where the finite becomes infinite, where the Uncreate becomes create, the Universal becomes individualized, the invisible becomes visible. It is the point at which life appears and there is no limit to the amount of life an individual may generate from this Solar center.

11. This center of energy is Omnipotent because it is the point of contact with all life and all intelligence. It can therefore accomplish whatever it is directed to accomplish, and herein lies the power of the conscious mind; the subconscious can and will carry out such plans and ideas as may be suggested to it by the conscious mind.

12. Conscious thought, then, is master of this sun center from which the life and energy of the entire body flows and the quality of the thought which we entertain determines the quality of the thought which this sun will radiate, and the character of the thought which our conscious mind entertains will determine the character of the thought which this sun will radiate, and the nature of the thought which our conscious mind entertains will determine the nature of thought which this sun will radiate, and consequently will determine the nature of the experience which will result.

13. It is evident, therefore, that all we have to do is let our light shine; the more energy we can radiate, the more rapidly shall we be enabled to transmute undesirable conditions into sources of pleasure and profit. The important question, then, is how to let this light shine; how to generate this energy.

14. Non-resistant thought expands the Solar Plexus; resistant thought contracts it. Pleasant thought expands it; unpleasant thought contracts it. Thoughts of courage, power, confidence and hope all produce a corresponding state, but the one arch enemy of the Solar Plexus which must be absolutely destroyed before there is any possibility of letting any light shine is fear. This enemy must be completely destroyed; he must be eliminated; he must be expelled forever; he is the cloud which hides the sun; which causes a perpetual gloom.

15. It is this personal devil which makes men fear the past, the present and the future; fear themselves, their friends and their enemies; fear everything and everybody. When fear is effectually and completely destroyed, your light will shine, the clouds will disperse and you will have found the source of power, energy and life.

16. When you find that you are really one with the Infinite power, and when you can consciously realize this power by a practical demonstration of your ability to overcome any adverse condition by the power of your thought, you will have nothing to fear; fear will have been destroyed and you will have come into possession of your birthright.

17. It is our attitude of mind toward life which determines the experiences with which we are to meet; if we expect nothing, we shall have nothing; if we demand much, we shall receive the greater portion. The world is harsh only as we fail to assert ourselves. The criticism of the world is bitter only to those who cannot compel room for their ideas. It is fear of this criticism that causes many ideas to fail to see the light of day.

18. But the man who knows that he has a Solar Plexus will not fear criticism or anything else; he will be too busy radiating courage, confidence, and power; he will anticipate success by his mental attitude; he will pound barriers to pieces, and leap over the chasm of doubt and hesitation which fear places in his path.

19. A knowledge of our ability to consciously radiate health, strength and harmony will bring us into a realization that there is nothing to fear because we are in touch with Infinite Strength.

20. This knowledge can be gained only by making practical application of this information. We learn by doing; through practice the athlete becomes powerful.

21. As the following statement is of considerable importance, I will put it in several ways, so that you cannot fail to get the full significance of it. If you are religiously inclined, I would say, you can let your light shine. If your mind has a bias toward physical science, I would say you can wake the Solar Plexus; or, if you prefer the strictly scientific interpretation, I will say that you can impress your subconscious mind.

22. I have already told you what the result of this impression will be. It is the method in which you are now interested. You have already learned that the subconscious is intelligent and that it is creative, and responsive to the will of the conscious mind. What, then, is the most natural way of making the desired impression? Mentally concentrate on the object of your desire; when you are concentrating you are impressing the subconscious.

23. This is not the only way, but it is a simple and effective way, and the most direct way, and consequently the way in which the best results are secured. It is the method which is producing such extraordinary results that many think that miracles are being accomplished.

24. It is the method by which every great inventor, every great financier, every great statesman has been enabled to convert the subtle and invisible force of desire, faith and confidence into actual, tangible, concrete facts in the objective world.

25. The subconscious mind is a part of the Universal mind. The Universal is the creative principle of the Universe, a part must be the same in kind and quality as the whole. This means that this creative power is absolutely unlimited; it is not bound by precedent of any kind, and consequently has no prior existing pattern by which to apply its constructive principle.

26. We have found that the subconscious mind is responsive to our conscious will, which means that the unlimited creative power of the Universal Mind is within control of the conscious mind of the individual.

27. When making a practical application of this principle, in accordance with the exercises given in the subsequent lessons, it is well to remember that it is not necessary to outline the method by which the subconscious will produce the results you desire. The finite cannot inform the Infinite. You are simply to say what you desire, not how you are to obtain it.

28. You are the channel by which the undifferentiated is being differentiated, and this differentiation is being accomplished by appropriation. It only requires recognition to set causes in motion which will bring about results in accordance with your desire, and this is accomplished because the Universal can act only through the individual, and the individual can act only through the Universal; they are one.

29. For your exercise this week, I will ask you to go one step further. I want you to not only be perfectly still, and inhibit all thought as far as possible, but relax, let go, let the muscles take their normal condition; this will remove all pressure from the nerves, and eliminate that tension which so frequently produces physical exhaustion.

30. Physical relaxation is a voluntary exercise of the will and the exercise will be found to be of great value, as it enables the blood to circulate freely to and from the brain and body.

31. Tension leads to mental unrest and abnormal mental activity of the mind; it produces worry, care, fear and anxiety. Relaxation is therefore an absolute necessity in order to allow the mental faculties to exercise the greatest freedom.

32. Make this exercise as thorough and complete as possible, mentally determine that you will relax every muscle and nerve, until you feel quiet and restful and at peace with yourself and the world.

33. The Solar Plexus will then be ready to function and you will be surprised at the result.

PART THREE:
STUDY QUESTIONS WITH ANSWERS

21. What system of nerves is the organ of the Conscious Mind?
  The Cerebro-spinal.

22. What system of nerves is the organ of the subconscious mind?
  The sympathetic.

23. What is the central point of distribution for energy which the body is constantly generating?
  The solar plexus.

24. How may this distribution be interrupted?
  By resistant, critical, discordant thoughts, but especially fear.

25. What is the result of such interruption?
    Every ill with which the human race is afflicted.

26. How may this energy be controlled and directed?
    By conscious thought.

27. How may fear be completely eliminated?
    By an understanding and recognition of the true source of all power.

28. What determines the experiences with which we meet in life?
    Our predominant mental attitude.

29. How may we awake the solar plexus?
    Mentally concentrate upon the condition which we desire to see manifested in our lives.

30. What is the creative principle of the Universe?
    The Universal Mind.

PART FOUR

Enclosed herewith I hand you Part Four. This part will show you why what you think, or do, or feel, is an indication of what you are.

Thought is energy and energy is power, and it is because all the religions, sciences and philosophies with which the world has heretofore been familiar have been based upon the manifestation of this energy instead of the energy itself, that the world has been limited to effects, while causes have been ignored or misunderstood.

For this reason we have God and the Devil in religion, positive and negative in science, and good and bad in philosophy.

The Master Key reverses the process; it is interested only in cause, and the letters received from students tell a marvelous story; they indicate conclusively that students are finding the cause whereby they may secure for themselves health, harmony, abundance, and whatever else may be necessary for their welfare and happiness.

Life is expressive and it is our business to express ourselves harmoniously and constructively. Sorrow, misery, unhappiness, disease and poverty are not necessities and we are constantly eliminating them.

But this process of eliminating consists in rising above and beyond limitation of any kind. He who has strengthened and purified his thought need *not concern himself about microbes, and he who has come into an understanding of the Law of Abundance will go at once to the source of supply.*

It is thus that fate, fortune, and destiny will be controlled as readily as a captain controls his ship, or an engineer, his train.

1. The "I" of you is not the physical body; that is simply an instrument which the "I" uses to carry out its purposes; the "I" cannot be the Mind, for the mind is simply another instrument which the "I" uses with which to think, reason, and plan.

2. The "I" must be something which controls and directs both the body and the mind; something which determines what they shall do and how they shall act. When you come into a realization of the true nature of this "I," you will enjoy a sense of power which you have never before known.

3. Your personality is made up of countless individual characteristics, peculiarities, habits, and traits of character; these are the result of your former method of thinking, but they have nothing to do with the real "I."

4. When you say "I think" the "I" tells the mind what it shall think; when you say "I go" the "I" tells the physical body where it shall go; the real nature of this "I" is spiritual, and is the source of the real power which comes to men and women when they come into a realization of their true nature.

5. The greatest and most marvelous power which this "I" has been given is the power to think, but few people know how to think constructively, or correctly, consequently they achieve only indifferent results. Most people allow their thoughts to dwell on selfish

purposes, the inevitable result of an infantile mind. When a mind becomes mature, it understands that the germ of defeat is in every selfish thought.

6. The trained mind knows that every transaction must benefit every person who is in any way connected with the transaction, and any attempt to profit by the weakness, ignorance or necessity of another will inevitably operate to his disadvantage.

7. This is because the individual is a part of the Universal. A part cannot antagonize any other part, but, on the contrary, the welfare of each part depends upon a recognition of the interest of the whole.

8. Those who recognize this principle have a great advantage in the affairs of life. They do not wear themselves out. They can eliminate vagrant thoughts with facility. They can readily concentrate to the highest possible degree on any subject. They do not waste time or money upon objects which can be of no possible benefit to them.

9. If you cannot do these things it is because you have thus far not made the necessary effort. Now is the time to make the effort. The result will be exactly in proportion to the effort expended. One of the strongest affirmations which you can use for the purpose of strengthening the will and realizing your power to accomplish, is, "I can be what I will to be."

10. Every time you repeat it realize who and what this "I" is; try to come into a thorough understanding of the true nature of the "I"; if you do, you will become invincible; that is, provided that your objects and purposes are constructive and are therefore in harmony with the creative principle of the Universe.

11. If you make use of this affirmation, use it continuously, night and morning, and as often during the day as you think of it, and continue to do so until it becomes a part of you; form the habit.

12. Unless you do this, you had better not start at all, because modern psychology tells us that when we start something and do not complete it, or make a resolution and do not keep it, we are forming the habit of failure; absolute, ignominious failure. If you do not intend to do a thing, do not start; if you do start, see it through even if the heavens fall; if you make up your mind to do something, do it; let nothing, no one, interfere; the "I" in you has determined, the thing is settled; the die is cast, there is no longer any argument.

13. If you carry out this idea, beginning with small things which you know you can control and gradually increase the effort, but never under any circumstances allowing your "I" to be overruled, you will find that you can eventually control yourself, and many men and women have found to their sorrow that it is easier to control a kingdom that to control themselves.

14. But when you have learned to control yourself you will have found the "World Within" which controls the world without; you will have become irresistible; men and things will respond to your every wish without any apparent effort on your part.

15. This is not so strange or impossible as it may appear when you remember that the "World Within" is controlled by the "I" and that this "I" is a part of or one with the Infinite "I" which is the Universal Energy or Spirit, usually called God.

16. This is not a mere statement or theory made for the purpose of confirming or establishing an idea, but it is a fact which has been accepted by the best religious thought as well as the best scientific thought.

17. Herbert Spender said: "Amid all the mysteries by which we are surrounded, nothing is more certain than that we are ever in the presence of an Infinite and Eternal Energy from which all things proceed."

18. Lyman Abbott, in an address delivered before the Alumni of Bangor Theological Seminary, said: "We are coming to think of God as dwelling in man rather than as operating on men from without."

19. Science goes a little way in its search and stops. Science finds the ever-present Eternal Energy, but Religion finds the Power behind this energy and locates it within man. But this is by no means a new discovery; the Bible says exactly the same thing, and the language is just as plain and convincing: "Know ye not that ye are the temple of the living God?" Here, then, is the secret of the wonderful creative power of the "World Within."

20. Here is the secret of power, of mastery. To overcome does not mean to go without things. Self-denial is not success. We cannot give unless we get; we cannot be helpful unless we are strong. The Infinite is not a bankrupt and we who are the representatives of Infinite power should not be bankrupts either, and if we wish to be of service to others we must have power and more power, but to get it we must give it; we must be of service.

21. The more we give the more we shall get; we must become a channel whereby the Universal can express activity. The Universal is constantly seeking to express itself, to be of service, and it seeks the channel whereby it can find the greatest activity, where it can do the most good, where it can be of greatest service to mankind.

22. The Universal cannot express through you as long as you are busy with your plans, your own purposes; quiet the senses, seek inspiration, focus the mental activity on the within, dwell in the consciousness of your unity with Omnipotence. "Still water runs deep"; contemplate the multitudinous opportunities to which you have spiritual access by the Omnipresence of power.

23. Visualize the events, circumstances and conditions which these spiritual connections may assist in manifesting. Realize the fact that the essence and soul of all things is spiritual and that the spiritual is the real, because it is the life of all there is; when the spirit is gone, the life is gone; it is dead; it has ceased to exist.

24. These mental activities pertain to the world within, to the world of cause; and conditions and circumstances which result are the effect. It is thus that you become a creator. This is important work, and the higher, loftier, grander and more noble ideals which you can conceive, the more important the work will become.

25. Over-work or over-play or over-bodily activity of any kind produces conditions of mental apathy and stagnation which make it impossible to do the more important work which results in a realization of conscious power. We should, therefore, seek the Silence frequently. Power comes through repose; it is in the Silence that we can be still, and when we are still, we can think, and thought is the secret of all attainment.

26. Thought is a mode of motion and is carried by the law of vibration the same as light or electricity. It is given vitality by the emotions through the law of love; it takes form and expression by the law of growth; it is a product of the spiritual "I," hence its Divine, spiritual, and creative nature.

27. From this it is evident that in order to express power, abundance or any other constructive purpose, the emotions must be called upon to give feeling to the thought so that it will take form. How may this purpose be accomplished? This is the vital point; how may we develop the faith, the courage, the feeling, which will result in accomplishment?

28. The reply is, by exercise; mental strength is secured in exactly the same way that physical strength is secured, by exercise. We think something, perhaps with difficulty the first time; we think the same thing again, and it becomes easier this time; we think it again and again; it then becomes a mental habit. We continue to think the same thing; finally it becomes automatic; we can no longer help thinking this thing; we are now positive of what we think; there is no longer any doubt about it. We are sure; we know.

29. Last week I asked you to relax, to let go physically. This week, I am going to ask you to let go mentally. If you practiced the exercise given you last week fifteen or twenty minutes a day in accordance with the instructions, you can no doubt relax physically; and anyone who cannot consciously do this quickly and completely is not a master of himself. He has not obtained freedom; he is still a slave to conditions. But I shall assume that you have mastered the exercise and are ready to take the next step, which is mental freedom.

30. This week, after taking your usual position, remove all tension by completely relaxing, then mentally let go of all adverse conditions, such as hatred, anger, worry, jealousy, envy, sorrow, trouble or disappointment of any kind.

31. You may say that you cannot "let go" of these things, but you can; you can do so by mentally determining to do so, by voluntary intention and persistence.

32. The reason that some cannot do this is because they allow themselves to be controlled by the emotions instead of by their intellect. But those who will be guided by the intellect will gain the victory. You will not succeed the first time you try, but practice makes perfect, in this as in everything else, and you must succeed in dismissing, eliminating and completely destroying these negative and destructive thoughts; because they are the seed which is constantly germinating into discordant conditions of every conceivable kind and description.

> *There is nothing truer than that the quality of thought which we entertain correlates certain externals in the outside world. This is the Law from which there is no escape. And it is this Law, this correlative of the thought with its object, that from time immemorial has led the people to believe in special providence.*

> —WILMANS

PART FOUR:
STUDY QUESTIONS WITH ANSWERS

31. What is thought?
Thought is spiritual energy.

32. How is it carried?
By the law of vibration.

33. How is it given vitality?
By the law of love.

34. How does it take form?
By the law of growth.

35. What is the secret of its creative power?
It is a spiritual activity.

36. How may we develop the faith, courage, and enthusiasm which will result in accomplishment?
By a recognition of our spiritual nature.

37. What is the secret of Power?
Service.

38. Why is this so?
Because we get what we give.

39. What is the Silence?
A physical stillness.

40. Of what value is it?
It is the first step to self-control, self-mastery.

PART FIVE

E nclosed herewith you will find Part Five. After studying this part carefully, you will see that every conceivable force or object or fact is the result of mind in action.

Mind in action is thought, and thought is creative. Men are thinking now as they never thought before.

Therefore, this is a creative age, and the world is awarding its richest prizes to the thinkers. Matter is powerless, passive, inert. Mind is force, energy, power. Mind shapes and controls matter. Every form which matter takes is but the expression of some pre-existing thought.

But thought works no magic transformations; it obeys natural laws; it sets in motion natural forces; it releases natural energies; it manifests itself in your conduct and actions, and these in turn react upon your friends and acquaintances, and eventually upon the whole of your environment. You can originate thought, and, since thoughts are creative, you can create for yourself the things you desire.

1. At least ninety per cent of our mental life is subconscious, so that those who fail to make use of this mental power live within very narrow limits.

2. The subconscious can and will solve any problem for us if we know how to direct it. The subconscious processes are always at work; the only question is, are we to be simply passive recipients of this activity, or are we to consciously direct the work? Shall we have a vision of the destination to be reached, the dangers to be avoided, or shall we simply drift?

3. We have found that mind pervades every part of the physical body and is always capable of being directed or impressed by authority coming from the objective or the more dominant portion of the mind.

4. The mind, which pervades the body, is largely the result of heredity, which, in turn, is simply the result of all the environments of all past generations on the responsive and ever-moving life forces. An understanding of this fact will enable us to use our authority when we find some undesirable trait of character manifesting itself.

5. We can consciously use all the desirable characteristics with which we have been provided and we can repress and refuse to allow the undesirable ones to be manifested.

6. Again, this mind which pervades our physical body is not only the result of hereditary tendencies, but is the result of home, business and social environment, where countless thousands of impressions, ideas, prejudices and similar thoughts have been received. Much of this has been received from others, the result of opinions, suggestions or statements; much of it is the result of our own thinking, but nearly all of it has been accepted with little or no examination or consideration.

7. The idea seemed plausible, the conscious received it, passed it on to the subconscious, where it was taken up by the Sympathetic Sys-

tem and passed on to be built into our physical body. "The word has become flesh."

8. This, then, is the way we are consistently creating and re-creating ourselves; we are today the result of our past thinking, and we shall be what we are thinking today, the Law of Attraction is bringing to us, not the things we should like, or the things we wish for, or the things someone else has, but it brings us "our own," the things which we have created by our thought processes, whether consciously or unconsciously. Unfortunately, many of us are creating these things unconsciously.

9. If either of us was building a home for ourself, how careful we would be in regard to the plans; how we should study every detail; how we should watch the material and select only the best of everything; and yet how careless we are when it comes to building our Mental Home, which is infinitely more important than any physical home, as everything which can possibly enter into our lives depends upon the character of the material which enters into the construction of our Mental Home.

10. What is the character of this material? We have seen that it is the result of the impressions which we have accumulated in the past and stored away in our subconscious Mentality. If these impressions have been of fear, of worry, of care, of anxiety; if they have been despondent, negative, doubtful, then the texture of the material which we are weaving today will be of the same negative material. Instead of being of any value, it will be mildewed and rotten and will bring us only more toil and care and anxiety. We shall be forever busy trying to patch it up and make it appear at least genteel.

11. But if we have stored away nothing but courageous thought, if we have been optimistic, positive, and have immediately thrown

any kind of negative thought on the scrap pile, have refused to have anything to do with it, have refused to associate with it or become identified with it in any way, what then is the result? Our mental material is now of the best kind; we can weave any kind of material we want; we can use any color we wish; we know that the texture is firm, that the material is solid, that it will not fade, and we have no fear, no anxiety concerning the future; there is nothing to cover, there are no patches to hide.

12. These are psychological facts; there is no theory or guesswork about these thinking processes; there is nothing secret about them; in fact, they are so plain that every one can understand them. The thing to do is to have a mental housecleaning, and to have this housecleaning every day, and keep the house clean. Mental, moral and physical cleanliness are absolutely indispensable if we are to make progress of any kind.

13. When this mental housecleaning process has been completed, the material which is left will be suitable for the making of the kind of ideals or mental images which we desire to realize.

14. There is a fine estate awaiting a claimant. Its broad acres, with abundant crops, running water and fine timber, stretch away as far as the eye can see. There is a mansion, spacious and cheerful, with rare pictures, a well-stocked library, rich hangings, and every comfort and luxury. All the heir has to do is to assert his heirship, take possession, and use the property. He must use it; he must not let it decay; for use is the condition on which he holds it. To neglect it is to lose possession.

15. In the domain of mind and spirit, in the domain of practical power, such an estate is yours. You are the heir! You can assert your

heirship and possess, and use this rich inheritance. Power over circumstances is one of its fruits, health, harmony and prosperity are assets upon its balance sheet. It offers you poise and peace. It costs you only the labor of studying and harvesting its great resources. It demands no sacrifice, except the loss of your limitations, your servitudes, your weakness. It clothes you with self-honor, and puts a scepter in your hands.

16. To gain this estate, three processes are necessary: You must earnestly desire it. You must assert your claim. You must take possession.

17. You admit that those are not burdensome conditions.

18. You are familiar with the subject of heredity. Darwin, Huxley, Haeckel, and other physical scientists have piled evidence mountain high that heredity is a law attending progressive creation. It is progressive heredity which gives man his erect attitude, his power of motion, the organs of digestion, blood circulation, nerve force, muscular force, bone structure and a host of other faculties on the physical side. There are even more impressive facts concerning heredity of mind force. All these constitute what may be called your human heredity.

19. But there is a heredity which the physical scientists have not compassed. It lies beneath and antecedent to all their researches. At a point where they throw up their hands in despair, saying they cannot account for what they see, this divine heredity is found in full sway.

20. It is the benignant force which decrees primal creation. It thrills down from the Divine, direct into every created being. It originates life, which the physical scientist has not done, nor ever can do. It stands out among all forces supreme, unapproachable. No human heredity can approach it. No human heredity measures up to it.

21. This Infinite Life flows through you; is you. Its doorways are but the faculties which comprise your consciousness. To keep open these doors is the Secret of Power. Is it not worthwhile to make the effort?

22. The great fact is, that the source of all life and all power is from within. Persons, circumstances and events may suggest need and opportunities, but the insight, strength and power to answer these needs will be found within.

23. Avoid counterfeits. Build firm foundations for your consciousness upon forces which flow direct from the Infinite source, the Universal Mind of which you are the image and likeness.

24. Those who have come into possession of this inheritance are never quite the same again. They have come into possession of a sense of power hitherto undreamed of. They can never again be timid, weak, vacillating, or fearful. They are indissolubly connected with Omnipotence. Something in them has been aroused; they have suddenly discovered that they possess a tremendous latent ability of which they were heretofore entirely unconscious.

25. This power is from within, but we cannot receive it unless we give it. Use is the condition upon which we hold this inheritance. We are each of us but the channel through which the Omnipotent power is being differentiated into form; unless we give, the channel is obstructed and we can receive no more. This is true on every plane of existence and in every field of endeavor and all walks of life.

The more we give, the more we get. The athlete who wishes to get strong must make use of the strength he has, and the more he gives the more he will get. The financier who wishes to make money must make use of the money he has, for only by using it can he get more.

26. The merchant who does not keep his goods going out will soon have none coming in; the corporation which fails to give efficient service will soon lack customers; the attorney who fails to get results will soon lack clients, and so it goes everywhere; power is contingent upon a proper use of the power already in our possession; what is true in every field of endeavor, every experience in life, is true of the power from which every other power known among men is begotten—spiritual power. Take away the spirit and what is left? Nothing.

27. If then the spirit is all there is, upon the recognition of this fact must depend the ability to demonstrate all power, whether physical, mental or spiritual.

28. All possession is the result of the accumulative attitude of mind, or the money consciousness; this is the magic wand which will enable you to receive the idea, and it will formulate plans for you to execute, and you will find as much pleasure in the execution as in the satisfaction of attainment and achievement.

29. Now, go to your room, take the same seat, the same position as heretofore, and mentally select a place which has pleasant associations. Make a complete mental picture of it, see the buildings, the grounds, the trees, friends, associations, everything complete. At first, you will find yourself thinking of everything under the sun, except the ideal upon which you desire to concentrate. But do not

let that discourage you. Persistence will win, but persistence requires that you practice these exercises every day without fail.

PART FIVE:
STUDY QUESTIONS WITH ANSWERS

41. What proportion of our mental life is subconscious?
At least ninety per cent.

42. Is this vast mental storehouse generally utilized?
No.

43. Why not?
Few understand or appreciate the fact that it is an activity which they may consciously direct.

44. Where has the conscious mind received its governing tendencies?
From heredity—which means that it is the result of all the environments of all past generations.

45. What is the Law of Attraction bringing to us?
Our "Own."

46. What is our "Own"?
What we inherently are, and is the result of our past thinking, both conscious and subconscious.

47. Of what is the material with which we construct our mental home composed?
The thoughts which we entertain.

48. What is the Secret of Power?
    A recognition of the omnipresence of omnipotence.

49. Where does it originate?
    All life and all power is from within.

50. Upon what is the possession of power contingent?
    Upon a proper use of the power already in our possession.

PART SIX

I t is my privilege to enclose Part Six. This part will give you an excellent understanding of the most wonderful piece of mechanism which has ever been created. A mechanism whereby you may create for yourself Health, Strength, Success, Prosperity or any other condition which you desire.

Necessities are demands, and demands create action, and actions bring about results. The process of evolution is constantly building our tomorrows out of our todays. Individual development, like Universal development, must be gradual with an ever-increasing capacity and volume.

The knowledge that if we infringe upon the rights of others, we become moral thorns and find ourselves entangled at every turn of the road, should be an indication that success is contingent upon the highest moral ideal, which is "The greatest good to the greatest number." Aspiration, desire and harmonious relations constantly and persistenly maintained will accomplish results. The greatest hindrance is erroneous and fixed ideas.

To be in tune with eternal truth we must possess poise and harmony within. In order to receive intelligence the receiver must be in tune with the transmitter.

Thought is a product of Mind and Mind is creative, but this does not mean that the Universal will change its modus operandi to suit us or our ideas, but it does mean that we can come into harmonious relationship with the Universal, and when we have accomplished this we may ask anything to which we are entitled, and the way will be made plain.

1. The Universal Mind is so wonderful that it is difficult to understand its utilitarian powers and possibilities and its unlimited producing effects.

2. We have found that this Mind is not only all intelligence but all substance. How, then, is it to be differentiated in form? How are we to secure the effect which we desire?

3. Ask any electrician what the effect of electricity will be and he will reply that "Electricity is a form of motion and its effect will depend upon the mechanism to which it is attached." Upon this mechanism will depend whether we shall have heat, light, power, music or any of the other marvelous demonstrations of power to which this vital energy has been harnessed.

4. What effect can be produced by thought? The reply is that thought is mind in motion (just as wind is air in motion), and its effect will depend entirely on the "mechanism to which it is attached."

5. Here, then, is the secret of all mental power; it depends entirely on the mechanism which we attach.

6. What is this mechanism? You know something of the mechanism which has been invented by Edison, Bell, Marconi and other electrical wizards, by which place and space and time have become only figures of speech, but did you ever stop to think that the mechanism which has been given you for transforming the Universal, Omnipresent Potential Power was invented by a greater inventor than Edison?

7. We are accustomed to examining the mechanism of the implements which we use for tilling the soil, and we try to get an understanding of the mechanism of the automobile which we drive, but most of us are content to remain in absolute ignorance of the greatest piece of mechanism which has ever come into existence, the brain of man.

8. Let us examine the wonders of this mechanism; perhaps we shall thereby get a better understanding of the various effects of which it is the cause.

9. In the first place, there is the great mental world in which we live and move and have our being; this world is omnipotent, omniscient and omnipresent; it will respond to our desire in direct ratio to our purpose and faith; the purpose must be in accordance with the law of our being, that is, it must be creative or constructive; our faith must be strong enough to generate a current of sufficient strength to bring our purpose into manifestation. "As thy faith is, so be it unto thee," bears the stamp of scientific test.

10. The effects which are produced in the world without are the result of the action and reaction of the individual upon the universal; that is the process which we call thinking; the brain is the organ through which this process is accomplished; think of the wonder of it all! Do you love music, flowers, literature, or are you inspired by the thought of ancient or modern genius? Remember, every beauty to which you respond must have its corresponding outline in your brain before you can appreciate it.

11. There is not a single virtue or principle in the storehouse of nature which the brain cannot express. The brain is an embryonic world, ready to develop at any time as necessity may arise. If you can comprehend that this is a scientific truth and one of the wonderful

laws of nature, it will be easier for you to get an understanding of the mechanism by which these extraordinary results are being accomplished.

12. The nervous system has been compared to an electric circuit with its battery of cells in which force is originated, and its white matter to insulated wires by which the current is conveyed; it is through these channels that every impulse or desire is carried through the mechanism.

13. The spinal cord is the great motor and sensory pathway by which messages are conveyed to and from the brain; then, there is the blood supply plunging through the veins and arteries, renewing our energy and strength, the perfectly arranged structure upon which the entire physical body rests, and, finally, the delicate and beautiful skin, clothing the entire mechanism in a mantle of beauty.

14. This then is the "Temple of the living God" and the individual "I" is given control and upon his understanding of the mechanism which is within his control will the result depend.

15. Every thought sets the brain cells in action; at first the substance upon which the thought is directed fails to respond, but if the thought is sufficiently refined and concentrated, the substance finally yields and expresses perfectly.

16. This influence of the mind can be exerted upon any part of the body, causing the elimination of any undesirable effect.

17. A perfect conception and understanding of the laws governing in the mental world cannot fail to be of inestimable value in the transaction of business, as it develops the power of discernment and gives a clearer understanding and appreciation of facts.

18. The man who looks within instead of without cannot fail to make use of the mighty forces which will eventually determine his course in life and so bring him into vibration with all that is best, strongest and most desirable.

19. Attention or concentration is probably the most important essential in the development of mind culture. The possibilities of attention when properly directed are so startling that they would hardly appear credible to the uninitiated. The cultivation of attention is the distinguishing characteristic of every successful man or woman, and is the very highest personal accomplishment which can be acquired.

20. The power of attention can be more readily understood by comparing it with a magnifying glass in which the rays of sunlight are focused; they possess no particular strength as long as the glass is moved about and the rays directed from one place to another; but let the glass be held perfectly still and let the rays be focused on one spot for any length of time, and the effect will become immediately apparent.

21. So with the power of thought; let power be dissipated by scattering the thought from one object to another, and no result is apparent; but focus this power through attention or concentration on any single purpose for any length of time and nothing becomes impossible.

22. A very simple remedy for a very complex situation, some will say. All right, try it, you who have had no experience in concentrating the thought on a definite purpose or object. Choose any single object and concentrate your attention on it for a definite purpose for even ten minutes; you cannot do it; the mind will wander a dozen times and it will be necessary to bring it back to the original purpose, and each time the effect will have been lost and at the end of the ten minutes nothing will have been gained, because you have not been able to hold your thought steadily to the purpose.

23. It is, however, through attention that you will finally be able to overcome obstacles of any kind that appear in your path onward and upward, and the only way to acquire this wonderful power is by practice—practice makes perfect, in this as in anything else.

24. In order to cultivate the power of attention, bring a photograph with you to the same seat in the same room in the same position as heretofore. Examine it closely at least ten minutes, note the expression of the eyes, the form of the features, the clothing, the way the hair is arranged; in fact, note every detail shown on the photograph carefully. Now cover it and close your eyes and try to see it mentally; if you can see every detail perfectly and can form a good mental image of the photograph, you are to be congratulated; if not, repeat the process until you can.

25. This step is simply for the purpose of preparing the soil; next week we shall be ready to sow the seed.

26. It is by such exercises as these that you will finally be able to control your mental moods, your attitude, your consciousness.

27. Great financiers are learning to withdraw from the multitude more and more, that they may have more time for planning, thinking and generating the right mental moods.

28. Successful businessmen are constantly demonstrating the fact that it pays to keep in touch with the thought of other successful businessmen.

29. A single idea may be worth millions of dollars, and these ideas can only come to those who are receptive, who are prepared to receive them, who are in a successful frame of mind.

30. Men are learning to place themselves in harmony with the Universal Mind; they are learning the unity of all things; they are learning the basic methods and principles of thinking, and this is changing conditions and multiplying results.

31. They are finding that circumstances and environment follow the trend of mental and spiritual progress; they find that growth follows knowledge; action follows inspiration; opportunity follows perception; always the spiritual first, then the transformation into the infinite and illimitable possibilities of achievement.

32. As the individual is but the channel for the differentiation of the Universal, these possibilities are necessarily inexhaustible.

33. Thought is the process by which we may absorb the Spirit of Power, and hold the result in our inner consciousness until it becomes a part of our ordinary consciousness. The method of accomplishing this result by the persistent practice of a few fundamental principles, as explained in this System, is the Master Key which unlocks the storehouse of Universal Truth.

34. The two great sources of human suffering at present are bodily disease and mental anxiety. These may be readily traced to the infringement of some natural law. This is, no doubt, owing to the fact that so far knowledge has largely remained partial, but the clouds of darkness which have accumulated through long ages are beginning to roll away and with them many of the miseries that attend imperfect information.

That a man can change himself, improve himself, re-create himself, control his environment, and master his own destiny is the conclusion of every mind who is wide-awake to the power of right thought in constructive action.

—LARSEN

PART SIX:
STUDY QUESTIONS WITH ANSWERS

51. What are some of the effects which can be produced by electricity?

Heat, light, power, music.

52. Upon what do these various effects depend?

Upon the mechanism to which electricity is attached.

53. What is the result of the action and interaction of the individual mind upon the Universal?

The conditions and experiences with which we meet.

54. How may these conditions be changed?

By changing the mechanism by which the Universal is differentiated in form.

55. What is this mechanism?

The brain.

56. How may it be changed?

By the process we call thinking. Thoughts produce brain cells, and these cells respond to the corresponding thought in the Universal.

57. Of what value is the power of concentration?

It is the very highest personal accomplishment which can be acquired, and the distinguishing characteristic of every successful man or woman.

58. How may it be acquired?

By faithfully practicing the exercises in this System.

59. Why is this so important?

Because it will enable us to control our thoughts, and since thoughts are causes conditions must be effects; if we can control the cause we can also control the effect.

60. What is changing conditions and multiplying results in the objective world?

Men are learning the basic methods of constructive thinking.

PART SEVEN

Through all the ages man has believed in an invisible power, through which and by which all things have been created and are continually being re-created. We may personalize this power and call it God, or we may think of it as the essence or spirit, which permeates all things, but in either case the effect is the same.

So far as the individual is concerned, the objective, the physical, the visible, is the personal, that which can be cognized by the senses. It consists of body, brain and nerves. The subjective is the spiritual, the invisible, the impersonal.

The personal is conscious because it is a personal entity. The impersonal, being the same in kind and quality as all other Being, is not conscious of itself and has therefore been termed the subconscious.

The personal, or conscious, has the power of will and choice, and can therefore exercise discrimination in the selection of methods whereby to bring about the solution of difficulties.

The impersonal, or spiritual, being a part or one with the source, and origin of all power, can necessarily exercise no such choice, but, on the contrary, it has Infinite resources at its command. It can and does bring about results by methods concerning which the human or individual mind can have no possible conception.

You will therefore see that it is your privilege to depend upon the human will with all its limitations and misconceptions, or you may utilize the potentialities of Infinity by making use of the subconscious mind. Here, then, is the scientific explanation of the wonderful power which has been put within your control, if you but understand, appreciate and recognize it.

One method of consciously utilizing this omnipotent power is outlined in Part Seven.

1. Visualization is the process of making mental images, and the image is the mold or model which will serve as a pattern from which your future will emerge.

2. Make the pattern clear and make it beautiful; do not be afraid; make it grand; remember that no limitation can be placed upon you by anyone but yourself; you are not limited as to cost or material; draw on the Infinite for your supply, construct it in your imagination; it will have to be there before it will ever appear anywhere else.

3. Make the image clear and clean-cut, hold it firmly in the mind and you will gradually and constantly bring the thing nearer to you. You can be what "you will to be."

4. This is another psychological fact which is well known, but unfortunately, reading about it will not bring about any result which you may have in mind; it will not even help you to form the mental image, much less bring it into manifestation. Work is necessary— labor, hard mental labor, the kind of effort which so few are willing to put forth.

5. The first step is idealization. It is likewise the most important step, because it is the plan on which you are going to build. It must be solid; it must be permanent. The architect, when he plans a

30-storey building, has every line and detail pictured in advance. The engineer, when he spans a chasm, first ascertains the strength requirements of a million separate parts.

6. They see the end before a single step is taken; so you are to picture in your mind what you want; you are sowing the seed, but before sowing any seed you want to know what the harvest is to be. This is Idealization. If you are not sure, return to the chair daily until the picture becomes plain; it will gradually unfold; first the general plan will be dim, but it will take shape, the outline will take form, then the details, and you will gradually develop the power by which you will be enabled to formulate plans which will eventually materialize in the objective world. You will come to know what the future holds for you.

7. Then comes the process of visualization. You must see the picture more and more complete, see the detail, and, as the details begin to unfold the ways and means for bringing it into manifestation will develop. One thing will lead to another. Thought will lead to action, action will develop methods, methods will develop friends, and friends will bring about circumstances, and, finally, the third step, or Materialization, will have been accomplished.

8. We all recognize the Universe must have been thought into shape before it ever could have become a material fact. And if we are willing to follow along the lines of the Great Architect of the Universe, we shall find our thoughts taking form, just as the universe took concrete form. It is the same mind operating through the individual. There is no difference in kind or quality, the only difference is one of degree.

9. The architect visualizes his building, he sees it as he wishes it to be. His thought becomes a plastic mold from which the building

will eventually emerge, a high one or a low one, a beautiful one or a plain one, his vision takes form on paper and eventually the necessary material is utilized and the building stands complete.

10. The inventor visualizes his idea in exactly the same manner, for instance, Nikola Tesla, he with the giant intellect, one of the greatest inventors of all ages, the man who has brought forth the most amazing realities, always visualizes his inventions before attempting to work them out. He did not rush to embody them in form and then spend his time in correcting defects. Having first built up the idea in his imagination, he held it there as a mental picture, to be reconstructed and improved by his thought. "In this way," he writes in the Electrical Experimenter. "I am enabled to rapidly develop and perfect a conception without touching anything. When I have gone so far as to embody in the invention every possible improvement I can think of, and see no fault anywhere, I put into concrete, the product of my brain. Invariably my device works as I conceived it should; in twenty years there has not been a single exception."

11. If you can conscientiously follow these directions, you will develop Faith, the kind of Faith that is the "Substance of things hoped for, the evidence of things not seen"; you will develop confidence, the kind of confidence that leads to endurance and courage; you will develop the power of concentration which will enable you to exclude all thoughts except the ones which are associated with your purpose.

12. The law is that thought will manifest itself in form, and only one who knows how to be the divine thinker of his own thoughts can ever take a Master's place and speak with authority.

13. Clearness and accuracy are obtained only by repeatedly having the image in mind. Each repeated action renders the image more

clear and accurate than the preceding, and in proportion to the clearness and accuracy of the image will the outward manifestation be. You must build it firmly and securely in your mental world, the world within, before it can take form in the world without, and you can build nothing of value, even in the mental world unless you have the proper material. When you have the material you can build anything you wish, but make sure of your material. You cannot make broadcloth from shoddy.

14. This material will be brought out by millions of silent mental workers and fashioned into the form of the image which you have in mind.

15. Think of it! You have over five million of these mental workers, ready and in active use; brain cells they are called. Besides this, there is another reserve force of at least an equal number, ready to be called into action at the slightest need. Your power to think, then, is almost unlimited, and this means that your power to create the kind of material which is necessary to build for yourself any kind of environment which you desire is practically unlimited.

16. In addition to these millions of mental workers, you have billions of mental workers in the body, every one of which is endowed with sufficient intelligence to understand and act upon any message or suggestion given. These cells are all busy creating and re-creating the body, but, in addition to this, they are endowed with psychic activity whereby they can attract to themselves the substance necessary for perfect development.

17. They do this by the same law and in the same manner that every form of life attracts to itself the necessary material for growth. The oak, the rose, the lily, all require certain material for their most perfect expression and they secure it by silent demand, the Law of Attraction, the most certain way for you to secure what you require for your most complete development.

18. Make the Mental Image; make it clear, distinct, perfect; hold it firmly; the ways and means will develop; supply will follow the demand; you will be led to do the right thing at the right time and in the right way. Earnest Desire will bring about Confident Expectation, and this in turn must be reinforced by Firm Demand. These three cannot fail to bring about Attainment, because the Earnest Desire is the feeling, the Confident Expectation is the thought, and the Firm Demand is the will, and, as we have seen, feeling gives vitality to thought and the will holds it steadily until the law of growth brings it into manifestation.

19. Is it not wonderful that man has such tremendous power within himself, such transcendental faculties concerning which he had no conception? Is it not strange that we have always been taught to look for strength and power "without"? We have been taught to look everywhere but "within" and whenever this power manifested itself in our lives we were told that it was something supernatural.

20. There are many who have come to an understanding of this wonderful power, and who make serious and conscientious efforts to realize health, power, and other conditions, and seem to fail. They do not seem able to bring the law into operation. The difficulty in nearly every case is that they are dealing with externals. They want money, power, health and abundance, but they fail to realize that these are effects and can come only when the cause is found.

21. Those who will give no attention to the world without will seek only to ascertain the truth, will look only for wisdom, will find that this wisdom will unfold and disclose the source of all power, that it will manifest itself in thought and purpose which will create the external conditions desired. This truth will find expression in noble purpose and courageous action.

22. Create ideals only, give no thought to external conditions, make the world within beautiful and opulent and the world without will express and manifest the condition which you have within. You will come into a realization of your power to create ideals and these ideals will be projected into the world of effect.

23. For instance, a man is in debt. He will be continually thinking about the debt, concentrating on it, and as thoughts are causes the result is that he not only fastens the debt closer to him, but actually creates more debt. He is putting the great Law of Attraction into operation with the usual and inevitable result—Loss leads to greater "Loss."

24. What, then, is the correct principle? Concentrate on the things you want, not on the things you do not want. Think of abundance; idealize the methods and plans for putting the Law of Abundance into operation. Visualize the condition which the Law of Abundance creates; this will result in manifestation.

25. If the law operates perfectly to bring about poverty, lack and every form of limitation for those who are continually entertaining thoughts of lack and fear, it will operate with the same certainty to bring about conditions of abundance and opulence for those who entertain thoughts of courage and power.

26. This is a difficult problem for many; we are too anxious; we manifest anxiety, fear, distress; we want to do something; we want to help; we are like a child who has just planted a seed and every

fifteen minutes goes and stirs up the earth to see if it is growing. Of course, under such circumstances, the seed will never germinate, and yet this is exactly what many of us do in the mental world.

27. We must plant the seed and leave it undisturbed. This does not mean that we are to sit down and do nothing, by no means; we will do more and better work than we have ever done before, new channels will constantly be provided, new doors will open; all that is necessary is to have an open mind, be ready to act when the time comes.

28. Thought force is the most powerful means of obtaining knowledge, and if concentrated on any subject will solve the problem. Nothing is beyond the power of human comprehension, but in order to harness thought force and make it do your bidding, work is required.

29. Remember that thought is the fire that creates the steam that turns the wheel of fortune, upon which your experiences depend.

30. Ask yourself a few questions and then reverently await the response; do you not now and then feel the self with you? Do you assert this self or do you follow the majority? Remember that majorities are always led, they never lead. It was the majority that fought, tooth and nail, against the steam engine, the power loom and every other advance or improvement ever suggested.

31. For your exercise this week, visualize your friend, see him exactly as you last saw him, see the room, the furniture, recall the conversation, now see his face, see it distinctly, now talk to him about some subject of mutual interest; see his expression change, watch him smile. Can you do this? All right, you can; then arouse

his interest, tell him a story of adventure, see his eyes light up with the spirit of fun or excitement. Can you do all of this? If so, your imagination is good, you are making excellent progress.

PART SEVEN:
STUDY QUESTIONS WITH ANSWERS

61. What is visualization?
    The process of making mental pictures.

62. What is the result of this method of thought?
    By holding the image or picture in mind, we can gradually but surely bring the thing nearer to us. We can be what we will to be.

63. What is Idealization?
    It is a process of visualizing or idealizing the plans which will eventually materialize in our objective world.

64. Why are clearness and accuracy necessary?
    Because "seeing" creates "feeling" and "feeling" creates "being." First the mental, then the emotional, then the illimitable possibilities of achievement.

65. How are they obtained?
    Each repeated action renders the image more accurate than the former one.

66. How is the material for the construction of your mental image secured?
    By millions of mental workers. Brain cells they are called.

67. How are the necessary conditions for bringing about the materialization of your ideal in the objective world secured?

By the Law of Attraction. The natural law by which all conditions and experiences are brought about.

68. What three steps are necessary in order to bring this law into operation?

Earnest Desire, Confident Expectation, Firm Demand.

69. Why do many fail?

Because they concentrate on loss, disease and disaster. The law is operating perfectly; the things they fear are coming upon them.

70. What is the alternative?

Concentrate on the ideals which you desire to see manifested in your life.

PART EIGHT

I n this Part you will find that you may freely choose what you think but the result of your thought is governed by an immutable law! Is not this a wonderful thought? Is it not wonderful to know that our lives are not subject to caprice or variability of any kind? That they are governed by law. This stability is our opportunity, because by complying with the law we can secure the desired effect with invariable precision.

It is the Law which makes the Universe one grand paean of Harmony. If it were not for law, the Universe would be a Chaos instead of a Cosmos.

Here, then, is the secret of the origin of both good and evil, this is all the good and evil there ever was or ever will be.

Let me illustrate. Thought results in action, if your thought is constructive and harmonious, the result will be good; if your thought is destructive or inharmonious, the result will be evil.

There is therefore but one law, one principle, on cause, one Source of Power, and good and evil are simply words which have been coined to indicate the result of our action, or our compliance or non-compliance with this law.

The importance of this is well illustrated in the lives of Emerson and Carlyle. Emerson loved the good and his life was a symphony of peace and harmony, Carlyle hated the bad, and his life was a record of perpetual discord and inharmony.

Here we have two grand men, each intent upon achieving the same ideal, but one makes use of constructive thought and is therefore in harmony with natural law, the other makes use of destructive thought and therefore brings upon himself discord of every kind and character.

It is evident therefore that we are to hate nothing, not even the "bad," because hatred is destructive, and we shall soon find that by entertaining destructive thought we are sowing the "wind" and in turn shall reap the "whirlwind."

1. Thought contains a vital principle, because it is the creative principle of the Universe and by its nature will combine with other similar thoughts.

2. As the one purpose of life is growth, all principles underlying existence must contribute to give it effect. Thought, therefore, takes form and the law of growth eventually brings it into manifestation.

3. You may freely choose what you think, but the result of your thought is governed by an immutable law. Any line of thought persisted in cannot fail to produce its result in the character, health and circumstances of the individual. Methods whereby we can substitute habits of constructive thinking for those which we have found produce only undesirable effects are therefore of primary importance.

4. We all know that this is by no means easy. Mental habits are difficult to control, but it can be done and the way to do it is to begin at once to substitute constructive thought for destructive thought. Form the habit of analyzing every thought. If it is necessary, if its manifestation in the objective will be a benefit, not only to yourself, but to all whom it may affect in any way, keep it; treasure it; it is of value; it is in tune with the Infinite; it will grow and develop and produce fruit a hundredfold. On the other hand, it will be well for

you to keep this quotation from George Matthews Adams, in mind, "Learn to keep the door shut, keep out of your mind, out of your office, and out of your world, every element that seeks admittance with no definite helpful end in view."

5. If your thought has been critical or destructive, and has resulted in any condition of discord or inharmony in your environment, it may be necessary for you to cultivate a mental attitude which will be conducive to constructive thought.

6. The imagination will be found to be a great assistance in this direction; the cultivation of the imagination leads to the development of the ideal out of which your future will emerge.

7. The imagination gathers up the material by which the Mind weaves the fabric in which your future is to be clothed.

8. Imagination is the light by which we can penetrate new worlds of thought and experience.

9. Imagination is the mighty instrument by which every discoverer, every inventor, opened the way from precedent to experience. Precedent said, "It cannot be done;" experience said, "It is done."

10. Imagination is a plastic power, molding the things of sense into new forms and ideals.

11. Imagination is the constructive form of thought which must precede every constructive form of action.

12. A builder cannot build a structure of any kind until he has first received the plans from the architect, and the architect must get them from his imagination.

13. The Captain of Industry cannot build a giant corporation which may coordinate hundreds of smaller corporations and thousands of employees, and utilize millions of dollars of capital until he has first created the entire work in his imagination. Objects in the material world are as clay in the potter's hand; it is in the Master Mind that the real things are created, and it is by the use of the imagination that the work is done. In order to cultivate the imagination it must be exercised. Exercise is necessary to cultivate mental muscle as well as physical muscle. It must be supplied with nourishment or it cannot grow.

14. Do not confuse Imagination with Fancy, or that form of daydreaming in which some people like to indulge. Daydreaming is a form of mental dissipation which may lead to mental disaster.

15. Constructive imagination means mental labor, by some considered to be the hardest kind of labor, but, if so, it yields the greatest returns, for all the great things in life have come to men and women who had the capacity to think, to imagine, and to make their dreams come true.

16. When you have become thoroughly conscious of the fact that Mind is the only creative principle, that it is Omnipotent, Omniscient and Omnipresent, and that you can consciously come into harmony with this Omnipotence through your power of thought, you will have taken a long step in the right direction.

17. The next step is to place yourself in position to receive this power. As it is Omnipresent, it must be within you. We know that this is so because we know that all power is from within, but it must be developed, unfolded, cultivated; in order to do this we must be receptive, and this receptivity is acquired just as physical strength is gained, by exercise.

18. The Law of Attraction will certainly and unerringly bring to you the conditions, environment, and experiences in life, corresponding with your habitual, characteristic, predominant mental attitude. Not what you think once in a while when you are in church, or have just read a good book, BUT your predominant mental attitude is what counts.

19. You cannot entertain weak, harmful, negative thoughts ten hours a day and expect to bring about beautiful, strong and harmonious conditions by ten minutes of strong, positive, creative thought.

20. Real power comes from within. All power that anybody can possibly use is within man, only waiting to be brought into visibility by his first recognizing it, and then affirming it as his, working it into his consciousness until he becomes one with it.

21. People say that they desire abundant life, and so they do, but so many interpret this to mean that if they will exercise their muscles or breathe scientifically, eat certain foods in certain ways, drink so many glasses of water every day of just a certain temperature, keep out of drafts, they will attain the abundant life they seek. The result of such methods is but indifferent. However, when man awakens to the truth, and affirms his oneness with all Life, he finds that he takes on the clear eye, the elastic step, the vigor of youth; he finds that he has discovered the source of all power.

22. All mistakes are but the mistakes of ignorance. Knowledge gaining and consequent power is what determines growth and evolution. The recognition and demonstration of knowledge is what constitutes power, and this power is spiritual power, and this spiritual power is the power which lies at the heart of all things; it is the soul of the universe.

23. This knowledge is the result of man's ability to think; thought is therefore the germ of man's conscious evolution. When man ceases to advance in his thoughts and ideals, his forces immediately begin to disintegrate and his countenance gradually registers these changing conditions.

24. Successful men make it their business to hold ideals of the conditions which they wish to realize. They constantly hold in mind the next step necessary to the ideal for which they are striving. Thoughts are the materials with which they build, and the imagination is their mental workshop. Mind is the ever-moving force with which they secure the persons and circumstance necessary to build their success structure, and imagination is the matrix in which all great things are fashioned.

25. If you have been faithful to your ideal, you will hear the call when circumstances are ready to materialize your plans and results will correspond in the exact ratio of your fidelity to your ideal. The ideal steadily held is what pre-determines and attracts the necessary conditions for its fulfillment.

26. It is thus that you may weave a garment of spirit and power into the web of your entire existence; it is thus that you may lead a charmed life and be forever protected from all harm; it is thus that you may become a positive force whereby conditions of opulence and harmony may be attracted to you.

27. This is the leaven which is gradually permeating the general consciousness and is largely responsible for the conditions of unrest which are everywhere evident.

28. In the last Part you created a mental image, you brought it from the invisible into the visible; this week I want you to take an object

and follow it back to its origination, see of what it really consists. If you do this you will develop imagination, insight, perception, and sagacity. These come not by the superficial observation of the multitude, but by a keen analytical observation which sees below the surface.

29. It is the few who know that the things which they see are only effects, and understand the causes by which these effects were brought into existence.

30. Take the same position as heretofore and visualize a battleship; see the grim monster floating on the surface of the water; there appears to be no life anywhere about; all is silence; you know that by far the largest part of the vessel is under water; out of sight; you know that the ship is as large and as heavy as a twenty-story skyscraper; you know that there are hundreds of men ready to spring to their appointed task instantly; you know that every department is in charge of able, trained, skilled officials who have proven themselves competent to take charge of this marvelous piece of mechanism; you know that although it lies apparently oblivious to everything else, it has eyes which see everything for miles around, and nothing is permitted to escape its watchful vision; you know that while it appears quiet, submissive and innocent, it is prepared to hurl a steel projectile weighing thousands of pounds at an enemy many miles away; this and much more you can bring to mind with comparatively no effort whatever. But how did the battleship come to be where it is; how did it come into existence in the first place? All of this you want to know if you are a careful observer.

31. Follow the great steel plates through the foundries, see the thousands of men employed in their production; go still further back, and see the ore as it comes from the mine, see it loaded on barges or cars, see it melted and properly treated; go back still further and see the architect and engineers who planned the vessel; let the thought carry you back still further in order to determine why they planned the vessel; you will see that you are now so far back that the vessel is something intangible, it no longer exists, it is now only a thought existing in the brain of the architect; but from where did the order come to plan the vessel? Probably from the Secretary of Defense; but probably this vessel was planned long before the war was thought of, and that Congress had to pass a bill appropriating the money; possibly there was opposition, and speeches for or against the bill. Whom do these Congressmen represent? They represent you and me, so that our line of thought begins with the battleship and ends with ourselves, and we find in the last analysis that our own thought is responsible for this and many other things, of which we seldom think, and a little further reflection will develop the most important fact of all and that is, if someone had not discovered the law by which this tremendous mass of steel and iron could be made to float upon the water, instead of immediately going to the bottom, the battleship could not have come into existence at all.

32. This law is that, "the specific gravity of any substance is the weight of any volume of it, compared with an equal volume of water." The discovery of this law revolutionized every kind of ocean travel, commerce and warfare, and made the existence of the battle-ship, aircraft carriers, and cruise ships possible.

33. You will find exercises of this kind invaluable. When the thought has been trained to look below the surface everything takes on a different appearance, the insignificant becomes significant, the uninteresting interesting; the things which we supposed to be of no importance are seen to be the only really vital things in existence.

*Look to This Day for it is Life, the very Life of Life. In Its brief course
lie all the Verities and Realities of your existence; The Bliss of Growth;*

The Glory of Action; The Splendor of Beauty; For Yesterday is but a Dream, And tomorrow is only a Vision: But Today well lived makes every Yesterday a Dream of Happiness, and Every Tomorrow a Vision of Hope. Look well, therefore, to This Day!

—From the Sanskrit

PART EIGHT:
STUDY QUESTIONS WITH ANSWERS

71. What is the imagination?

A form of constructive thought. The light by which we penetrate new worlds of thought and experience. The mighty instrument by which every inventor or discoverer opened the way from precedent to experience.

72. What is the result of imagination?

The cultivation of the imagination leads to the development of the ideal out of which your future will emerge.

73. How may it be cultivated?

By exercise; it must be supplied with nourishment or it cannot live.

74. How does imagination differ from daydreaming?

Daydreaming is a form of mental dissipation, while imagination is a form of constructive thought which must precede every constructive action.

75. What are mistakes?

The result of ignorance.

76. What is knowledge?

The result of man's ability to think.

77. What is the power with which successful men build?

 Mind is the very moving force with which they secure the persons and circumstances necessary to complete their plans.

78. What pre-determines the result?

 The ideal held steadily in mind attracts the necessary conditions for its fulfillment.

79. What is the result of a keen analytical observation?

 The development of imagination, insight, perception and sagacity.

80. To what do these lead?

 Opulence and harmony.

PART NINE

In this Part you may learn to fashion the tools by which you may build for yourself any condition you desire. If you wish to change conditions you must change yourself. Your whims, your wishes, your fancies, your ambitions may be thwarted at every step, but your inmost thoughts will find expression just as certainly as the plant springs from the seed.

Suppose, then, we desire to change conditions, how are we to bring this about? The reply is simple: By the law of growth. Cause and effect are as absolute and undeviating in the hidden realm of thought as in the world of material things.

Hold in mind the condition desired; affirm it as an already existing fact. This indicates the value of a powerful affirmation. By constant repetition it becomes a part of ourselves. We are actually changing ourselves; are making ourselves what we want to be.

Character is not a thing of chance, but it is the result of continued effort. If you are timid, vacillating, self-conscious, or if you are over-anxious or harassed by thoughts of fear or impending danger, remember that it is axiomatic that "two things cannot exist in the same place at the same time."

Exactly the same thing is true in the mental and spiritual world; so that your remedy is plainly to substitute thoughts of courage, power, self-reliance and confidence, for those of fear, lack and limitation.

The easiest and most natural way to do this is to select an affirmation which seems to fit your particular case.

The positive thought will destroy the negative as certainly as light destroys darkness, and the results will be just as effectual.

Act is the blossom of thought, and conditions are the result of action, so that you constantly have in your possession the tools by which you will certainly and inevitably make or unmake yourself, and joy or suffering will be the reward.

1. There are only three things which can possibly be desired in the "world without" and each of them can be found in the "world within." The secret of finding them is simply to apply the proper "mechanism" of attachment to the omnipotent power to which each individual has access.

2. The three things which all mankind desires and which are necessary for his highest expression and complete development are Health, Wealth and Love. All will admit that Health is absolutely essential; no one can be happy if the physical body is in pain. All will not so readily admit that Wealth is necessary, but all must admit that a sufficient supply at least is necessary, and what would be considered sufficient for one, would be considered absolute and painful lack for another; and as nature provides not only enough but abundantly, wastefully, lavishly, we realize that any lack or limitation is only the limitation which has been made by an artificial method of distribution.

3. All will probably admit that Love is the third, or maybe some will say the first essential necessary to the happiness of mankind; at any rate, those who possess all three, Health, Wealth, and Love, find nothing else which can be added to their cup of happiness.

4. We have found that the Universal substance is "All Health," "All Substance" and "All Love" and that the mechanism of attachment whereby we can consciously connect with this Infinite supply is in

our method of thinking. To think correctly is therefore to enter into the "Secret Place of the Most High."

5. What shall we think? If we know this we shall have found the proper mechanism of attachment which will relate us to "Whatsoever things we desire." This mechanism may seem very simple when I give it to you, but read on; you will find that it is in reality the "Master Key," the "Aladdin's lamp," if you please; you will find that it is the foundation, the imperative condition, the absolute law of well-doing, which means, well-being.

6. To think correctly, accurately, we must know the "Truth." The truth then is the underlying principle in every business or social relation. It is a condition precedent to every right action. To know the truth, to be sure, to be confident, affords a satisfaction beside which no other is at all comparable; it is the only solid ground in a world of doubt, conflict and danger.

7. To know the Truth is to be in harmony with the Infinite and Omnipotent power. To know the truth is, therefore, to connect yourself with a power which is irresistible and which will sweep away every kind of discord, inharmony, doubt or error of any kind, because the "Truth is mighty and will prevail."

8. The humblest intellect can readily foretell the result of any action when he knows that it is based on truth, but the mightiest intellect, the most profound and penetrating mind loses its way hopelessly and can form no conception of the results which may ensue when his hopes are based on a premise which he knows to be false.

9. Every action which is not in harmony with Truth, whether through ignorance or design, will result in discord, and eventual loss in proportion to its extent and character.

10. How then are we to know the truth in order to attach this mechanism which will relate us to the Infinite?

11. We can make no mistake about this if we realize that truth is the vital principle of the Universal Mind and is Omnipresent. For instance, if you require health, a realization of the fact that the "I" in you is spiritual and that all spirit is one; that wherever a part is the whole must be, will bring about a condition of health, because every cell in the body must manifest the truth as you see it. If you see sickness; they will manifest sickness; if you see perfection they must manifest perfection. The affirmation, "I am whole, perfect, strong, powerful, loving, harmonious and happy" will bring about harmonious conditions. The reason for this is because the affirmation is in strict accordance with the Truth, and when truth appears every form of error or discord must necessarily disappear.

12. You have found that the "I" is spiritual, it must necessarily then always be no less than perfect, the affirmation. "I am whole, perfect, strong, powerful, loving, harmonious and happy" is therefore an exact scientific statement.

13. Thought is a spiritual activity and spirit is creative, therefore the result of holding this thought in mind, must necessarily bring about conditions in harmony with the thought.

14. If you require Wealth a realization of the fact that the "I" in you is one with the Universal mind which is all substance, and is Omnipotent, will assist you in bringing into operation the Law of Attraction which will bring you into vibration with those forces which make for success and bring about conditions of power and affluence in direct proportion with the character and purpose of your affirmation.

15. Visualization is the mechanism of the attachment which you require. Visualization is a very different process from seeing; seeing is physical, and is therefore related to the objective world, the "world without," but Visualization is a product of the imagination, and is therefore a product of the subjective mind, the "world within." It therefore possesses vitality; it will grow. The thing visualized will manifest itself in form. The mechanism is perfect; it was created by the Master Architect who "doeth all things well," but unfortunately sometimes the operator is inexperienced or inefficient, but practice and determination will overcome this defect.

16. If you require Love try to realize that the only way to get love is by giving it, that the more you give the more you will get, and the only way in which you can give it, is to fill yourself with it, until you become a magnet. The method was explained in another lesson.

17. He who has learned to bring the greatest spiritual truths into touch with the so-called lesser things of life has discovered the secret of the solution of his problem. One is always quickened, made more thoughtful, by his nearness of approach to great ideas, great events, great natural objects, and great men. Lincoln is said to have begotten in all who came near him the feeling awakened when one approaches a mountain, and this sense asserts itself most keenly when one comes to realize that he has laid hold upon things that are eternal, the power of Truth.

18. It is sometimes an inspiration to hear from someone who has actually put these principles to the test, someone who has demonstrated them in their own life. A letter from Frederick Andrews offers the following insight:

19. I was about thirteen years old when Dr. T. W. Marsee, since passed over, said to my mother: "There is no possible chance,

Mrs. Andrews. I lost my little boy the same way, after doing everything for him that it was possible to do. I have made a special study of these cases, and I know there is no possible chance for him to get well."

20. She turned to him and said: "Doctor, what would you do if he were your boy?" and he answered, "I would fight, fight, as long as there is a breath of life to fight for."

21. That was the beginning of a long, drawn-out battle, with many ups and downs, the doctors all agreeing that there was no chance for a cure, though they encouraged and cheered us the best they could.

22. But at last the victory came, and I have grown from a little, crooked, twisted, cripple, going about on my hands and knees, to a strong, straight, well-formed man.

23. Now, I know you want the formula, and I will give it to you as briefly and quickly as I can.

24. I built up an affirmation for myself, taking the qualities I most needed, and affirming for myself over and over again, "I am whole, perfect, strong, powerful, loving, harmonious and happy." I kept up this affirmation, always the same, never varying, till I could wake up in the night and find myself repeating, "I am whole, perfect, strong, powerful, loving, harmonious and happy." It was the last thing on my lips at night and the first thing in the morning.

25. Not only did I affirm it for myself, but for others that I knew needed it. I want to emphasize this point. Whatever you desire for yourself, affirm it for others, and it will help you both. We reap what we sow. If we send out thoughts of love and health, they return

to us like bread cast upon the waters; but if we send out thoughts of fear, worry, jealousy, anger, hate, etc., we will reap the results in our own lives.

26. It used to be said that man is completely built over every seven years, but some scientists now declare that we build ourselves over entirely every eleven months; so we are really only eleven months old. If we build the defects back into our bodies year after year, we have no one to blame but ourselves.

27. Man is the sum total of his own thoughts; so the question is, how are we going to entertain only the good thoughts and reject the evil ones? At first we can't keep the evil thoughts from coming, but we can keep from entertaining them. The only way to do this is to forget them—which means, get something for them. This is where the ready-made affirmation comes into play.

28. When a thought of anger, jealousy, fear or worry creeps in, just start your affirmation going. The way to fight darkness is with light—the way to fight cold is with heat—the way to overcome evils is with good. For myself, I never could find any help in denials. Affirm the good, and the bad will vanish.—Frederick Elias Andrews.

29. If there is anything you require, it will be well for you to make use of this affirmation; it cannot be improved upon. Use it just as it is; take it into the silence with you, until it sinks into your subconsciousness, so that you can use it anywhere, in your car, in the office, at home; this is the advantage of spiritual methods; they are always available. Spirit is omnipresent, ever ready; all that is required is a proper recognition of its omnipotence, and a willingness or desire to become the recipient of its beneficent effects.

30. If our predominant mental attitude is one of power, courage, kindliness and sympathy, we shall find that our environment will reject conditions in correspondence with these thoughts; if it is weak, critical, envious and destructive, we shall find our environment reflecting conditions corresponding to these thoughts.

31. Thoughts are causes and conditions are effects. Herein is the explanation of the origin of both good and evil. Thought is creative and will automatically correlate with its object. This is a cosmological law (a universal law), the Law of Attraction, the law of cause and effect; the recognition and application of this law will determine both beginning and end; it is the law by which in all ages and in all times the people were led to believe in the power of prayer. "As thy faith is, so be it unto thee," is simply another, shorter and a better way of stating it.

32. This week visualize a plant; take a flower, the one you most admire, bring it from the unseen into the seen, plant the tiny seed, water it, care for it, place it where it will get the direct rays of the morning sun, see the seed burst; it is now a living thing, something which is alive and beginning to search for the means of subsistence. See the roots penetrating the earth, watch them shoot out in all directions and remember that they are living cells dividing and subdividing, and that they will soon number millions, that each cell is intelligent, that it knows what is wants and knows how to get it. See the stem shoot forward and upward, watch it burst through the surface of the earth, see it divide and form branches, see how perfect and symmetrical each branch is formed, see the leaves begin to form, and then the tiny stems, each one holding aloft a bud, and as you watch you see the bud begin to unfold and your favorite flower comes to view; and now if you will concentrate intently you will become conscious of a fragrance; it is the fragrance of the

flower as the breeze gently sways the beautiful creation which you have visualized.

33. When you are enabled to make your vision clear and complete you will be enabled to enter into the spirit of a thing; it will become very real to you; you will be learning to concentrate and the process is the same, whether you are concentrating on health, a favorite flower, an ideal, a complicated business proposition or any other problem of life.

34. Every success has been accomplished by persistent concentration upon the object in view.

PART NINE:
STUDY QUESTIONS WITH ANSWERS

81. What is the imperative condition of all well-being?
   Well doing.

82. What is the condition precedent to every right action?
   Right thinking.

83. What is the underlying condition necessary in every business transaction or social relation?
   To know the Truth.

84. What is the result of a knowledge of the Truth?
   We can readily predict the result of any action that is based upon a true premise.

85. What is the result of any action based upon a false premise?
    We can form no conception of the results which may ensue.

86. How may we know the Truth?
    By a realization of the fact that Truth is the vital principle of the Universe and is therefore omnipresent.

87. What is the nature of Truth?
    It is spiritual.

88. What is the secret of the solution to every problem?
    To apply spiritual Truth.

89. What is the advantage of spiritual methods?
    They are always available.

90. What are the necessary requirements?
    A recognition of the omnipotence of spiritual power and a desire to become the recipient of its beneficent effects.

Thought means life, since those who do not think do not live in any high or real sense. Thinking makes the man.

—A. B. ALCOTT

PART TEN

If you get a thorough understanding of the thought contained in Part Ten, you will have learned that nothing happens without a definite cause. You will be enabled to formulate your plans in accordance with exact knowledge. You will know how to control any situation by bringing adequate causes into play. When you win, as you will, you will know exactly why.

The ordinary man, who has no definite knowledge of cause and effect, is governed by his feelings or emotions.

He thinks chiefly to justify his action. If he fails as a businessman, he says that luck is against him. If he dislikes music, he says that music is an expensive luxury. If he is a poor office man, he says that he could succeed better at some outdoor work. If he lacks friends, he says his individuality is too fine to be appreciated.

He never thinks his problem through to the end. In short, he does not know that every effect is the result of a certain definite cause, but he seeks to console himself with explanations and excuses. He thinks only in self-defense.

On the contrary, the man who understands that there is no effect without an adequate cause thinks impersonally. He gets down to bedrock facts regardless of consequences. He is free to follow the trail of truth wherever it may lead. He sees the issue clear to the end, and he meets the requirements fully *and fairly, and the result is that the world gives him all that it has to give, in friendship, honor, love and approval.*

1. Abundance is a natural law of the Universe. The evidence of this law is conclusive; we see it on every hand. Everywhere, nature is lavish, wasteful, extravagant. Nowhere is economy observed in any created thing. Profusion is manifested in everything. The millions and millions of trees and flowers and plants and animals and the vast scheme of reproduction where the process of creating and re-creating is forever going on, all indicate the lavishness with which nature has made provision for man. That there is an abundance for everyone is evident, but that many fail to participate in this abundance is also evident; they have not yet come into a realization of the Universality of all substance, and that mind is the active principle whereby we are related to the things we desire.

2. All wealth is the offspring of power; possessions are of value only as they confer power. Events are significant only as they affect power; all things represent certain forms and degrees of power.

3. Knowledge of cause and effect as shown by the laws governing electricity, chemical affinity and gravitation, enables man to plan courageously and execute fearlessly. These laws are called natural laws, because they govern in the physical world, but all power is not physical power; there is also mental power, and there is moral and spiritual power.

4. Spiritual power is superior because it exists on a higher plane. It has enabled man to discover the law by which these wonderful forces of Nature could be harnessed and made to do the work of hundreds and thousands of men. It has enabled man to discover laws whereby time and space have been annihilated and the law of

gravitation to be overcome. The operation of this law is dependent upon spiritual contact, as Henry Drummond well says:

5. "In the physical world as we know it, there exists the organic and the inorganic. The inorganic of the mineral world is absolutely cut off from the plant or animal world; the passage is hermetically sealed. These barriers have never yet been crossed. No change of substance, no modification of environment, no chemistry, no electricity, no form of energy, no evolution of any kind can ever endow a single atom of the mineral world with the attribute of Life."

6. "Only by the bending down into this dead world of some living form can those dead atoms be gifted with the properties of vitality; without this contact with life they remain fixed in the inorganic sphere forever. Huxley says that the doctrine of Biogenesis (or life only from life) is victorious all along the line, and Tyndall is compelled to say: 'I affirm that no shred of trustworthy evidence exists to prove that life in our day has ever appeared independent of antecedent life.'

7. "Physical laws may explain the inorganic, Biology explains and accounts for the development of the organic, but of the point of contact Science is silent. A similar passage exists between the natural world and the spiritual world; this passage is hermetically sealed on the natural side. The door is closed; no man can open it, no organic change, no mental energy, no moral effort, no progress of any kind can enable any human being to enter the spiritual world."

8. But as the plant reaches down into the mineral world and touches it with the mystery of Life, so the Universal Mind reaches down into the human mind and endows it with new, strange, wonderful and even marvelous qualities. All men or women who have ever

accomplished anything in the world of industry, commerce or art have accomplished because of this process.

9. Thought is the connecting link between the Infinite and the finite, between the Universal and the individual. We have seen that there is an impassable barrier between the organic and the inorganic, and that the only way that matter can unfold is to be impregnated with life; as a seed reaches down into the mineral world and begins to unfold and reach out, the dead matter begins to live, a thousand invisible fingers begin to weave a suitable environment for the new arrival, and as the law of growth begins to take effect, we see the process continue until the Lily finally appears, and even "Solomon in all his glory was not arrayed like one of these."

10. Even so, a thought is dropped into the invisible substance of the Universal Mind, that substance from which all things are created, and as it takes root, the law of growth begins to take effect and we find that conditions and environment are but the objective form of our thought.

11. The law is that Thought is an active vital form of dynamic energy which has the power to correlate with its object and bring it out of the invisible substance from which all things are created into the visible or objective world. This is the law by which, and through which all things come into manifestation; it is the Master Key by which you are admitted into the Secret Place of the Most High and are "given dominion over all things." With an understanding of this law you may "decree a thing and it shall be established unto thee."

12. It could not be otherwise; if the soul of the Universe as we know it is the Universal Spirit, then the Universe is simply the condition which the Universal Spirit has made for itself. We are simply

individualized spirit and are creating the conditions for our growth in exactly the same way.

13. This creative power depends upon our recognition of the potential power of spirit or mind and must not be confused with Evolution. Creation is the calling into existence of that which does not exist in the objective world. Evolution is simply the unfolding of potentialities involved in things which already exist.

14. In taking advantage of the wonderful possibilities opened up to us through the operation of this law, we must remember that we ourselves contribute nothing to its efficacy as the Great Teacher said: "It is not I that doeth the works, but the Father that dwelleth in me, He doeth the works." We must take exactly the same position; we can do nothing to assist in the manifestation, we simply comply with the law, and the All-originating Mind will bring about the result.

15. The great error of the present day is the idea that Man has to originate the intelligence whereby the Infinite can proceed to bring about a specific purpose or result. Nothing of this kind is necessary; the Universal Mind can be depended upon to find the ways and means for bringing about any necessary manifestation. We must, however, create the ideal, and this ideal should be perfect.

16. We know that the laws governing Electricity have been formulated in such a way that this invisible power can be controlled and used for our benefit and comfort in thousands of ways. We know that messages are carried around the world, that ponderous machinery does its bidding, that it now illuminates practically the whole world, but we know too that if we consciously or ignorantly violate its law by touching a live wire, when it is not properly insulated,

the result will be unpleasant and possibly disastrous. A lack of understanding of the laws governing in the invisible world has the same result, and many are suffering the consequences all the time.

17. It has been explained that the law of causation depends upon polarity, a circuit must be formed; this circuit cannot be formed unless we operate in harmony with the law. How shall we operate in harmony with the law unless we know what the law is? How shall we know what the law is? By study, by observation.

18. We see the law in operation everywhere; all nature testifies to the operation of the law by silently, constantly expressing itself in the law of growth. Where there is growth, there must be life; where there is life there must be harmony, so that everything that has life is constantly attracting to itself the conditions and the supply which is necessary for its most complete expression.

19. If your thought is in harmony with the creative principle of nature, it is in tune with the Infinite Mind, and it will form the circuit, it will not return to you void; but it is possible for you to think thoughts that are not in tune with the Infinite, and when there is no polarity, the circuit is not formed. What, then, is the result? What is the result when a dynamo is generating electricity, the circuit is cut off and there is no outlet? The dynamo stops.

20. It will be exactly the same with you, if you entertain thoughts which are not in accordance with the Infinite and cannot therefore be polarized; there is no circuit, you are isolated, the thoughts cling to you, harass you, worry you, and finally bring about disease and possibly death; the physician may not diagnose the case exactly in this way, he may give it some fancy name which has been manufactured for the various ills which are the result of wrong thinking, but the cause is the same nevertheless.

21. Constructive thought must necessarily be creative, but creative thought must be harmonious, and this eliminates all destructive or competitive thought.

22. Wisdom, strength, courage and all harmonious conditions are the result of power and we have seen that all power is from within; likewise, every lack, limitation or adverse circumstance is the result of weakness, and weakness is simply absence of power; it comes from nowhere, it is nothing—the remedy then is simply to develop power, and this is accomplished in exactly the same manner that all power is developed, by exercise.

23. This exercise consists in making an application of your knowledge. Knowledge will not apply itself. You must make the application. Abundance will not come to you out of the sky, neither will it drop into your lap, but a conscious realization of the law of attraction and the intention to bring it into operation for a certain, definite and specific purpose, and the will to carry out this purpose will bring about the materialization of your desire by a natural law of transference. If you are in business, it will increase and develop along regular channels, possibly new or unusual channels of distribution will be opened and when the law becomes fully operative, you will find that the things you seek are seeking you.

24. This week select a blank space on the wall, or any other convenient spot, from where you usually sit, mentally draw a black horizontal line about six inches long, try to see the line as plainly as though it were painted on the wall; now mentally draw two vertical lines connecting with this horizontal line at either end; now draw another horizontal line connecting with the two vertical lines; now you have a square. Try to see the square perfectly; when you can do so draw a circle within the square; now place a point in the center of the circle; now draw the point toward you about 10 inches; now you have a cone on a square base; you will remember that your work was all in black; change it to white, to red, to yellow.

25. If you can do this, you are making excellent progress and will soon be enabled to concentrate on any problem you may have in mind.

> *When any object or purpose is clearly held in thought, its precipitation, in tangible and visible form, is merely a question of time. The vision always precedes and itself determines the realization.*
>
> —LILLIAN WHITING

PART TEN:
STUDY QUESTIONS WITH ANSWERS

91. What is Wealth?
   Wealth is the offspring of power.

92. Of what value are possessions?
   Possessions are of value only as they confer power.

93. Of what value is a knowledge of cause and effect?
   It enables men to plan courageously and execute fearlessly.

94. How does life originate in the inorganic world?
   Only by the introduction of some living form. There is no other way.

95. What is the connecting link between the finite and the Infinite?
   Thought is the connecting link.

96. Why is that so?

Because the Universal can manifest itself only through the individual.

97. Upon what does causation depend?

Upon polarity; a circuit must be formed; the Universal is the positive side of the battery of life, the individual is the negative, and thought forms the circuit.

98. Why do many fail to secure harmonious conditions?

They do not understand the law; there is no polarity; they have not formed the circuit.

99. What is the remedy?

A conscious recognition of the Law of Attraction with the intention of bringing it into existence for a definite purpose.

100. What will be the result?

Thought will correlate with its object and bring it into manifestation, because thought is a product of the spiritual man, and spirit is the creative Principle of the Universe.

A vivid thought brings the power to paint it; and in proportion to the depth of its source is the force of its projection.

—EMERSON

PART ELEVEN

Your life is governed by law—by actual, immutable principles that never vary. Law is in operation at all times; in all places. Fixed laws underlie all human actions. For this reason, men who control giant industries are enabled to determine with absolute precision just what percentage of every hundred thousand people will respond to any given set of conditions.

It is well, however, to remember that while every effect is the result of a cause, the effect in turn becomes a cause, which creates other effects, which in turn create still other causes; so that when you put the Law of Attraction into operation you must remember that you are starting a train of causation for good or otherwise which may have endless possibilities.

We frequently hear it said, "A very distressing situation came into my life, which could not have been the result of my thought, as I certainly never entertained any thought which could have such a result." We fail to remember that like attracts like in the mental world, and that the thought which we entertain brings to us certain friendships, companionships of a particular kind, and these in turn bring about conditions and environment, which in turn are responsible for the conditions of which we complain.

1. Inductive reasoning is the process of the objective mind by which we compare a number of separate instances with one another until we see the common factor that gives rise to them all.

2. Induction proceeds by comparison of facts; it is this method of studying nature which has resulted in the discovery of a reign of law which has marked an epoch in human progress.

3. It is the dividing line between superstition and intelligence; it has eliminated the elements of uncertainty and caprice from men's lives and substituted law, reason, and certitude.

4. It is the "Watchman at the Gate" mentioned in a former lesson.

5. When, by virtue of this principle, the world to which the senses were accustomed had been revolutionized; when the sun had been arrested in his course, the apparently flat earth had been shaped into a ball and set whirling around him; when the inert matter had been resolved into active elements, and the universe presented itself wherever we directed the telescope and microscope, full of force, motion and life; we are constrained to ask by what possible means the delicate forms of organization in the midst of it are kept in order and repair.

6. Like poles and like forces repel themselves or remain impenetrable to each other, and this cause seems in general sufficient to assign a proper place and distance to stars, men and forces. As men of different virtues enter into partnership, so do opposite poles attract each other, elements that have no property in common like acids and gases cling to each other in preference and a general exchange is kept up between the surplus and the demand.

7. As the eye seeks and receives satisfaction from colors complementary to those which are given, so do need, want and desire, in the largest sense, induce, guide and determine action.

8. It is our privilege to become conscious of the principle and act in accordance with it. Cuvier sees a tooth belonging to an extinct race of animals. This tooth wants a body for the performance of its function, and it defines the peculiar body it stands in need of with such precision that Cuvier is able to reconstruct the frame of this animal.

9. Perturbations are observed in the motion of Uranus. Leverrier needs another planet at a certain place to keep the solar system in order, and Neptune appears in the place and hour appointed.

10. The instinctive wants of the animal and the intellectual wants of Cuvier, the wants of nature and of the mind of Leverrier were alike, and thus the results; here the thoughts of an existence, there an existence. A well-defined lawful want, therefore, furnishes the reason for the more complex operations of nature.

11. Having recorded correctly the answers furnished by nature and stretched our senses with the growing science over her surface; having joined hands with the levers that move the earth; we become conscious of such a close, varied and deep contact with the world without, that our wants and purposes become no less identified with the harmonious operations of this vast organization, than the life, liberty, and happiness of the citizen is identified with the existence of his government.

12. As the interests of the individual are protected by the arms of the country, added to his own; and his needs may depend upon certain supply in the degree that they are felt more universally and steadily; in the same manner does conscious citizenship in the Republic of

nature secure us from the annoyances of subordinate agents by alliance with superior powers; and by appeal to the fundamental laws of resistance or inducement offered to mechanical or chemical agents, distribute the labor to be performed between them and man to the best advantage of the inventor.

13. If Plato could have witnessed the pictures executed by the sun with the assistance of the photographer, or a hundred similar illustrations of what man does by induction, he would perhaps have been reminded of the intellectual midwifery of his master and, in his own mind might have arisen the vision of a land where all manual, mechanical labor and repetition is assigned to the power of nature, where our wants are satisfied by purely mental operations set in motion by the will, and where the supply is created by the demand.

14. However distant that land may appear, induction has taught men to make strides toward it and has surrounded him with benefits which are, at the same time, rewards for past fidelity and incentives for more assiduous devotion.

15. It is also an aid in concentrating and strengthening our faculties for the remaining part, giving unerring solution for individual as well as universal problems, by the mere operations of mind in the purest form.

16. Here we find a method, the spirit of which is, to believe that what is sought has been accomplished, in order to accomplish it: a method, bequeathed upon us by the same Plato who, outside of this sphere, could never find how the ideas became realities.

17. This conception is also elaborated by Swedenborg in his doctrine of correspondences; and a still greater teacher has said, "What things soever ye desire, when ye pray, believe that ye receive them, and ye shall have them." (Mark 11:24) The difference of the tenses in this passage is remarkable.

18. We are first to believe that our desire has already been fulfilled, its accomplishment will then follow. This is a concise direction for making use of the creative power of thought by impressing on the Universal subjective mind, the particular thing which we desire as an already existing fact.

19. We are thus thinking on the plane of the absolute and eliminating all consideration of conditions of limitation and are planting a seed which, if left undisturbed, will finally germinate into external fruition.

20. To review: Inductive reasoning is the process of the objective mind, by which we compare a number of separate instances with one another until we see the common factor that gives rise to them all. We see people in every civilized country on the globe, securing results by some process which they do not seem to understand themselves, and to which they usually attach more or less mystery. Our reason is given to us for the purpose of ascertaining the law by which these results are accomplished.

21. The operation of this thought process is seen in those fortunate natures that possess everything that others must acquire by toil, who never have a struggle with conscience because they always act correctly, and can never conduct themselves otherwise than with tact, learn everything easily, complete everything they begin with a happy knack, live in eternal harmony with themselves, without ever reflecting much what they do, or ever experiencing difficulty or toil.

22. The fruit of this thought is, as it were, a gift of the gods, but a gift which few as yet realize, appreciate, or understand. The recognition of the marvelous power which is possessed by the mind under proper conditions and the fact that this power can be utilized, directed, and made available for the solution of every human problem is of transcendental importance.

23. All truth is the same, whether stated in modern scientific terms or in the language of apostolic times. There are timid souls who fail to realize that the very completeness of truth requires various statements—that no one human formula will show every side of it.

24. Changing, emphasis, new language, novel interpretations, unfamiliar perspectives, are not, as some suppose, signs of departure from truth but on the contrary, they are evidence that the truth is being apprehended in new relations to human needs, and is becoming more generally understood.

25. The truth must be told to each generation and to every people in new and different terms, so that when the Great Teacher said—"Believe that ye receive and ye shall receive" or, when Paul said—"Faith is the substance of things hoped for, the evidence of things not seen" or, when modern science says—"The Law of Attraction is the law by which thought correlates with its object," each statement when subjected to analysis, is found to contain exactly the same truth. The only difference being in the form of presentation.

26. We are standing on the threshold of a new era. The time has arrived when man has learned the secrets of mastery and the way is being prepared for a new social order, more wonderful than anything ever heretofore dreamed of. The conflict of modern science with theology, the study of comparative religions, the tremendous

power of new social movements, all of these are but clearing the way for the new order. They may have destroyed traditional forms which have become antiquated and impotent, but nothing of value has been lost.

27. A new faith has been born, a faith which demands a new form of expression, and this faith is taking form in a deep consciousness of power which is being manifested, in the present spiritual activity found on every hand.

28. The spirit which sleeps in the mineral, breathes in the vegetable, moves in the animal and reaches its highest development in man is the Universal Mind, and it behooves us to span the gulf between being and doing, theory and practice, by demonstrating our understanding of the dominion which we have been given.

29. By far the greatest discovery of all the centuries is the power of thought. The importance of this discovery has been a little slow in reaching the general consciousness, but it has arrived, and already in every field of research the importance of this greatest of all great discoveries is being demonstrated.

30. You ask in what does the creative power of thought consist? It consists in creating ideas, and these in turn objectify themselves by appropriating, inventing, observing, discerning, discovering, analyzing, ruling, governing, combining, and applying matter and force. It can do this because it is an intelligent creative power.

31. Thought reaches its loftiest activity when plunged into its own mysterious depth; when it breaks through the narrow compass of self and passes from truth to truth to the region of eternal light, where all which is, was or ever will be, melt into one grand harmony.

32. From this process of self-contemplation comes inspiration which is creative intelligence, and which is undeniably superior to every element, force or law of nature, because it can understand, modify, govern and apply them to its own ends and purposes and therefore possess them.

33. Wisdom begins with the dawn of reason, and reason is but an understanding of the knowledge and principles whereby we may know the true meaning of things. Wisdom, then, is illuminated reason, and this wisdom leads to humility, for humility is a large part of Wisdom.

34. We all know many who have achieved the seemingly impossible, who have realized lifelong dreams, who have changed everything including themselves. We have sometimes marveled at the demonstration of an apparently irresistible power, which seemed to be ever available just when it was most needed, but it is all clear now. All that is required is an understanding of certain definite fundamental principles and their proper application.

35. For your exercise this week, concentrate on the quotation taken from the Bible, "Whatsoever things ye desire, when ye pray, believe that ye receive them and ye shall have them"; notice that there is no limitation, "Whatsoever things" is very definite and implies that the only limitation which is placed upon us in our ability to think, to be equal to the occasion, to rise to the emergency, to remember that Faith is not a shadow, but a substance, "the substance of things hoped for, the evidence of things not seen."

> *Death is but the natural process whereby all material forms are thrown into the crucible for reproduction in fresh diversity.*

PART ELEVEN:
STUDY QUESTIONS WITH ANSWERS

101. What is inductive reasoning?

The process of the objective mind by which we compare a number of separate instances with each other until we see the common factor which gives rise to them all.

102. What has this method of studying accomplished?

It has resulted in the discovery of a reign of law which has marked an epoch in human progress.

103. What is it that guides and determines action?

It is need, want and desire which in the largest sense induce, guide and determine action.

104. What is the formula for the unerring solution of every individual problem?

We are to believe that our desire has already been fulfilled; its accomplishment will then follow.

105. What great Teachers advocated it?

Jesus, Plato, Swedenborg.

106. What is the result of this thought process?

We are thinking on the plane of the absolute and planting a seed, which if left undisturbed will germinate into fruition.

107. Why is it scientifically exact?

Because it is natural law.

108. What is Faith?

"Faith is the substance of things hoped for, the evidence of things unseen."

109. What is the Law of Attraction?

The law by which Faith is brought into manifestation.

110. What importance do you attach to an understanding of this law?

It has eliminated the elements of uncertainty and caprice from men's lives and substituted law, reason, and certitude.

PART TWELVE

P art Twelve is enclosed herewith. In the fourth paragraph you will find the following statement: "You must first have the knowledge of your power; second, the courage to dare; third, the faith to do." If you concentrate upon the thoughts given, if you give them your entire attention, you will find a world of meaning in each sentence, and will attract to yourself other thoughts in harmony with them, and you will soon grasp the full significance of the vital knowledge upon which you are concentrating.

Knowledge does not apply itself; we as individuals must make the application, and the application consists in fertilizing the thought with a living purpose.

The time and thought which most persons waste in aimless effort would accomplish wonders if properly directed with some special object in view. In order to do this, it is necessary to center your mental force upon a specific thought and hold it there, to the exclusion of all other thoughts. If you have ever looked through the viewfinder of a camera, you found that when the object was not in focus, the impression was indistinct and possibly blurred, but when the proper focus was obtained the picture was clear and distinct. This illustrates the power of concentration. Unless you can concentrate upon the object which you have in view, you will have but a hazy, indifferent, vague, *indistinct and blurred outline of your ideal and the results will be in accordance with your mental picture.*

1. There is no purpose in life that cannot be best accomplished through a scientific understanding of the creative power of thought.

2. This power to think is common to all. Man is, because he thinks. Man's power to think is infinite, consequently his creative power is unlimited.

3. We know that thought is building for us the thing we think of and actually bringing it nearer, yet we find it difficult to banish fear, anxiety or discouragement, all of which are powerful thought forces, and which continually send the things we desire further away, so that it is often one step forward and two steps backward.

4. The only way to keep from going backward is to keep going forward. Eternal vigilance is the price of success. There are three steps, and each one is absolutely essential. You must first have the knowledge of your power; second, the courage to dare; third, the faith to do.

5. With this as a basis you can construct an ideal business, an ideal home, ideal friends, and an ideal environment. You are not restricted as to material or cost. Thought is omnipotent and has the power to draw on the Infinite bank of primary substance for all that it requires. Infinite resources are therefore at your command.

6. But your ideal must be sharp, clear-cut, definite; to have one ideal today, another tomorrow, and a third next week, means to scatter your forces and accomplish nothing; your result will be a meaningless and chaotic combination of wasted material.

7. Unfortunately this is the result which many are securing, and the cause is self-evident. If a sculptor started out with a piece of marble and a chisel and changed his ideal every fifteen minutes, what result could he expect? And why should you expect any different result in molding the greatest and most plastic of all substances, the only real substance?

8. The result of this indecision and negative thought is often found in the loss of material wealth. Supposed independence which required many years of toil and effort suddenly disappears. It is often found then that money and property are not independence at all. On the contrary, the only independence is found to be a practical working knowledge of the creative power of thought.

9. This practical working method cannot come to you until you learn that the only real power which you can have is the power to adjust yourself to Divine and unchangeable principles. You cannot change the Infinite, but you can come into an understanding of natural laws. The reward of this understanding is a conscious realization of your ability to adjust your thought faculties with the Universal Thought which is Omnipresent. Your ability to cooperate with this Omnipotence will indicate the degree of success with which you meet.

10. The power of thought has many counterfeits which are more or less fascinating, but the results are harmful instead of helpful.

11. Of course, worry, fear, and all negative thoughts produce a crop after their kind; those who harbor thoughts of this kind must inevitably reap what they have sown.

12. Again, there are the Phenomena seekers who gormandize on the so-called proofs and demonstration obtained at materializing séances.

They throw open their mental doors and soak themselves in the most poisonous currents which can be found in the psychic world. They do not seem to understand that it is the ability to become negative, receptive and passive, and thus drain themselves of all their vital force, which enables them to bring about these vibratory thought forms.

13. There are also the Hindu worshippers, who see in the materializing phenomena which are performed by the so-called adepts, a source of power, forgetting, or never seeming to realize that as soon as the will is withdrawn the forms wither, and the vibratory forces of which they are composed vanish.

14. Telepathy, or thought transference, has received considerable attention, but as it requires a negative mental state on the part of the receiver, the practice is harmful. A thought may be sent with the intention of hearing or seeing, but it will bring the penalty attached to the inversion of the principle involved.

15. In many instances, hypnotism is positively dangerous to the subject as well as the operator. No one familiar with the laws governing in the mental world would think of attempting to dominate the will of another, for by so doing, he will gradually (but surely) divest himself of his own power.

16. All of these perversions have their temporary satisfaction and for some a keen fascination, but there is an infinitely greater fascination in a true understanding of the world of power within, a power which increases with use; is permanent instead of fleeting; which not only is potent as a remedial agency to bring about the remedy for past error or results of wrong thinking, but is a prophylactic agency protecting us from all manner and form of danger, and finally is an actual creative force with which we can build new conditions and new environment.

17. The law is that thought will correlate with its object and bring forth in the material world the correspondence of the thing thought or produced in the mental world. We then discern the absolute necessity of seeing that every thought has the inherent germ of truth in order that the law of growth will bring into manifestation good, for good alone can confer any permanent power.

18. The principle which gives the thought the dynamic power to correlate with its object, and therefore to master every adverse human experience, is the Law of Attraction, which is another name for love. This is an eternal and fundamental principle, inherent in all things, in every system of Philosophy, in every Religion, and in every Science. There is no getting away from the law of love. It is feeling that imparts vitality to thought. Feeling is desire, and desire is love. Thought impregnated with love becomes invincible.

19. We find this truth emphasized wherever the power of thought is understood, the Universal Mind is not only Intelligence, but it is substance, and this substance is the attractive force which brings electrons together by the Law of Attraction so that they form atoms; the atoms in turn are brought together by the same law and form molecules; molecules take objective forms; and so we find that the law of love is the creative force behind every manifestation, not only of atoms, but of worlds, of the Universe, of everything of which the imagination can form any conception.

20. It is the operation of this marvelous Law of Attraction which has caused men in all ages and all times to believe that there must be some personal being who responded to their petitions and desires, and manipulated events in order to comply with their requirements.

21. It is the combination of Thought and Love which forms the irresistible force called the Law of Attraction. All natural laws are

irresistible, the law of gravitation, or electricity, or any other law operates with mathematical exactitude. There is no variation; it is only the channel of distribution which may be imperfect. If a bridge falls, we do not attribute the collapse to any variation of the law of gravitation. If a light fails us, we do not conclude that the laws governing electricity cannot be depended upon, and if the Law of Attraction seems to be imperfectly demonstrated by an inexperienced or uninformed person, we are not to conclude that the greatest and most infallible law upon which the entire system of creation depends has been suspended. We should rather conclude that a little more understanding of the law is required, for the same reason that a correct solution of a difficult problem in Mathematics is not always readily and easily obtained.

22. Things are created in the mental or spiritual world before they appear in the outward act or event; by the simple process of governing our thought forces today, we help create the events which will come into our lives in the future, perhaps even tomorrow. Educated desire is the most potent means of bringing into action the Law of Attraction.

23. Man is so constituted that he must first create the tools, or implements by which he gains the power to think. The mind cannot comprehend an entirely new idea until a corresponding vibratory brain cell has been prepared to receive it. This explains why it is so difficult for us to receive or appreciate an entirely new idea; we have no brain cell capable of receiving it; we are therefore incredulous; we do not believe it.

24. If, therefore, you have not been familiar with the omnipotence of the Law of Attraction, and the scientific method by which it can be put into operation, or if you have not been familiar with the unlimited possibilities which it opens to those who are enabled to

take advantage of the resources it offers, begin now and create the necessary brain cells which will enable you to comprehend the unlimited powers which may be yours by cooperating with natural law. This is done by concentration or attention.

25. The intention governs the attention. Power comes through repose. It is by concentration that deep thoughts, wise speech, and all forces of high potentiality are accomplished.

26. It is in the Silence that you get into touch with the Omnipotent power of the subconscious mind from which all power is evolved.

27. He who desires wisdom, power, or permanent success of any kind will find it only within; it is an unfoldment. The unthinking may conclude that the silence is very simple and easily attained, but it should be remembered that only in absolute silence may one come into contact with Divinity itself; may learn of the unchangeable law and open for himself the channels by which persistent practice and concentration lead to perfection.

28. This week go to the same room, take the same chair, the same position as previously; be sure to relax, let go, both mentally and physically; always do this; never try to do any mental work under pressure; see that there are no tense muscles or nerves, that you are entirely comfortable. Now realize your unity with omnipotence; get into touch with this power, come into a deep and vital understanding, appreciation, and realization of the fact that your ability to think is your ability to act upon the Universal Mind, and bring it into manifestation, realize that it will meet any and every requirement; that you have exactly the same potential ability which any individual ever did have or ever will have, because each is but an expression or manifestation of the One, all are parts of the whole, there is no difference in kind or quality, the only difference being one of degree.

Thought cannot conceive of anything that may not be brought to expression. He who first uttered it may be only the suggester, but the doer will appear.

—WILSON

PART TWELVE:
STUDY QUESTIONS WITH ANSWERS

111. How may any purpose in life be best accomplished?
Through a scientific understanding of the spiritual nature of thought.

112. What three steps are absolutely essential?
The knowledge of our power, the courage to dare, the faith to do.

113. How is the practical working knowledge secured?
By an understanding of natural laws.

114. What is the reward of an understanding of these laws?
A conscious realization of our ability to adjust ourselves to Divine and unchanging principle.

115. What will indicate the degree of success with which we meet?
The degree in which we realize that we cannot change the Infinite but must cooperate with it.

116. What is the principle which gives thought its dynamic power?
The Law of Attraction, which rests on vibration, which in turn rests upon the law of love. Thought impregnated with love becomes invincible.

117. Why is this law irresistible?
Because it is a natural law. All natural laws are irresistible and unchange-

able and act with mathematical exactitude. There is no deviation or variation.

118. Why then does it sometimes seem to be difficult to find the solution to our problems in life?

For the same reason that it is sometimes difficult to find the correct solution to a difficult mathematical problem. The operator is uninformed or inexperienced.

119. Why is it impossible for the mind to grasp an entirely new idea?

We have no corresponding vibratory brain cell capable of receiving the idea.

120. How is wisdom secured?

By concentration; it is an unfoldment; it comes from within.

PART THIRTEEN

Physical science is responsible for the marvelous age of invention in which we are now living, but spiritual science is now setting out on a career whose possibilities no one can foretell.

Spiritual science has previously been the football of the uneducated, the superstitious, the mystical, but men are now interested in definite methods and demonstrated facts only.

We have come to know that thinking is a spiritual process, that vision and imagination preceded action and event, that the day of the dreamer has come.

The following lines by Mr. Herbert Kaufman are interesting in this connection.

"They are the architects of greatness, their vision lies within their souls, they peer beyond the veils and mists of doubt and pierce the walls of unborn Time. The belted wheel, the trail of steel, the churning screw, are shuttles in the loom on which they weave their magic tapestries. Makers of Empire, they have fought for bigger things than crowns and higher seats than thrones. Your homes are set upon the land a dreamer found. The pictures on its walls are visions from a dreamer's soul. They are the chosen few—the blazers of the way. Walls crumble and Empires fall, the tidal wave sweeps from the sea and tears a fortress from its rocks. The rotting nations drop off from Time's bough, and only things the dreamers make live on."

Part Thirteen, which follows, tells why the dreams of the dreamer come true. It explains the law of causation by which dreamers, inventors, authors, financiers, bring about the realization of their desires. It explains the law by which the thing pictured upon our mind eventually becomes our own.

1. It has been the tendency, and, as might be proved, a necessity for science to seek the explanation of everyday facts by a generalization of those others which are less frequent and form the exception. Thus does the eruption of the volcano manifest the heat which is continually at work in the interior of the earth and to which the latter owes much of her configuration.

2. Thus does the lightning reveal a subtle power constantly busy to produce changes in the inorganic world, and, as dead languages now seldom heard were once ruling among the nations, so does a giant tooth in Siberia, or a fossil in the depth of the earth not only bear record of the evolution of past ages but thereby explain to us the origin of the hills and valleys which we inhabit today.

3. In this way a generalization of facts which are rare, strange, or form the exception, has been the magnetic needle guiding to all the discoveries of inductive science.

4. This method is founded upon reason and experience and thereby destroyed superstition, precedent and conventionality.

5. It is almost three hundred years since Lord Bacon recommended this method of study, to which the civilized nations owe the greater part of their prosperity and the more valuable part of their knowledge; purging the mind from narrow prejudices, denominated theories, more effectually than by the keenest irony; calling the attention of men from heaven to earth more successfully by surprising experiments than by the most forcible demonstration of their

ignorance; educating the inventive faculties more powerfully by the near prospect of useful discoveries thrown open to all, than by talk of bringing to light the innate laws of our mind.

6. The method of Bacon has seized the spirit and aim of the great philosophers of Greece and carried them into effect by the new means of observation which another age offered; thus gradually revealing a wondrous field of knowledge in the infinite space of astronomy, in the microscopic egg of embryology, and the dim age of geology; disclosing an order of the pulse which the logic of Aristotle could never have unveiled, and analyzing into formerly unknown elements the material combinations which no dialectic of the scholastics could force apart.

7. It has lengthened life; it has mitigated pain; it has extinguished diseases; it has increased the fertility of the soil; it has given new securities to the mariner; it has spanned great rivers with bridges of form unknown to our fathers; it has guided the thunderbolt from heaven to earth; it has lighted up night with the splendor of day; it has extended the range of human vision; it has multiplied the power of the human muscles; it has accelerated motion; it has annihilated distance; it has facilitated intercourse, correspondence, all friendly offices, all dispatch of business; it has enabled men to descend into the depths of the sea, to soar into the air, to penetrate securely into the noxious recesses of the earth.

8. This then is the true nature and scope of induction. But the greater the success which men have achieved in the inductive science, the more does the whole tenor of their teachings and example impress us with the necessity of observing carefully, patiently, accurately, with all the instruments and resources at our command the individual facts before venturing upon a statement of general laws.

9. To ascertain the bearing of the spark drawn from the electric machine under every variety of circumstances, that we thus may be emboldened with Franklin to address, in the form of a kite, the question to the cloud about the nature of the lightning. To assure ourselves of the manner in which bodies fall with the exactness of a Galileo, that with Newton we may dare to ask the moon about the force that fastens it to the earth.

10. In short, by the value we set upon truth, by our hope in a steady and universal progress, not to permit a tyrannical prejudice to neglect or mutilate unwelcome facts, but to rear the superstructure of science upon the broad and unchangeable basis, of full attention paid to the most isolated as well as the most frequent phenomena.

11. An ever-increasing material may be collected by observation, but the accumulated facts are of very different value for the explanation of nature, and as we esteem most highly those useful qualities of men which are of the rarest occurrence, so does natural philosophy sift the facts and attach a pre-eminent importance to that striking class which cannot be accounted for by the usual and daily observation of life.

12. If then, we find that certain persons seem to possess unusual power, what are we to conclude? First, we may say, it is not so, which is simply an acknowledgment of our lack of information because every honest investigator admits that there are many strange and previously unaccountable phenomena constantly taking place. Those, however, who become acquainted with the creative power of thought, will no longer consider them unaccountable.

13. Second, we may say that they are the result of supernatural interference, but a scientific understanding of natural laws will convince us that there is nothing supernatural. Every phenomenon is the result of an accurate definite cause, and the cause is an immutable law or principle, which operates with invariable precision, whether the law is put into operation consciously or unconsciously.

14. Third, we may say that we are on "forbidden ground," that there are some things which we should not know. This objection was used against every advance in human knowledge. Every individual who ever advanced a new idea, whether a Columbus, a Darwin, a Galileo, a Fulton or an Emerson, was subjected to ridicule or persecution; so that this objection should receive no serious consideration; but, on the contrary, we should carefully consider every fact which is brought to our attention; by doing this we will more readily ascertain the law upon which it is based.

15. It will be found that the creative power of thought will explain every possible condition or experience, whether physical, mental or spiritual.

16. Thought will bring about conditions in correspondence with the predominant mental attitude. Therefore, if we fear disaster, as fear is a powerful form of thought, disaster will be the certain result of our thinking. It is this form of thought which frequently sweeps away the result of many years of toil and effort.

17. If we think of some form of material wealth we may secure it. By concentrated thought the required conditions will be brought about, and the proper effort put forth, which will result in bringing about the circumstances necessary to realize our desires; but we often find that when we secure the things we thought we wanted, they do not have the effect we expected. That is, the satisfaction is only temporary, or possibly is the reverse of what we expected.

18. What, then, is the proper method of procedure? What are we to think in order to secure what we really desire? What you and I desire, what we all desire, what every one is seeking, is Happiness and Harmony. If we can be truly happy we shall have everything the world can give. If we are happy ourselves we can make others happy.

19. But we cannot be happy unless we have health, strength, congenial friends, pleasant environment, sufficient supply, not only to take care of our necessities but to provide for those comforts and luxuries to which we are entitled.

20. The old orthodox way of thinking was to be "a worm," to be satisfied with our portion whatever it is; but the modern idea is to know that we are entitled to the best of everything, that the "Father and I are one" and that the "Father" is the Universal Mind, the Creator, the Original Substance from which all things proceed.

21. Now admitting that this is all true in theory, and it has been taught for two thousand years, and is the essence of every system of Philosophy or Religion, how are we to make it practical in our lives? How are we to get the actual, tangible results here and now?

22. In the first place, we must put our knowledge into practice. Nothing can be accomplished in any other way. The athlete may read books and lessons on physical training all his life, but unless he begins to give out strength by actual work he will never receive any strength; he will eventually get exactly what he gives; but he will have to give it first. It is exactly the same with us; we will get exactly what we give, but we shall have to give it first. It will then return to us many fold, and the giving is simply a mental process, because thoughts are causes and conditions are effects; therefore in giving thoughts of courage, inspiration, health or help of any kind we are setting causes in motion which will bring about their effect.

23. Thought is a spiritual activity and is therefore creative, but make no mistake, thought will create nothing unless it is consciously, systematically, and constructively directed; and herein is the difference between idle thinking, which is simply a dissipation of effort, and constructive thinking, which means practically unlimited achievement.

24. We have found that everything we get comes to us by the Law of Attraction. A happy thought cannot exist in an unhappy consciousness; therefore the consciousness must change, and, as the consciousness changes, all conditions necessary to meet the changed consciousness must gradually change, in order to meet the requirements of the new situation.

25. In creating a Mental Image or an Ideal, we are projecting a thought into the Universal Substance from which all things are created. This Universal Substance is Omnipresent, Omnipotent and Omniscient. Are we to inform the Omniscient as to the proper channel to be used to materialize our demand? Can the finite advise the Infinite? This is the cause of failure; of every failure. We recognize the Omnipresence of the Universal Substance, but we fail to appreciate the fact that this substance is not only Omnipresent, but is Omnipotent and Omniscient, and consequently will set causes in motion concerning which we may be entirely ignorant.

26. We can best conserve our interests by recognizing the Infinite Power and Infinite Wisdom of the Universal Mind, and in this way become a channel whereby the Infinite can bring about the realization of our desire. This means that recognition brings about realization, therefore for your exercise this week make use of the principle, recognize the fact that you are a part of the whole, and that a part must be the same in kind and quality as the whole; the only difference there can possibly be, is in degree.

27. When this tremendous fact begins to permeate your consciousness, when you really come into a realization of the fact that you (not your body, but the Ego), the "I," the spirit which thinks is an integral part of the great whole, that it is the same in substance, in quality, in kind, that the Creator could create nothing different from Himself, you will also be able to say, "The Father and I are one" and you will come into an understanding of the beauty, the grandeur, the transcendental opportunities which have been placed at your disposal.

Increase in me that wisdom which discovers my truest interest, strengthen my resolution to perform that which wisdom dictates.

—FRANKLIN

PART THIRTEEN:
STUDY QUESTIONS WITH ANSWERS

121. What is the method by which natural philosophers obtain and apply their knowledge?

To observe individual facts carefully, patiently, accurately, with all the instruments and resources at their command, before venturing upon a statement of general laws.

122. How may we be certain that this method is correct?

By not permitting a tyrannical prejudice to neglect or mutilate unwelcome facts.

123. What classes of facts are esteemed most highly?

Those which cannot be accounted for by the usual daily observation of life.

124. Upon what is this principle founded?

Upon reason and experience.

125. What does it destroy?

Superstition, precedent and conventionality.

126. How have these laws been discovered?

By a generalization of facts which are uncommon, rare, strange and form the exception.

127. How may we account for much of the strange and heretofore unexplainable phenomena which are constantly taking place?

By the creative power of thought.

128. Why is this so?

Because when we learn of a fact we can be sure that it is the result of a certain definite cause and that this cause will operate with invariable precision.

129. What is the result of this knowledge?

It will explain the cause of every possible condition, whether physical, mental or spiritual.

130. How will our best interest be conserved?

By a recognition of the fact that a knowledge of the creative nature of thought puts us in touch with Infinite power.

PART FOURTEEN

You have found from your study thus far that thought is a spiritual activity and is therefore endowed with creative power. This does not mean that some thought is creative, but that all thought is creative. This same principle can be brought into operation in a negative way, through the process of denial.

The conscious and subconscious are but two phases of action in connection with one mind. The relation of the subconscious to the conscious is quite analogous to that existing between a weather vane and the atmosphere.

Just as the least pressure of the atmosphere causes an action on the part of the weather vane, so does the least thought entertained by the conscious mind produce within your subconscious mind action in exact proportion to the depth of feeling characterizing the thought and the intensity with which the thought is indulged.

It follows that if you deny unsatisfactory conditions, you are withdrawing the creative power of your thought from these conditions. You are cutting them away at the root. You are sapping their vitality.

Remember that the law of growth necessarily governs every manifestation in the objective, so that a denial of unsatisfactory conditions will not bring about instant change. A plant will remain visible for some time after its roots have been cut, but it will gradually fade away and eventually disappear, so

the withdrawal of your thought from the contemplation of unsatisfactory con-
ditions will gradually, but surely, terminate these conditions.

You will see that this is an exactly opposite course from the one which we
would naturally be inclined to adopt.

It will therefore have an exactly opposite effect to the one usually secured.
Most persons concentrate intently upon unsatisfactory conditions, thereby giv-
ing the condition that measure of energy and vitality which is necessary in
order to supply a vigorous growth.

1. The Universal Energy in which all motion, light, heat, and color have their origin, does not partake of the limitation of the many effects of which it is the cause, but it is supreme over them all. This Universal Substance is the source of all Power, Wisdom and Intelligence.

2. To recognize this Intelligence is to acquaint yourself with the knowing quality of Mind and through it to move upon the Universal Substance, and bring it into harmonious relations in your affairs.

3. This is something that the most learned physical science teacher has not attempted—a field of discovery upon which he has not yet launched; in fact, but few of the materialistic schools have ever caught the first ray of this light. It does not seem to have dawned upon them that wisdom is just as much present everywhere as are force and substance.

4. Some will say, if these principles are true, why are we not demonstrating them? As the fundamental principle is obviously correct, why do we not get proper results? We do. We get results in exact accordance with our understanding of the law and our ability to make the proper application. We secured no results from the laws governing electricity until someone formulated the law and showed us how to apply it.

5. This puts us in an entirely new relation to our environment, opening up possibilities previously undreamed of, and this by an orderly sequence of law which is naturally involved in our new mental attitude.

6. Mind is creative and the principle upon which this law is based is sound and legitimate and is inherent in the nature of things; but this creative power does not originate in the individual, but in the Universal, which is the source and fountain of all energy and substance, the individual is simply the channel for the distribution of this energy. The individual is the means by which the Universal produces the various combinations which result in the formation of phenomena.

7. We know that scientists have resolved matter into an immense number of molecules; these molecules have been resolved into atoms, and the atoms into electrons. The discovery of electrons in high vacuum glass tubes containing fused terminals of hard metal, indicates conclusively that these electrons fill all space; that they exist everywhere, that they are omnipresent. They fill all material bodies and occupy the whole of what we call empty space. This, then, is the Universal Substance from which all things proceed.

8. Electrons would forever remain electrons unless directed where to go to be assembled into atoms and molecules, and this director is Mind. A number of electrons revolving around a center of force constitutes an atom; atoms unite in absolutely regular mathematical ratios and form molecules, and these unite with each other to form a multitude of compounds which unite to build the Universe.

9. The lightest known atom is hydrogen and this is 1,700 times heavier than an electron. An atom of mercury is 300,000 times heavier than an electron. Electrons are pure negative electricity, and

as they have the same potential velocity as all other cosmic energy, such as heat, light, electricity and thought, neither time nor space require consideration. The manner in which the velocity of light was ascertained is interesting.

10. The velocity of light was obtained by the Danish astronomer Roemer in 1676, by observing the eclipses of Jupiter's moons. When the earth was nearest to Jupiter, the eclipse appeared about eight and one-half minutes too soon for the calculations, and when the earth was most remote from Jupiter, they were about eight and one-half minutes too late. Roemer concluded the reason to be that it required 17 minutes for light from the planet to traverse the diameter of the earth's orbit, which measured the difference of the distances of the earth from Jupiter. This calculation has since been verified, and proves that light travels about 186,000 miles a second.

11. Electrons manifest in the body as cells, and possess mind and intelligence sufficient for them to perform their functions in the human physical anatomy. Every part of the body is composed of cells, some of which operate independently; others in communities. Some are busy building tissue, while others are engaged in forming the various secretions necessary for the body. Some act as carriers of material; others are the surgeons whose work it is to repair damage; others are scavengers, carrying off waste; others are constantly ready to repel invaders or other undesirable intruders of the germ family.

12. All these cells are moving for a common purpose and each one is not only a living organism, but has sufficient intelligence to enable it to perform its necessary duties. It is also endowed with sufficient intelligence to conserve the energies and perpetuate its own life. It must, therefore, secure sufficient nourishment and it has been found that it exercises choice in the selection of such nourishment.

13. Each cell is born, reproduces itself, dies and is absorbed. The maintenance of health and life itself depends upon the constant regeneration of these cells.

14. It is therefore apparent that there is mind in every atom of the body; this mind is negative mind, and the power of the individual to think makes him positive, so that he can control this negative mind. This is the scientific explanation for metaphysical healing, and will enable anyone to understand the principle upon which this remarkable phenomenon rests.

15. This negative mind, which is contained in every cell of the body, has been called the subconscious mind, because it acts without our conscious knowledge. We have found that this subconscious mind is responsive to the will of the conscious mind.

16. All things have their origin in mind, and appearances are the result of thought. So that we see that things in themselves have no origin, permanency, or reality. Since they are produced by thought, they can be erased by thought.

17. In mental, as in natural science, experiments are being made and each discovery lifts man one step higher toward his possible goal. We find that every man is the reflection of the thought he has entertained during his lifetime. This is stamped on his face, his form, his character, his environment.

18. Back of every effect there is a cause, and if we follow the trail to its starting point, we shall find the creative principle out of which it grew. Proofs of this are now so complete that this truth is generally accepted.

19. The objective world is controlled by an unseen and, heretofore, unexplainable power. We have, heretofore, personalized this power and called it God. We have now, however, learned to look upon it as the permeating essence or Principle of all that exists—the Infinite or Universal Mind.

20. The Universal Mind, being infinite and omnipotent, has unlimited resources at its command, and when we remember that it is also omnipresent, we cannot escape the conclusion that we must be an expression or manifestation of that Mind.

21. A recognition and understanding of the resources of the subconscious mind will indicate that the only difference between the subconscious and the Universal is one of degree. They differ only as a drop of water differs from the ocean. They are the same in kind and quality, the difference is one of degree only.

22. Do you, can you, appreciate the value of this all-important fact; do you realize that a recognition of this tremendous fact places you in touch with Omnipotence? The subconscious mind being the connecting link between the Universal Mind and the conscious mind, is it not evident that the conscious mind can consciously suggest thoughts which the subconscious mind will put into action, and as the subconscious is one with the Universal, is it not evident that no limit can be placed upon its activities?

23. A scientific understanding of this principle will explain the wonderful results which are secured through the power of prayer. The results which are secured in this way are not brought about by any special dispensations of providence, but on the contrary, they are the result of the operation of a perfectly natural law. There is, therefore, nothing either religious or mysterious about it.

24. Yet there are many who are not ready to enter into the discipline necessary to think correctly, even though it is evident that wrong thinking has brought failure.

25. Thought is the only reality; conditions are but the outward manifestations; as the thought changes, all outward or material conditions must change in order to be in harmony with their creator, which is thought.

26. But the thought must be clear-cut, steady, fixed, definite, unchangeable; you cannot take one step forward and two steps backward, neither can you spend twenty or thirty years of your life building up negative conditions as the result of negative thoughts, and then expect to see them all melt away as the result of fifteen or twenty minutes of right thinking.

27. If you enter into the discipline necessary to bring about a radical change in your life, you must do so deliberately, after giving the matter careful thought and full consideration, and then you must allow nothing to interfere with your decision.

28. This discipline, this change of thought, this mental attitude will not only bring you the material things which are necessary for your highest and best welfare, but will bring health and harmonious conditions generally.

29. If you wish harmonious conditions in your life, you must develop a harmonious mental attitude.

30. Your world without will be a reflection of your world within.

31. For your exercise this week, concentrate on Harmony, and when I say concentrate, I mean all that the word implies; concentrate so deeply, so earnestly, that you will be conscious of nothing but harmony. Remember, we learn by doing. Reading these lessons will get you nowhere. It is in the practical application that the value consists.

Learn to keep the door shut, keep out of your mind and out of your world, every element that seeks admittance with no definite helpful end in view.
—GEORGE MATHEW ADAMS

PART FOURTEEN:
STUDY QUESTIONS WITH ANSWERS

131. What is the source of all Wisdom, Power, and Intelligence?
The Universal Mind.

132. Where do all motion, light, heat, and color have their origin?
In the Universal Energy, which is one manifestation of the Universal Mind.

133. Where does the creative power of thought originate?
In the Universal Mind.

134. What is thought?
Mind in motion.

135. How is the Universal differentiated in form?
The individual is the means by which the Universal produces the various combinations which result in formation of phenomena.

136. How is this accomplished?
The power of the individual to think is his ability to act upon the Universal and bring it into manifestation.

137. What is the first form which the Universal takes so far as we know?

Electrons, which fill all space.

138. Where do all things have their origin?

In mind.

139. What is the result of a change of thought?

A change in conditions.

140. What is the result of a harmonious mental attitude?

Harmonious conditions in life.

Thought, immaterial though it may be, is the matrix that shapes the issues of life. The mind has been active in all fields during this fruitful century, but it is to science we must look for the thoughts that have shaped all thinking.

PART FIFTEEN

Experiments with parasites found on plants indicate that even the lowest order of life is enabled to take advantage of natural law. This experiment was made by Jacques Loch, M.D., Ph.D., a member of the Rockefeller Institute.

"In order to obtain the material, potted rose bushes are brought into a room and placed in front of a closed window. If the plants are allowed to dry out, the aphids (parasites), previously wingless, change to winged insects. After the metamorphosis, the animals leave the plants, fly to the window and then creep upward on the glass."

It is evident that these tiny insects found that the plants on which they had been thriving were dead, and that they could therefore secure nothing more to eat and drink from this source. The only method by which they could save themselves from starvation was to grow temporary wings and fly, which they did.

Experiments such as these indicate that Omniscience as well as Omnipotence is omnipresent and that the tiniest living thing can take advantage of it in an emergency.

Part Fifteen will tell you more about the law under which we live. It will explain that these laws operate to our advantage; that all conditions and experiences that come to us are for our benefit; that we gain strength in *proportion to the effort expended, and that our happiness is best attained through a conscious cooperation with natural laws.*

1. The laws under which we live are designed solely for our advantage. These laws are immutable and we cannot escape from their operation.

2. All the great eternal forces act in solemn silence, but it is in our power to place ourselves in harmony with them and thus express a life of comparative peace and happiness.

3. Difficulties, inharmonies, and obstacles, indicate that we are either refusing to give out what we no longer need, or refusing to accept what we require.

4. Growth is attained through an exchange of the old for the new, of the good for the better; it is a conditional or reciprocal action, for each of us is a complete thought entity and this completeness makes it possible for us to receive only as we give.

5. We cannot obtain what we lack if we tenaciously cling to what we have. We are able to consciously control our conditions as we come to sense the purpose of what we attract, and are able to extract from each experience only what we require for our further growth. Our ability to do this determines the degree of harmony or happiness we attain.

6. The ability to appropriate what we require for our growth, continually increases as we reach higher planes and broader visions, and the greater our abilities to know what we require, the more certain we shall be to discern its presence, to attract it and to absorb it. Nothing may reach us except what is necessary for our growth.

7. All conditions and experiences that come to us do so for our benefit. Difficulties and obstacles will continue to come until we absorb their wisdom and gather from them the essentials of further growth.

8. That we reap what we sow is mathematically exact. We gain permanent strength exactly to the extent of the effort required to overcome difficulties.

9. The inexorable requirements of growth demand that we exert the greatest degree of attraction for what is perfectly in accord with us. Our highest happiness will be best attained through our understanding of, and conscious cooperation with natural laws.

10. In order to possess vitality thought must be impregnated with love. Love is a product of the emotions. It is therefore essential that the emotions be controlled and guided by the intellect and reason.

11. It is love which imparts vitality to thought and thus enables it to germinate. The Law of Attraction, or the law of love, for they are one and the same, will bring to it the necessary material for its growth and maturity.

12. The first form which thought will find is language, or words; this determines the importance of words; they are the first manifestation of thought—the vessels in which thought is carried. They take hold of the ether and by setting it in motion reproduce the thought to others in the form of sound.

13. Thought may lead to action of any kind, but whatever the action, it is simply the thought attempting to express itself in visible form. It is evident, therefore, that if we wish desirable conditions, we can afford to entertain only desirable thoughts.

14. This leads to the inevitable conclusion that if we wish to express abundance in our lives, we can afford to think abundance only, and as words are only thoughts taking form, we must be especially careful to use nothing but constructive and harmonious language, which when finally crystallized into objective forms, will prove to our advantage.

15. We cannot escape from the pictures we incessantly photograph on the mind, and this photography of erroneous conceptions is exactly what is being done by the use of words, when we use any form of language which is not identified with our welfare.

16. We manifest more and more life as our thought becomes clarified and takes higher planes. This is obtained with greater facility as we use word pictures that are clearly defined, and relieved of the conceptions attached to them on lower planes of thought.

17. It is with words that we must express our thoughts, and if we are to make use of higher forms of truth, we may use only such material as has been carefully and intelligently selected with this purpose in view.

18. This wonderful power of clothing thoughts in the form of words is what differentiates man from the rest of the animal kingdom; by the use of the written word he has been enabled to look back over the centuries and see the stirring scenes by which he has come into his present inheritance.

19. He has been enabled to come into communion with the greatest writers and thinkers of all time, and the combined record which we possess today is therefore the expression of Universal Thought as it has been seeking to take form in the mind of Man.

20. We know that the Universal Thought has for its goal the creation of form, and we know that the individual thought is likewise forever attempting to express itself in form, and we know that the word is a thought form, and a sentence is a combination of thought forms, therefore, if we wish our ideal to be beautiful or strong, we must see that the words out of which this temple will eventually be created are exact, that they are put together carefully, because accuracy in building words and sentences is the highest form of architecture in civilization and is a passport to success.

21. Words are thoughts and are therefore an invisible and invincible power which will finally objectify themselves in the form they are given.

22. Words may become mental places that will live forever, or they may become shacks which the first breeze will carry away. They may delight the eye as well as the ear; they may contain all knowledge; in them we find the history of the past as well as the hope of the future; they are living messengers from which every human and superhuman activity is born.

23. The beauty of the word consists in the beauty of the thought; the power of the word consists in the power of the thought, and the power of the thought consists in its vitality. How shall we identify a vital thought? What are its distinguishing characteristics? It must have principle. How shall we identify principle?

24. There is a principle of Mathematics, but none of error; there is a principle of health, but none of disease; there is a principle of truth, but none of dishonesty; there is a principle of light, but none of darkness, and there is a principle of abundance, but none of poverty.

25. How shall we know that this is true? Because if we apply the principle of Mathematics correctly we shall be certain of our results. Where there is health there will be no disease. If we know the Truth we cannot be deceived by error. If we let in light there can be no darkness, and where there is abundance there can be no poverty.

26. These are self-evident facts, but the all-important truth that a thought containing principle is vital and therefore contains life and consequently takes root, and eventually but surely and certainly displaces the negative thoughts, which by their very nature can contain no vitality, is one which seems to have been overlooked.

27. But this is a fact which will enable you to destroy every manner of discord, lack and limitation.

28. There can be no question but that he who "is wise enough to understand" will readily recognize that the creative power of thought places an invincible weapon in his hands and makes him a master of destiny.

29. In the physical world there is a law of compensation which is that "the appearance of a given amount of energy anywhere means the disappearance of the same amount somewhere else," and so we find that we can get only what we give; if we pledge ourselves to a certain action we must be prepared to assume the responsibility for the development of that action. The subconscious cannot reason. It takes us at our word; we have asked for something; we are now to receive it; we have made our bed, we are now to lie in it; the die has been cast; the threads will carry out the pattern we have made.

30. For this reason Insight must be exercised so that the thought which we entertain contains no mental, moral or physical germ which we do not wish objectified in our lives.

31. Insight is a faculty of the mind whereby we are enabled to examine facts and conditions at long range, a kind of human telescope; it enables us to understand the difficulties, as well as the possibilities, in any undertaking.

32. Insight enables us to be prepared for the obstacles which we shall meet; we can therefore overcome them before they have any opportunity of causing difficulty.

33. Insight enables us to plan to advantage and turn our thought and attention in the right direction, instead of into channels which can yield no possible return.

34. Insight is therefore absolutely essential for the development of any great achievement, but with it we may enter, explore and possess any mental field.

35. Insight is a product of the world within and is developed in the Silence, by concentration.

36. For your exercise this week, concentrate on Insight; take your accustomed position and focus the thought on the fact that to have a knowledge of the creative power of thought does not mean to possess the art of thinking. Let the thought dwell on the fact that knowledge does not apply itself. That our actions are not governed by knowledge, but by custom, precedent and habit. That the only way we can get ourselves to apply knowledge is by a determined conscious effort. Call to mind the fact that knowledge unused passes from the mind, that the value of the information is in the application of the principle; continue this line of thought until you gain sufficient insight to formulate a definite program for applying this principle to your own particular problem.

Think truly, and thy thoughts shall the world's famine feed; Speak truly, and each word of thine shall be a fruitful seed; Live truly, and thy life shall be a great and noble creed.

—Horatio Bonar

PART FIFTEEN:
STUDY QUESTIONS WITH ANSWERS

141. What determines the degree of harmony which we attain?

Our ability to appropriate what we require for our growth from each experience.

142. What do difficulties and obstacles indicate?

That they are necessary for our wisdom and spiritual growth.

143. How may these difficulties be avoided?

By a conscious understanding of and cooperation with natural laws.

144. What is the principle by which thought manifests itself in form?

The Law of Attraction.

145. How is the necessary material secured by which the growth, development and maturity of the idea take form?

The law of love, which is the creative principle of the Universe, imparts vitality to the thought, and the Law of Attraction brings the necessary substance by the law of growth.

146. How are desirable conditions secured?

By entertaining desirable thoughts only.

147. How are undesirable conditions brought about?

By thinking, discussing and visualizing conditions of lack, limitation, disease, inharmony and discord of every kind. This mental photography of erroneous conceptions is taken up by the subconscious and the law of attraction will inevitably crystallize it into objective form. That we reap what we sow is scientifically exact.

148. How can we overcome every kind of fear, lack, limitation, poverty, and discord?

By substituting principle for error.

149. How may we recognize principle?

By a conscious realization of the fact that Truth invariably destroys error. We do not have to laboriously shovel the darkness out; all that is necessary is to turn on the light. The same principle applies to every form of negative thought.

150. What is the value of Insight?

It enables us to understand the value of making application of the knowledge which we gain. Many seem to think that knowledge will automatically apply itself, which is by no means true.

To every man there openeth a way, And the high soul climbs the high way, And the low soul gropes the low; And in between on the misty flats, The rest drift to and fro. But to every man there openeth A high way and a low And every man decideth The way his soul shall go.

PART SIXTEEN

The vibratory activities of the planetary Universe are governed by a law of periodicity. Everything that lives has periods of birth, growth, fruitage, and decline. These periods are governed by the Septimal Law.

The Law of Sevens governs the days of the week, the phases of the moon, the harmonies of sound, light, heat, electricity, magnetism, atomic structure. It governs the life of individuals and of nations, and it dominates the activities of the commercial world.

Life is growth, and growth is change; each seven-year period takes us into a new cycle. The first seven years is the period of infancy. The next seven the period of childhood, representing the beginning of individual responsibility. The next seven represents the period of adolescence. The fourth period marks the attainment of full growth. The fifth period is the constructive period, when men begin to acquire property, possessions, a home and family. The next from 35 to 42, is a period of reactions and changes, and this in turn is followed by a period of reconstruction, adjustment and recuperation, so as to be ready for a new cycle of sevens, beginning with the fiftieth year.

There are many who think that the world is just about to pass out of the *sixth period; that it will soon enter into the seventh period, the period of re-adjustment, reconstruction and harmony; the period which is frequently referred to as the Millennium.*

Those familiar with these cycles will not be disturbed when things seem to go wrong, but can apply the principle outlined in these lessons with the full assurance that a higher law will invariably control all other laws, and that through an understanding and conscious operation of spiritual laws, we can convert every seeming difficulty into a blessing.

1. Wealth is a product of labor. Capital is an effect, not a cause; a servant, not a master; a means, not an end.

2. The most commonly accepted definition of wealth is that it consists of all useful and agreeable things which possess exchange value. It is this exchange value which is the predominant characteristic of wealth.

3. When we consider the small addition made by wealth to the happiness of the possessor, we find that the true value consists not in its utility but in its exchange.

4. This exchange value makes it a medium for securing the things of real value whereby our ideals may be realized.

5. Wealth should then never be desired as an end, but simply as a means of accomplishing an end. Success is contingent upon a higher ideal than the mere accumulation of riches, and he who aspires to such success must formulate an ideal for which he is willing to strive.

6. With such an ideal in mind, the ways and means can and will be provided, but the mistake must not be made of substituting the means for the end. There must be a definite fixed purpose, an ideal.

7. Prentice Mulford said: "The man of success is the man possessed of the greatest spiritual understanding and every great fortune comes of superior and truly spiritual power." Unfortunately, there are those who fail to recognize this power; they forget that Andrew Carnegie's mother had to help support the family when they came to America, that Harriman's father was a poor clergyman with a salary of only $200 a year, that Sir Thomas Lipton started with only 25 cents. These men had no other power to depend upon, but it did not fail them.

8. The power to create depends entirely upon spiritual power; there are three steps, idealization, visualization and materialization. Every captain of industry depends upon this power exclusively. In an article in *Everybody's Magazine,* Henry M. Flagler, the Standard Oil multi-millionaire, admitted that the secret of his success was his power to see a thing in its completeness. The following conversation with the reporter shows his power of idealization, concentration and visualization, all spiritual powers:

9. "Did you actually vision to yourself the whole thing? I mean, did you, or could you, really close your eyes and see the tracks? And the trains running? And hear the whistles blowing? Did you go as far as that?" "Yes." "How clearly?" "Very clearly."

10. Here we have a vision of the law, we see "cause and effect," we see that thought necessarily precedes and determines action. If we are wise, we shall come into a realization of the tremendous fact that no arbitrary condition can exist for a moment, and that human experience is the result of an orderly and harmonious sequence.

11. The successful businessman is more often than not an idealist and is ever striving for higher and higher standards. The subtle

forces of thought as they crystallize in our daily moods is what constitutes life.

12. Thought is the plastic material with which we build images of our growing conception of life. Use determines its existence. As in all other things our ability to recognize it and use it properly is the necessary condition for attainment.

13. Premature wealth is but the forerunner of humiliation and disaster, because we cannot permanently retain anything which we do not merit or which we have not earned.

14. The conditions with which we meet in the world without, correspond to the conditions which we find in the world within. This is brought about by the Law of Attraction. How then shall we determine what is to enter into the world within?

15. Whatever enters the mind through the senses or the objective mind will impress the mind and result in a mental image which will become a pattern for the creative energies. These experiences are largely the result of environment, chance, past thinking and other forms of negative thought, and must be subjected to careful analysis before being entertained. On the other hand, we can form our own mental images, through our own interior processes of thought regardless of the thoughts of others, regardless of exterior conditions, regardless of environment of every kind, and it is by the exercise of this power that we can control our own destiny, body, mind and soul.

16. It is by the exercise of this power that we take our fate out of the hands of chance, and consciously make for ourselves the experiences which we desire, because when we consciously realize a condition, that condition will eventually manifest itself in our lives; it is therefore evident that in the last analysis thinking is the one great cause in life.

17. Therefore, to control thought is to control circumstances, conditions, environment, and destiny.

18. How then are we to control thought; what is the process? To think is to create a thought, but the result of the thought will depend upon its form, its quality and its vitality.

19. The form will depend upon the mental images from which it emanates; this will depend upon the depth of the impression, the predominance of the idea, the clarity of the vision, the boldness of the image.

20. The quality depends upon its substance, and this depends upon the material of which the mind is composed; if this material has been woven from thoughts of vigor, strength, courage, determination, the thought will possess these qualities.

21. And finally, the vitality depends upon the feeling with which the thought is impregnated. If the thought is constructive, it will possess vitality; it will have life, it will grow, develop, expand, it will be creative; it will attract to itself everything necessary for its complete development.

22. If the thought is destructive, it will have within itself the germ of its own dissolution; it will die, but in the process of dying, it will bring sickness, disease, and every other form of discord.

23. This we call evil, and when we bring it upon ourselves, some of us are disposed to attribute our difficulties to a Supreme Being, but this supreme being is simply Mind in equilibrium.

24. It is neither good nor bad, it simply is.

25. Our ability to differentiate it into form is our ability to manifest good or evil.

26. Good and evil therefore are not entities, they are simply words which we use to indicate the result of our actions, and these actions are in turn predetermined by the character of our thought.

27. If our thought is constructive and harmonious we manifest good; if it is destructive and discordant we manifest evil.

28. If you desire to visualize a different environment, the process is simply to hold the ideal in mind, until your vision has been made real; give no thought to persons, places or things; these have no place in the absolute; the environment you desire will contain everything necessary; the right persons, and the right things will come at the right time and in the right place.

29. It is sometimes not plain how character, ability, attainment, achievement, environment and destiny can be controlled through the power of visualization, but this is an exact scientific fact.

30. You will readily see that what we think determines the quality of mind, and that the quality of mind in turn determines our ability and mental capacity, and you can readily understand that the improvement in our ability will naturally be followed by increase in attainment and a greater control of circumstances.

31. It will thus be seen that natural laws work in a perfectly natural and harmonious manner; everything seems to "just happen." If you want any evidence of this fact simply compare results of your efforts in your own life, when your actions were prompted by high ideals and when you had selfish or ulterior motives in mind. You will need no further evidence.

32. If you wish to bring about the realization of any desire, form a mental picture of success in your mind, by consciously visualizing your desire; in this way you will be compelling success, you will be externalizing it in your life by scientific methods.

33. We can only see what already exists in the objective world, but what we visualize, already exists in the spiritual world, and this visualization is a substantial token of what will one day appear in the objective world, if we are faithful to our ideal. The reason for this is not difficult; visualization is a form of imagination; this process of thinking forms impressions on the mind, and these impressions in turn form concepts and ideals, and they in turn are the plans from which the Master architect will weave the future.

34. The psychologists have come to the conclusion that there is but one sense, the sense of feeling, and that all other senses are but modifications of this one sense; this being true, we know why feeling is the very fountainhead of power, why the emotions so easily overcome the intellect, and why we must put feeling into our thought, if we wish results. Thought and feeling is the irresistible combination.

35. Visualization must, of course, be directed by the will; we are to visualize exactly what we want; we must be careful not to let the imagination run riot. Imagination is a good servant but a poor master, and unless it is controlled it may easily lead us into all kinds of speculations and conclusions which have no basis or foundation of fact whatever. Every kind of plausible opinion is liable to be accepted without any analytical examination and the inevitable result is mental chaos.

36. We must therefore construct only such mental images as are known to be scientifically true. Subject every idea to a searching analysis and accept nothing which is not scientifically exact. When you do this you will attempt nothing but what you know you can carry out and success will crown your efforts; this is what businessmen call far-sightedness; it is much the same as insight, and is one of the great secrets of success in all important undertakings.

37. For your exercise this week, try to bring yourself to a realization of the important fact that harmony and happiness are states of consciousness and do not depend upon the possession of things. That things are effects and come as a consequence of correct mental states. So that if we desire material possession of any kind our chief concern should be to acquire the mental attitude which will bring about the result desired. This mental attitude is brought about by a realization of our spiritual nature and our unity with the Universal Mind which is the substance of all things. This realization will bring about everything which is necessary for our complete enjoyment. This is scientific or correct thinking. When we succeed in bringing about this mental attitude it is comparatively easy to realize our desire as an already accomplished fact; when we can do this we shall have found the "Truth" which makes us "free" from every lack or limitation of any kind.

A man might frame and let loose a star, to roll in its orbit, and yet not have done so memorable a thing before God as he who lets a golden-orbed thought to roll through the generations of time.

—H. W. BEECHER

PART SIXTEEN:
STUDY QUESTIONS WITH ANSWERS

151. Upon what does wealth depend?
Upon an understanding of the creative nature of thought.

152. Upon what does its true value consist?
Upon its exchange value.

153. Upon what does success depend?
Upon spiritual power.

154. Upon what does this power depend?
Upon use; use determines its existence.

155. How may we take our fate out of the hands of chance?
By consciously realizing the conditions which we desire to see manifested in our lives.

156. What then is the great business of life?
Thinking.

157. Why is this so?
Because thought is spiritual and therefore creative. To consciously control thought is therefore to control circumstances, conditions, environment and destiny.

158. What is the source of all evil?
Destructive thinking.

159. What is the source of all good?
Scientific correct thinking.

160. What is scientific thinking?

A recognition of the creative nature of spiritual energy and our ability to control it.

The greatest events of an age are its best thoughts. It is the nature of thought to find its way into action.

—BOVEE

PART SEVENTEEN

The kind of Deity which a man, consciously or unconsciously, worships, indicates the intellectual status of the worshipper.

Ask the Indian of God, and he will describe to you a powerful chieftain of a glorious tribe. Ask the Pagan of God, and he will tell you of a God of fire, a God of water, a god of this, that, and the other.

Ask the Israelite of God, and he will tell you of the God of Moses, who conceived it expedient to rule by coercive measures; hence, the Ten Commandments. Or of Joshua, who led the Israelites into battle, confiscated property, murdered the prisoners, and laid waste to cities.

The so-called heathen made "graven images" of their Gods, whom they were accustomed to worship, but among the most intelligent, at least, these images were but the visible fulcrums with which they were enabled to mentally concentrate on the qualities which they desired to externalize in their lives.

We of the twentieth century worship a God of Love in theory, but in practice we make for ourselves "graven images" of "Wealth," "Power," "Fashion," "Custom" and "Conventionality." We "fall down" before them and worship them. We concentrate on them and they are thereby externalized in our lives.

The student who masters the contents of Part Seventeen will not mistake the symbols for the reality; he will be interested in causes, rather than effects.

He will concentrate on the realities of life, and will then not be disappointed in the results.

1. We are told that Man has "dominion over all things"; this dominion is established through Mind. Thought is the activity which controls every principle beneath it. The highest principle by reason of its superior essence and qualities necessarily determines the circumstances, aspects and relation of everything with which it comes in contact.

2. The vibrations of mental forces are the finest and consequently the most powerful in existence. To those who perceive the nature and transcendency of mental force, all physical power sinks into insignificance.

3. We are accustomed to look upon the Universe with a lens of five senses, and from these experiences our anthropomorphic conceptions originate, but true conceptions are only secured by spiritual insight. This insight requires a quickening of the vibrations of the Mind, and is only secured when the mind is continuously concentrated in a given direction.

4. Continuous concentration means an even, unbroken flow of thought and is the result of patient, persistent, persevering and well-regulated system.

5. Great discoveries are the result of long-continued investigation. The science of mathematics requires years of concentrated effort to master it, and the greatest science—that of the Mind—is revealed only through concentrated effort.

6. Concentration is much misunderstood; there seems to be an idea of effort or activity associated with it, when just the contrary is

necessary. The greatness of an actor lies in the fact that he forgets himself in the portrayal of his character, becoming so identified with it, that the audience is swayed by the realism of the performance. This will give you a good idea of true concentration; you should be so interested in your thought, so engrossed in your subject, as to be conscious of nothing else. Such concentration leads to intuitive perception and immediate insight into the nature of the object concentrated upon.

7. All knowledge is the result of concentration of this kind; it is thus that the secrets of Heaven and Earth have been wrested; it is thus that the mind becomes a magnet and the desire to know draws the knowledge, irresistibly attracts it, makes it your own.

8. Desire is largely subconscious; conscious desire rarely realizes its object when the latter is out of immediate reach. Subconscious desire arouses the latent faculties of the mind, and difficult problems seem to solve themselves.

9. The subconscious mind may be aroused and brought into action in any direction and made to serve us for any purpose, by concentration. The practice of concentration requires the control of the physical, mental, and physical being; all modes of consciousness whether physical, mental, or physical, must be under control.

10. Spiritual Truth is therefore the controlling factor; it is this which will enable you to grow out of limited attainment and reach a point where you will be able to translate modes of thought into character and consciousness.

11. Concentration does not mean mere thinking of thoughts, but the transmutation of these thoughts into practical values; the average person has no conception of the meaning of concentration.

There is always the cry "to have" but never the cry "to be"; they fail to understand that they cannot have one without the other, that they must first find the "kingdom" before they can have the "things added." Momentary enthusiasm is of no value; it is only with unbounded self-confidence that the goal is reached.

12. The mind may place the ideal a little too high and fall short of the mark; it may attempt to soar on untrained wings and instead of flying, fall to earth; but that is no reason for not making another attempt.

13. Weakness is the only barrier to mental attainment; attribute your weakness to physical limitations or mental uncertainties and try again; ease and perfection are gained by repetition.

14. The astronomer centers his mind on the stars and they give forth their secrets; the geologist centers his mind on the construction of the earth and we have geology; so with all things. Men center their minds on the problems of life, and the result is apparent in the vast and complex social order of the day.

15. All mental discovery and attainment are the result of desire plus concentration; desire is the strongest mode of action; the more persistent the desire, the more authoritative the revelation. Desire added to concentration will wrench any secret from nature.

16. In realizing great thoughts, in experiencing great emotions that correspond with great thoughts, the mind is in a state where it appreciates the value of higher things.

17. The intensity of one moment's earnest concentration and the intense longing to become and to attain may take you further than years of slow normal and forced effort; it will unfasten the prison

bars of unbelief, weakness, impotence and self-belittlement, and you will come into a realization of the joy of overcoming.

18. The spirit of initiative and originality is developed through persistence and continuity of mental effort. Business teaches the value of concentration and encourages decision of character; it develops practical insight and quickness of conclusion. The mental element in every commercial pursuit is dominant as the controlling factor, and desire is the predominating force; all commercial relations are the externalization of desire.

19. Many of the sturdy and substantial virtues are developed in commercial employment; the mind is steadied and directed; it becomes efficient. The principal necessity is the strengthening of the mind so that it rises superior to the distractions and wayward impulses of instinctive life and thus successfully overcomes in the conflict between the higher and lower self.

20. All of us are dynamos, but the dynamo of itself is nothing; the mind must work the dynamo; then it is useful and its energy can be definitely concentrated. The mind is an engine whose power is undreamed; thought is an omni-working power. It is the ruler and creator of all form and all events occurring in form. Physical energy is nothing in comparison with the omnipotence of thought, because thought enables man to harness all other natural power.

21. Vibration is the action of thought; it is vibration which reaches out and attracts the material necessary to construct and build. There is nothing mysterious concerning the power of thought; concentration simply implies that consciousness can be focalized to the point where it becomes identified with the object of its attention. As food absorbed is the essence of the body, so the mind absorbs the object of its attention, gives it life and being.

22. If you concentrate on some matter of importance, the intuitive power will be set in operation, and help will come in the nature of information which will lead to success.

23. Intuition arrives at conclusions without the aid of experience or memory. Intuition often solves problems that are beyond the grasp of the reasoning power. Intuition often comes with a suddenness that is startling; it reveals the truth for which we are searching, so directly that it seems to come from a higher power. Intuition can be cultivated and developed; in order to do this it must be recognized and appreciated; if the intuitive visitor is given a royal welcome when he comes, he will come again; the more cordial the welcome the more frequent his visits will become, but if he is ignored or neglected he will make his visits few and far apart.

24. Intuition usually comes in the Silence; great minds seek solitude frequently; it is here that all the larger problems of life are worked out. For this reason every businessman who can afford it has a private office, where he will not be disturbed; if you cannot afford a private office you can at least find somewhere, where you can be alone a few minutes each day, to train the thought along lines which will enable you to develop that invincible power which is necessary to achieve.

25. Remember that fundamentally the subconscious is omnipotent; there is no limit to the things that can be done when it is given the power to act. Your degree of success is determined by the nature of your desire. If the nature of your desire is in harmony with natural law or the Universal Mind, it will gradually emancipate the mind and give you invincible courage.

26. Every obstacle conquered, every victory gained, will give you more faith in your power, and you will have greater ability to win.

Your strength is determined by your mental attitude; if this attitude is one of success, and is permanently held with an unswerving purpose, you will attract to you from the invisible domain the things you silently demand.

27. By keeping the thought in mind, it will gradually take tangible form. A definite purpose sets causes in motion which go out in the invisible world and find the material necessary to serve your purpose.

28. You may be pursuing the symbols of power, instead of power itself. You may be pursuing fame instead of honor, riches instead of wealth, position instead of servitude; in either event you will find that they turn to ashes just as you overtake them.

29. Premature wealth or position cannot be retained because it has not been earned; we get only what we give, and those who try to get without giving always find that the law of compensation is relentlessly bringing about an exact equilibrium.

30. The race has usually been for money and other mere symbols of power, but with an understanding of the true source of power, we can afford to ignore the symbols. The man with a large bank account finds it unnecessary to load his pockets down with gold; so with the man who has found the true source of power; he is no longer interested in its shams or pretensions.

31. Thought ordinarily leads outwardly in evolutionary directions, but it can be turned within where it will take hold of the basic principles of things, the heart of things, the spirit of things. When you get to the heart of things it is comparatively easy to understand and command them.

32. This is because the Spirit of a thing is the thing itself, the vital part of it, the real substance. The form is simply the outward manifestation of the spiritual activity within.

33. For your exercise this week concentrate as nearly as possible in accordance with the method outlined in this lesson; let there be no conscious effort or activity associated with your purpose. Relax completely, avoid any thought of anxiety as to results. Remember that power comes through repose. Let the thought dwell upon your object, until it is completely identified with it, until you are conscious of nothing else.

34. If you wish to eliminate fear, concentrate on courage.

35. If you wish to eliminate lack, concentrate on abundance.

36. If you wish to eliminate disease, concentrate on health.

37. Always concentrate on the ideal as an already existing fact; this is the germ cell, the life principle which goes forth and sets in motion those causes which guide, direct and bring about the necessary relation, which eventually manifests itself in form.

Thought is the property of those only who can entertain it.

—EMERSON

PART SEVENTEEN:
STUDY QUESTIONS WITH ANSWERS

161. What is the true method of concentration?

To become so identified with the object of your thought that you are conscious of nothing else.

162. What is the result of this method of concentration?

Invisible forces are set in motion which irresistibly bring about conditions in correspondence with your thought.

163. What is the controlling factor in this method of thought?

Spiritual Truth.

164. Why is this so?

Because the nature of our desire must be in harmony with natural law.

165. What is the practical value of this method of concentration?

Thought is transmuted into character, and character is the magnet which creates the environment of the individual.

166. What is the controlling factor in every commercial pursuit?

The mental element.

167. Why is this so?

Because Mind is the ruler and creator of all form and all events occurring in form.

168. How does concentration operate?

By the development of the powers of perception, wisdom, intuition, and sagacity.

169. Why is intuition superior to reason?

Because it does not depend upon experience or memory and frequently brings about the solution to our problems by methods concerning which we are in entire ignorance.

170. What is the result of pursuing the symbol of the reality?

They frequently turn to ashes just as we overtake them, because the symbol is only the outward form of the spiritual activity within, therefore unless we can possess the spiritual reality, the form disappears.

PART EIGHTEEN

In order to grow we must obtain what is necessary for our growth. This is brought about through the Law of Attraction. This principle is the sole means by which the individual is differentiated from the Universal.

Think for a moment, what would a man be if he were not a husband, father, or brother, if he were not interested in the social, economical, political or religious world. He would be nothing but an abstract theoretical ego. He exists, therefore, only in his relation to the whole, in his relation to other men, in his relation to society. This relation constitutes his environment and in no other way.

It is evident, therefore, that the individual is simply the differentiation of the one Universal Mind "which lighteth every man that cometh into the world," and his so-called individuality or personality consists of nothing but the manner in which he relates with the whole.

This we call his environment and is brought about by the Law of Attraction. Part Eighteen, which follows, has something more to say concerning this important law.

1. There is a change in the thought of the world. This change is silently transpiring in our midst, and is more important than any which the world has undergone since the downfall of Paganism.

2. The present revolution in the opinions of all classes of men, the highest and most cultured of men as well as those of the laboring class, stands unparalleled in the history of the world.

3. Science has of late made such vast discoveries, has revealed such an infinity of resources, has unveiled such enormous possibilities and such unsuspected forces, that scientific men more and more hesitate to affirm certain theories as established and beyond doubt or to deny other theories as absurd or impossible.

4. A new civilization is being born; customs, creeds, and precedent are passing; vision, faith and service are taking their place. The fetters of tradition are being melted off from humanity, and as the impurities of materialism are being consumed, thought is being liberated and truth is rising full robed before an astonished multitude.

5. The whole world is on the eve of a new consciousness, a new power, and a new realization within the self.

6. Physical Science has resolved matter into molecules, molecules into atoms, atoms into energy, and it has remained for Mr. J. A. Fleming, in an address before the Royal Institution, to resolve this energy into mind. He says, "In its ultimate essence, energy may be incomprehensible by us except as an exhibition of the direct operation of that which we call Mind or Will."

7. And this mind is the indwelling and ultimate. It is imminent in matter as in spirit. It is the sustaining, energizing, all-pervading Spirit of the universe.

8. Every living thing must be sustained by this omnipotent Intelligence, and we find the difference in individual lives to be largely measured by the degree of this intelligence, which they manifest. It is greater intelligence that places the animal in a higher scale of being than the plant, the man higher than the animal, and we find that this increased intelligence is again indicated by the power of the individual to control modes of action and thus to consciously adjust himself to his environment.

9. It is this adjustment that occupies the attention of the greatest minds, and this adjustment consists in nothing else than the recognition of an existing order in the Universal Mind, for it is well known that this mind will obey us precisely in proportion as we first obey it.

10. It is the recognition of natural laws that has enabled us to annihilate time and space, to soar in the air and to make iron float, and the greater the degree of intelligence the greater will be our recognition of these natural laws and the greater will be the power we can possess.

11. It is the recognition of the self as an individualization of this Universal Intelligence that enables the individual to control those forms of intelligence which have not yet reached this level of self-recognition; they do not know that this Universal Intelligence permeates all things ready to be called into action; they do not know that it is responsive to every demand, and they are therefore in bondage to the law of their own being.

12. Thought is creative and the principle on which the law is based is sound and legitimate and is inherent in the nature of things; but this creative power does not originate in the individual, but in the Universal, which is the source and foundation of all energy and substance; the individual is simply the channel for the distribution of this energy.

13. The individual is simply the means by which the Universal produces the various combinations which result in the formation of phenomena, which depends upon the law of vibration, whereby various rates of rapidity of motion in the primary substance form new substances only in certain exact numerical ratios.

14. Thought is the invisible link by which the individual comes into communication with the Universal, the finite with the Infinite, the seen with the Unseen. Thought is the magic by which the human is transformed into a being who thinks and knows and feels and acts.

15. As the proper apparatus has enabled the eye to discover worlds without number millions of miles away, so, with the proper understanding, man has been enabled to communicate with the Universal Mind, the source of all power.

16. The Understanding which is usually developed is about as valuable as a VCR without a videotape; in fact, it is usually nothing more than a "belief," which means nothing at all. The savages of the Cannibal Islands believe something; but that proves nothing.

17. The only belief which is of any value to anyone is a belief that has been put to a test and demonstrated to be a fact; it is then no longer a belief, but has become a living Faith or Truth.

18. And this Truth has been put to the test by hundreds of thousands of people and has been found to be the Truth exactly in proportion to the usefulness of the apparatus which they used.

19. A man would not expect to locate stars hundreds of millions of miles away without a sufficiently strong telescope, and for this reason Science is continually engaged in building larger and more powerful telescopes and is continually rewarded by additional knowledge of the heavenly bodies.

20. So with understanding; men are continually making progress in the methods which they use to come into communication with the Universal Mind and its infinite possibilities.

21. The Universal Mind manifests itself in the objective, through the principle of attraction that each atom has for every other atom, in infinite degrees of intensity.

22. It is by this principle of combining and attracting that things are brought together. This principle is of universal application and is the sole means whereby the purpose of existence is carried into effect.

23. The expression of growth is met in a most beautiful manner through the instrumentality of this Universal Principle.

24. In order to grow we must obtain what is essential for our growth, but as we are at all times a complete thought entity, this completeness makes it possible for us to receive only as we give; growth is therefore conditioned on reciprocal action, and we find that on the mental plane like attracts like, that mental vibrations respond only to the extent of their vibratory harmony.

25. It is clear, therefore, that thoughts of abundance will respond only to similar thoughts; the wealth of the individual is seen to be what he inherently is. Affluence within is found to be the secret of attraction for affluence without. The ability to produce is found to be the real source of wealth of the individual. It is for this reason that he who has his heart in his work is certain to meet with unbounded success. He will give and continually give; and the more he gives, the more he will receive.

26. What do the great financiers of Wall Street, the captains of industry, the statesmen, the great corporation attorneys, the inventors, the physicians, the authors—what do each of these contribute to the sum of human happiness but the power of their thought?

27. Thought is the energy by which the Law of Attraction is brought into operation, which eventually manifests itself in abundance.

28. The Universal Mind is static Mind or Substance in equilibrium. It is differentiated into form by our power to think. Thought is the dynamic phase of mind.

29. Power depends upon consciousness of power; unless we use it, we shall lose it, and unless we are conscious of it, we cannot use it.

30. The use of this power depends upon attention; the degree of attention determines our capacity for the acquirement of knowledge which is another name for power.

31. Attention has been held to be the distinguishing mark of genius. The cultivation of attention depends upon practice.

32. The incentive of attention is interest; the greater the interest, the greater the attention; the greater the attention, the greater the interest, action and reaction; begin by paying attention; before long you will have aroused interest; this interest will attract more attention, and this attention will produce more interest, and so on. This practice will enable you to cultivate the power of attention.

33. This week concentrate upon your power to create; seek insight, perception; try to find a logical basis for the faith which is in you. Let the thought dwell on the fact that the physical man lives and moves and has his being in the sustainer of all organic life air, that he must breathe to live. Then let the thought rest on the fact that the spiritual man also lives and moves and has his being in a similar but subtler energy upon which he must depend for life, and that as in the physical world no life assumes form until after a seed is sown, and no higher fruit than that of the parent stock can be produced; so in the spiritual world no effect can be produced until the seed is sown and the fruit will depend upon the nature of the seed, so that the results which you secure depend upon your perception of law in the mighty domain of causation, the highest evolution of human consciousness.

There is no thought in my mind but it quickly tends to convert itself into a power and organizes a huge instrumentality of means.

—EMERSON

PART EIGHTEEN:
STUDY QUESTIONS WITH ANSWERS

171. How is the difference in individual lives measured?
By the degree of intelligence which they manifest.

172. What is the law by which the individual may control other forms of intelligence?
A recognition of the self as an individualization of the Universal Intelligence.

173. Where does the creative power originate?
In the Universal.

174. How does the Universal create form?
By means of the individual.

175. What is the connecting link between the individual and the Universal?

Thought.

176. What is the principle by which the means of existence is carried into effect?

The law of love.

177. How is this principle brought into expression?

By the law of growth.

178. Upon what condition does the law of growth depend?

Upon reciprocal action. The individual is complete at all times and this makes it possible to receive only as we give.

179. What is it that we give?

Thought.

180. What do we receive?

Thought, which is substance in equilibrium and which is constantly being differentiated in form by what we think.

PART NINETEEN

Fear is a powerful form of thought. It paralyzes the nerve centers, thus affecting the circulation of the blood.

This, in turn, paralyzes the muscular system, so that fear affects the entire being, body, brain and nerve, physical, mental, and muscular.

Of course the way to overcome fear is to become conscious of power. What is this mysterious vital force which we call power? We do not know, but then, neither do we know what electricity is.

But we do know that by conforming to the requirements of the law by which electricity is governed, it will be our obedient servant; that it will light our homes, our cities, run our machinery, and serve us in many useful capacities.

And so it is with vital force. Although we do not know what it is, and possibly may never know, we do know that it is a primary force which manifests itself through living bodies, and that by complying with the laws and principles by which it is governed, we can open ourselves to a more abundant inflow of this vital energy, and thus express the highest possible degree of mental, moral, and spiritual efficiency.

This part tells of a very simple way of developing this vital force. If you put into practice the information outlined in this lesson you will soon develop the sense of power which has ever been the distinguishing mark of genius.

1. The search for truth is no longer a haphazard adventure, but it is a systematic process, and is logical in its operation. Every kind of experience is given a voice in shaping its decision.

2. In seeking the truth we are seeking ultimate cause; we know that every human experience is an effect; then if we may ascertain the cause, and if we shall find that this cause is one which we can consciously control, the effect or the experience will be within our control also.

3. Human experience will then no longer be the football of fate; a man will not be the child of fortune, but destiny. Fate and fortune will be controlled as readily as a captain controls his ship, or an engineer his train.

4. All things are finally resolvable into the same element and as they are thus translatable, one into the other, they must ever be in relation and may never be in opposition to one another.

5. In the physical world there are innumerable contrasts, and these may for convenience's sake, be designated by distinctive names. There are sizes, colors, shades or ends to all things. There is a North Pole, and a South Pole, an inside and an outside, a seen and an unseen, but these expressions merely serve to place extremes in contrast.

6. They are names given to two different parts of one quantity. The two extremes are relative; they are not separate entities, but are two parts or aspects of the whole.

7. In the mental world we find the same law; we speak of knowledge and ignorance, but ignorance is but a lack of knowledge and is therefore found to be simply a word to express the absence of knowledge; it has no principle in itself.

8. In the Moral World we again find the same law; we speak of good and evil, but Good is a reality, something tangible, while Evil is found to be simply a negative condition, the absence of Good. Evil is sometimes thought to be a very real condition, but it has no principle, no vitality, no life; we know this because it can always be destroyed by Good; just as Truth destroys Error and light destroys darkness, so Evil vanishes when Good appears; there is therefore but one principle in the Moral World.

9. We find exactly the same law obtaining in the spiritual world; we speak of Mind and Matter as two separate entities, but clearer insight makes it evident that there is but one operative principle and that is Mind.

10. Mind is the real and the eternal. Matter is forever changing; we know that in the eons of time a hundred years is but as a day. If we stand in any large city and let the eye rest on the innumerable large and magnificent buildings, the vast array of modern automobiles, telephones, the electric lights, and all the other conveniences of modern civilization, we may remember that not one of them was there just over a century ago, and if we could stand on the same spot in a hundred years from now, in all probability we should find that but few of them remained.

11. In the animal kingdom we find the same law of change. The millions and millions of animals come and go, a few years constituting their span of life. In the plant world the change is still more rapid. Many plants and nearly all grasses come and go in a single year. When we pass to the inorganic, we expect to find something more substantial, but as we gaze on the apparently solid continent, we are told that it arose from the ocean; we see the giant mountain and are told that the place where it now stands was once a lake; and as we stand in awe before the great cliffs in the Yosemite

Valley we can easily trace the path of the glaciers which carried all before them.

12. We are in the presence of continual change, and we know that this change is but the evolution of the Universal Mind, the grand process whereby all things are continually being created anew, and we come to know that matter is but a form which Mind takes and is therefore simply a condition. Matter has no principle; Mind is the only principle.

13. We have then come to know that Mind is the only principle which is operative in the physical, mental, moral and spiritual world.

14. We also know that this mind is static, mind at rest; we also know that the ability of the individual to think is his ability to act upon the Universal Mind and convert it into dynamic mind, or mind in motion.

15. In order to do this fuel must be applied in the form of food, for man cannot think without eating, and so we find that even a spiritual activity such as thinking cannot be converted into sources of pleasure and profit except by making use of material means.

16. It requires energy of some kind to collect electricity and convert it into a dynamic power, it requires the rays of the sun to give the necessary energy to sustain plant life, so it also requires energy in the form of food to enable the individual to think and thereby act upon the Universal Mind.

17. You may know that thought constantly, eternally is taking form, is forever seeking expression, or you may not, but the fact remains that if your thought is powerful, constructive, and positive, this will be plainly evident in the state of your health, your business and your

environment; if your thought is weak, critical, destructive and negative generally, it will manifest itself in your body as fear, worry and nervousness, in your finance as lack and limitation, and in discordant conditions in your environment.

18. All wealth is the offspring of power; possessions are of value only as they confer power. Events are significant only as they affect power; all things represent certain forms and degrees of power.

19. A knowledge of cause and effect as shown by the laws governing steam, electricity, chemical affinity and gravitation enables men to plan courageously and to execute fearlessly. These laws are called natural laws, because they govern the physical world, but all power is not physical power; there is also mental power, and there is moral and spiritual power.

20. What are our schools, our universities, but mental powerhouses, places where mental power is being developed?

21. As there are many mighty powerhouses for the application of power to ponderous machinery, whereby raw material is collected and converted into the necessities and comforts of life, so the mental powerhouses collect the raw material and cultivate and develop it into a power which is infinitely superior to all the forces of nature, marvelous though they may be.

22. What is this raw material which is being collected in these thousands of mental powerhouses all over the world and developed into a power which is evidently controlling every other power? In its static form it is Mind—in its dynamic form, it is Thought.

23. This power is superior because it exists on a higher plane, because it has enabled man to discover the law by which these wonderful forces of nature could be harnessed and made to do the work of hundreds and thousands of men. It has enabled man to discover laws whereby time and space have been annihilated, and the law of gravitation overcome.

24. Thought is the vital force or energy which is being developed and which has produced such startling results in the last half century as to bring about a world which would be absolutely inconceivable to a man existing only 50 or 25 years ago. If such results have been secured by organizing these mental powerhouses in 50 years, what may not be expected in another 50 years?

25. The substance from which all things are created is infinite in quantity; we know that light travels at the rate of 186,000 miles per second, and we know that there are stars so remote that it takes light 2,000 years to reach us, and we know that such starts exist in all parts of the heaven; we know, too, that this light comes in waves, so that if the ether on which these waves travel was not continuous the light would fail to reach us; we can then only come to the conclusion that this substance, or ether, or raw material, is universally present.

26. How, then, does it manifest itself in form? In electrical science a battery is formed by connecting the opposite poles of zinc and copper, which causes a current to flow from one to the other and so provides energy. This same process is repeated in respect to every polarity, and as all form simply depends upon the rate of vibration and consequent relations of atoms to each other, if we wish to change the form of manifestation we must change the polarity. This is the principle of causation.

27. For your exercise this week, concentrate, and when I use the word concentrate, I mean all that the word implies; become so absorbed in the object of your thought that you are conscious of nothing else, and do this a few minutes every day. You take the necessary time to eat in order that the body may be nourished, why not take the time to assimilate your mental food?

28. Let the thought rest on the fact that appearances are deceptive. The earth is not flat, neither is it stationary; the sky is not a dome, the sun does not move, the stars are not small specks of light, and matter which was once supposed to be fixed has been found to be in a state of perpetual flux.

29. Try to realize that the day is fast approaching—its dawn is now at hand—when modes of thought and action must be adjusted to rapidly increasing knowledge of the operation of eternal principles.

> *Silent thought, is, after all, the mightiest agent in human affairs.*
>
> —CHANNING

PART NINETEEN:
STUDY QUESTIONS WITH ANSWERS

181. How are extremes placed in contrast?

They are designated by distinctive names, such as inside and outside, top and bottom, light and dark, good and bad.

182. Are these separate entities?

No, they are parts or aspects of one Whole.

183. What is the one creative Principle in the physical, mental and spiritual world?

The Universal Mind, or the Eternal Energy from which all things proceed.

184. How are we related to this creative Principle?

By our ability to think.

185. How does this creative Principle become operative?

Thought is the seed, which results in action and action results in form.

186. Upon what does form depend?

Upon the rate of vibration.

187. How may the rate of vibration be changed?

By mental action.

188. Upon what does mental action depend?

Upon polarity, action and reaction, between the individual and the Universal.

189. Does the creative energy originate in the individual or the Universal?

In the Universal, but the Universal can manifest itself only through the individual.

190. Why is the individual necessary?

Because the Universal is static, and requires energy to start it in motion. This is furnished by food which is converted into energy, which in turn enables the individual to think. When the individual stops eating he stops thinking; then he no longer acts upon the Universal; there is consequently no longer any action or reaction; the Universal is then only pure mind in static form—mind at rest.

PART TWENTY

For many years there has been an endless discussion as to the origin of evil. Theologians have told us that God is Love, and that God is Omnipresent. If this be true, there is no place where God is not. Where, then, are Evil, Satan, and Hell?

Let us see:

God is Spirit.

Spirit is the Creative Principle of the Universe.

Man is made in the image and likeness of God.

Man is therefore a spiritual being.

The only activity which spirit possesses is the power to think.

Thinking is therefore a creative process.

All form is therefore the result of the thinking process.

The destruction of form must also be a result of the thinking process.

Fictitious representations of form are the result of the creative power of thought, as in Hypnotism.

Apparent representations of form are the result of the creative power of thought, as in Spiritualism.

Invention, organization and constructive work of all kinds are the result of the creative power of thought, as in concentration.

When the creative power of thought is manifested for the benefit of
humanity, we call the result good.
When the creative power of thought is manifested in a destructive or
evil manner, we call the result evil.

This indicates the origin of both good and evil; they are simply words
which have been coined in order to indicate the nature of the result of the
thinking or creative process. Thought necessarily precedes and predetermines
action; action precedes and predetermines condition.
Part Twenty will throw more light upon this important subject.

1. The spirit of a thing is that thing; it is necessarily fixed, changeless
and eternal. The spirit of you is—you; without the spirit you would
be nothing. It becomes active through your recognition of it and its
possibilities.

2. You may have all the wealth in Christendom, but unless you recognize it and make use of it, it will have no value; so with your spiritual wealth: unless you recognize it and use it, it will have no value.
The one and only condition of spiritual power is use or recognition.

3. All great things come through recognition; the scepter of power
is consciousness, and thought is its messenger, and this messenger is
constantly molding the realities of the invisible world into the conditions and environments of your objective world.

4. Thinking is the true business of life, power is the result. You are
at all times dealing with the magical power of thought and consciousness. What results can you expect so long as you remain
oblivious to the power which has been placed within your control?

5. So long as you do this you limit yourself to superficial conditions,
and make of yourself a beast of burden for those who think; those

who recognize their power; those who know that unless we are willing to think we shall have to work, and the less we think the more we shall have to work, and the less we shall get for our work.

6. The secret of power is a perfect understanding of the principles, forces, methods and combinations of Mind, and a perfect understanding of our relationship to the Universal Mind. It is well to remember that this principle is unchangeable; if this were not so, it would not be reliable; all principles are changeless.

7. This stability is your opportunity; you are its active attribute, the channel for its activity; the Universal can act only through the individual.

8. When you begin to perceive that the essence of the Universal is within yourself—is you—you begin to do things; you begin to feel your power; it is the fuel which fires the imagination; which lights the torch of inspiration; which gives vitality to thought; which enables you to connect with all the invisible forces of the Universe. It is this power which will enable you to plan fearlessly, to execute masterfully.

9. But perception will come only in the Silence; this seems to be the condition required for all great purposes. You are a visualizing entity. Imagination is your workshop. It is here that your ideal is to be visualized.

10. As a perfect understanding of the nature of this power is a primary condition for its manifestation, visualize the entire method over and over again, so that you may use it whenever occasion requires. The infinity of wisdom is to follow the method whereby we may have the inspiration of the omnipotent Universal Mind on demand at any time.

11. We can fail to recognize this world within, and so exclude it from our consciousness, but it will still be the basic fact of all existence; and when we learn to recognize it, not only in ourselves, but in all persons, events, and things and circumstances we shall have found the "Kingdom of heaven" which we are told is "within" us.

12. Our failures are a result of the operation of exactly the same principle; the principle is unchangeable; its operation is exact, there is no deviation; if we think lack, limitation, discord, we shall find their fruits on every hand; if we think poverty, unhappiness or disease, the thought messengers will carry the summons as readily as any other kind of thought and the result will be just as certain. If we fear a coming calamity, we shall be able to say with Job, "the thing I feared has come upon me"; if we think unkindly or ignorantly we shall thus attract to ourselves the results of our ignorance.

13. This power of thought, if understood and correctly used, is the greatest labor-saving device ever dreamed of, but if not understood or improperly used, the result will in all probability be disastrous, as we have already seen; by the help of this power you can confidently undertake things that are seemingly impossible, because this power is the secret of all inspiration, all genius.

14. To become inspired means to get out of the beaten path, out of the rut, because extraordinary results require extraordinary means. When we come into a recognition of the Unity of all things and that the source of all power is within, we tap the source of inspiration.

15. Inspiration is the art of imbibing, the art of self-realization; the art of adjusting the individual mind to that of the Universal Mind; the art of attaching the proper mechanism to the source of all power; the art of differentiating the formless into form; the art of becoming a channel for the flow of Infinite Wisdom; the art of visualizing perfection; the art of realizing the omnipresence of Omnipotence.

16. An understanding and appreciation of the fact that the infinite power is omnipresent and is therefore in the infinitely small as well as the infinitely large will enable us to absorb its essence; a further understanding of the fact that this power is spirit and therefore indivisible will enable us to appreciate its presence at all points at the same time.

17. An understanding of these facts, first intellectually and then emotionally, will enable us to drink deeply from this ocean of infinite power. An intellectual understanding will be of no assistance; the emotions must be brought into action; thought without feeling is cold. The required combination is thought and feeling.

18. Inspiration is from within. The Silence is necessary, the senses must be stilled, the muscles relaxed, repose cultivated. When you have thus come into possession of a sense of poise and power you will be ready to receive the information or inspiration or wisdom which may be necessary for the development of your purpose.

19. Do not confuse these methods with those of the clairvoyant; they have nothing in common. Inspiration is the art of receiving and makes for all that is best in life; your business in life is to understand and command these invisible forces instead of letting them command and rule you. Power implies service; inspiration implies power; to understand and apply the method of inspiration is to become a superman.

20. We can live more abundantly every time we breathe, if we consciously breathe with that intention. The IF is a very important condition in this case, as the intention governs the attention, and

without the attention you can secure only the results which everyone else secures. That is, a supply equal to the demand.

21. In order to secure the larger supply your demand must be increased, and as you consciously increase the demand the supply will follow, you will find yourself coming into a larger and larger supply of life, energy and vitality.

22. The reason for this is not difficult to understand, but it is another of the vital mysteries of life which do not seem to be generally appreciated. If you make it your own, you will find it one of the great realities of life.

23. We are told that "In Him we live and move and have our being," and we are told that "He" is a Spirit, and again that "He" is Love, so that every time we breathe, we breathe this life, love, and spirit. This is Pranic Energy, or Pranic Ether; we could not exist a moment without it. It is the Cosmic Energy; it is the Life of the Solar Plexus.

24. Every time we breathe we fill our lungs with air and at the same time vitalize our body with this Pranic Ether which is Life itself, so that we have the opportunity of making a conscious connection with All Life, All Intelligence and All Substance.

25. A knowledge of your relation and oneness with this Principle that governs the Universe and the simple method whereby you can consciously identify yourself with it gives you a scientific understanding of a law whereby you may free yourself from disease, from lack or limitation of any kind; in fact, it enables you to breathe the "breath of life" into your own nostrils.

26. This "breath of life" is a superconscious reality. It is the essence of the "I am." It is pure "Being" or Universal Substance, and our

conscious unity with it enables us to localize it, and thus exercise the powers of this creative energy.

27. Thought is creative vibration and the quality of the conditions created will depend upon the quality of our thought, because we cannot express powers which we do not possess. We must "be" before we can "do" only to the extent to which we "are," and so what we do will necessarily coincide with what we "are" and what we are depends upon what we "think."

28. Every time you think you start a train of causation which will create a condition in strict accordance with the quality of the thought which originated it. Thought which is in harmony with the Universal Mind will result in corresponding conditions. Thought which is destructive or discordant will produce corresponding results. You may use thought constructively or destructively, but the immutable law will not allow you to plant a thought of one kind and reap the fruit of another. You are free to use this marvelous creative power as you will, but you must take the consequences.

29. This is the danger from what is called Will Power. There are those who seem to think that by force of will they can coerce this law; that they can sow seed of one kind and by "Will Power" make it bear fruit of another, but the fundamental principle of creative power is in the Universal, and therefore the idea of forcing a compliance with our wishes by the power of the individual will is an inverted conception which may appear to succeed for a while but is eventually doomed to failure—because it antagonizes the very power which it is seeking to use.

30. It is the individual attempting to coerce the Universal, the finite in conflict with the Infinite. Our permanent well-being will be best

conserved by a conscious cooperation with the continuous forward movement of the Great Whole.

31. For your exercise this week, go into the Silence and concentrate on the fact that "In him we live and move and have our being" is literally and scientifically exact! That you ARE because He IS, that if He is Omnipresent He must be in you. That if He is all in all you must be in Him! That He is Spirit and you are made in "His image and likeness" and that the only difference between His spirit and your spirit is one of degree, that a part must be the same in kind and quality as the whole. When you can realize this clearly you will have found the secret of the creative power of thought, you will have found the origin of both good and evil, you will have found the secret of the wonderful power of concentration, you will have found the key to the solution of every problem whether physical, financial, or environmental.

> *The power to think consecutively and deeply and clearly, is an avowed and deadly enemy to mistakes and blunders, superstitions, unscientific theories, irrational beliefs, unbridled enthusiasm, fanaticism.*
>
> —HADDOCK

PART TWENTY:
STUDY QUESTIONS WITH ANSWERS

191. Upon what condition does power depend?
Upon recognition and use.

192. What is recognition?
Consciousness.

193. How do we become conscious of power?

By thinking.

194. What then is the true business of life?

Correct scientific thinking.

195. What is correct scientific thinking?

The ability to adjust our thought processes to the will of the Universal. In other words, to cooperate with natural laws.

196. How is this accomplished?

By securing a perfect understanding of the principles, forces, methods and combinations of mind.

197. What is this Universal Mind?

The basic fact of all existence.

198. What is the cause of all lack, limitation, disease and discord?

It is due to the operation of exactly the same law; the law operates relentlessly and is continually bringing about conditions in correspondence with the thought which originated or created them.

199. What is inspiration?

The art of realizing the omnipresence of Omniscience.

200. Upon what do the conditions with which we meet depend?

Upon the quality of our thought. Because what we do depends upon what we are and what we are depends upon what we think.

PART TWENTY-ONE

I t is my privilege to enclose Part Twenty-one. In paragraph 7 you will find that one of the secrets of success, one of the methods of organizing victory, one of the accomplishments of the Master Mind is to think big thoughts.

In paragraph 8 you will find that everything which we hold in our consciousness for any length of time becomes impressed upon our subconsciousness and so becomes a pattern which the creative energy will wave into our life and environment. This is the secret of the wonderful power of prayer.

We know that the universe is governed by law; that for every effect there must be a cause, and that the same cause, under the same conditions, will invariably produce the same effect.

Consequently, if prayer has ever been answered, it will always be answered, if the proper conditions are complied with. This must necessarily be true; otherwise the universe would be a chaos instead of a cosmos. The answer to prayer is therefore subject to law, and this law is definite, exact and scientific, just as are the laws governing gravitation and electricity. An understanding of this law takes the foundation of Christianity out of the realm of superstition and credulity and places it upon the firm rock of scientific understanding.

But, unfortunately, there are comparatively few persons who know how to pray.

They understand that there are laws governing electricity, mathematics, and chemistry, but, for some inexplicable reason, it never seems to occur to them that there are also spiritual laws, and that these laws are also definite, scientific, exact, and operate with immutable precision.

1. The real secret of power is consciousness of power. The Universal Mind is unconditional; therefore, the more conscious we become of our unity with this mind, the less conscious we shall become of conditions and limitations, and as we become emancipated or freed from conditions we come into a realization of the unconditional. We have become free!

2. As soon as we become conscious of the inexhaustible power in the world within, we begin to draw on this power and apply and develop the greater possibilities which this discernment has realized, because whatever we become conscious of, is invariably manifested in the objective world, is brought forth into tangible expression.

3. This is because the Infinite Mind, which is the source from which all things proceed, is one and indivisible, and each individual is a channel whereby this Eternal Energy is being manifested. Our ability to think is our ability to act upon this Universal Substance, and what we think is what is created or produced in the objective world.

4. The result of this discovery is nothing less than marvelous, and means that mind is extraordinary in quality, limitless in quantity, and contains possibilities without number. To become conscious of this power is to become a "live wire"; it has the same effect as placing an ordinary wire in contact with a wire that is charged. The Universal is the live wire. It carries power sufficient to meet every situation which may arise in the life of every individual. When the individual mind touches the Universal Mind it receives all the power it requires. This is the world within. All science recognizes the reality of this world, and all power is contingent upon our recognition of this world.

5. The ability to eliminate imperfect conditions depends upon mental action, and mental action depends upon consciousness of power; therefore, the more conscious we become of our unity with the source of all power, the greater will be our power to control and master every condition.

6. Large ideas have a tendency to eliminate all smaller ideas so that it is well to hold ideas large enough to counteract and destroy all small or undesirable tendencies. This will remove innumerable petty and annoying obstacles from your path. You also become conscious of a larger world of thought, thereby increasing your mental capacity as well as placing yourself in position to accomplish something of value.

7. This is one of the secrets of success, one of the methods of organizing victory, one of the accomplishments of the Master-Mind. He thinks big thoughts. The creative energies of mind find no more difficulty in handling large situations, than small ones. Mind is just as much present in the Infinitely large as in the Infinitely small.

8. When we realize these facts concerning mind we understand how we may bring ourselves any condition by creating the corresponding conditions in our consciousness, because everything which is held for any length of time in the consciousness, eventually becomes impressed upon the subconscious and thus becomes a pattern which the creative energy will wave into the life and environment of the individual.

9. In this way conditions are produced and we find that our lives are simply the reflection of our predominant thoughts, our mental

attitude; we see then that the science of correct thinking is the one science, that it includes all other sciences.

10. From this science we learn that every thought creates an impression on the brain, that these impressions create mental tendencies, and these tendencies create character, ability and purpose, and that the combined action of character, ability and purpose determines the experiences with which we shall meet in life.

11. These experiences come to us through the Law of Attraction; through the action of this law we meet in the world without the experiences which correspond to our world within.

12. The predominant thought or the mental attitude is the magnet, and the law is that "like attracts like"; consequently the mental attitude will invariably attract such conditions as correspond to its nature.

13. This mental attitude is our personality and is composed of the thoughts which we have been creating in our own mind; therefore, if we wish a change in conditions all that is necessary is to change our thought; this will in turn change our mental attitude, which will in turn change our personality, which will in turn change the persons, things and conditions or the experiences with which we meet in life.

14. It is, however, no easy matter to change the mental attitude, but by persistent effort it may be accomplished; the mental attitude is patterned after the mental pictures which have been photographed on the brain; if you do not like the pictures, destroy the negatives and create new pictures; this is the art of visualization.

15. As soon as you have done this you will begin to attract new things, and the new things will correspond to the new pictures. To do this: impress on the mind a perfect picture of the desire which you wish to have objectified and continue to hold the picture in mind until results are obtained.

16. If the desire is one which requires determination, ability, talent, courage, power or any other spiritual power, these are necessary essentials for your picture; build them in; they are the vital part of the picture; they are the feeling which combines with thought and creates the irresistible magnetic power which draws the things you require to you. They give your picture life, and life means growth, and as soon as it begins to grow, the result is practically assured.

17. Do not hesitate to aspire to the highest possible attainments in anything you may undertake, for the mind forces are ever ready to lend themselves to a purposeful will in the effort to crystallize its highest aspirations into acts, accomplishments, and events.

18. An illustration of how these mind forces operate is suggested by the method in which all our habits are formed. We do a thing, then do it again, and again, and again, until it becomes easy and perhaps almost automatic; and the same rule applies in breaking any and all bad habits; we stop doing a thing, and then avoid it again, and again until we are entirely free from it; and if we do fail now and then, we should by no means lose hope, for the law is absolute and invincible and gives us credit for every effort and every success, even though our efforts and successes are perhaps intermittent.

19. There is no limit to what this law can do for you; dare to believe in your own idea; remember that nature is plastic to the ideal; think of the ideal as an already accomplished fact.

20. The real battle of life is one of ideas; it is being fought out by the few against the many; on the one side is the constructive and creative thought, on the other side the destructive and negative thought; the creative thought is dominated by an ideal, the passive thought is dominated by appearances. On both sides are men of science, men of letters, and men of affairs.

21. On the creative side are men who spend their time in laboratories, or over microscopes and telescopes, side by side with the men who dominate the commercial, political, and scientific world; on the negative side are men who spend their time investigating law and precedent, men who mistake theology for religion, statesmen who mistake might for right, and all the millions who seem to prefer precedent to progress, who are eternally looking backward instead of forward, who see only the world without, but know nothing of the world within.

22. In the last analysis there are but these two classes; all men will have to take their place on one side or the other; they will have to go forward, or go back; there is no standing still in a world where all is motion; it is this attempt to stand still that gives sanction and force to arbitrary and unequal codes of law.

23. That we are in a period of transition is evidenced by the unrest which is everywhere apparent. The complaint of humanity is as a roll of heaven's artillery, commencing with low and threatening notes and increasing until the sound is sent from cloud to cloud, and the lightning splits the air and earth.

24. The sentries who patrol the most advanced outposts of the Industrial, Political, and Religious world are calling anxiously to each other. What of the night? The danger and insecurity of the position they occupy and attempt to hold is becoming more apparent every hour. The dawn of a new era necessarily declares that the existing order of things cannot much longer be.

25. The issue between the old regime and the new, the crux of the social problem, is entirely a question of conviction in the minds of the people as to the nature of the Universe. When they realize that the transcendent force of spirit or mind of the Cosmos is within each individual, it will be possible to frame laws that shall consider the liberties and rights of the many instead of the privileges of the few.

26. As long as the people regard the Cosmic power as a power non-human and alien to humanity, so long will it be comparatively easy for a supposed privileged class to rule by Divine right in spite of every protest of social sentiment. The real interest of democracy is therefore to exalt, emancipate and recognize the divinity of the human spirit. To recognize that all power is from within. That no human being has any more power than any other human being, except such as may willingly be delegated to him. The old regime would have us believe that the law was superior to the law-makers; herein is the gist of the social crime of every form of privilege and personal inequality, the institutionalizing of the fatalistic doctrine of Divine election.

27. The Divine Mind is the Universal Mind; it makes no exceptions, it plays no favorites; it does not act through sheer caprice or from anger, jealousy or wrath; neither can it be flattered, cajoled or moved by sympathy or petition to supply man with some need which he thinks necessary for his happiness or even his existence. The Divine Mind makes no exceptions to favor any individual; but when the individual understands and realizes his Unity with the Universal principle he will appear to be favored because he will have found the source of all health, all wealth, and all power.

28. For your exercise this week, concentrate on the Truth. Try to realize that the Truth shall make you free, that is, nothing can permanently stand in the way of your perfect success when you learn to apply the scientifically correct thought methods and principles. Realize that you are externalizing in your environment your inherent soul potencies. Realize that the Silence offers an ever-available and almost unlimited opportunity for awakening the highest conception of Truth. Try to comprehend that Omnipotence itself is absolute silence, all else is change, activity, limitation. Silent thought concentration is therefore the true method of reaching, awakening, and then expressing the wonderful potential power of the world within.

> *The possibilities of thought training are infinite, its consequence eternal, and yet few take the pains to direct their thinking into channels that will do them good, but instead leave all to chance.*
>
> —MARDEN

PART TWENTY-ONE:
STUDY QUESTIONS WITH ANSWERS

201. What is the real secret of power?

The consciousness of power, because whatever we become conscious of, is invariably manifested in the objective world, is brought forth into tangible expression.

202. What is the source of this power?

The Universal Mind, from which all things proceed, and which is one and indivisible.

203. How is this power being manifested?

Through the individual; each individual is a channel whereby this energy is being differentiated in form.

204. How may we connect with this Omnipotence?

Our ability to think is our ability to act on this Universal Energy, and what we think is what is produced or created in the objective world.

205. What is the result of this discovery?

The result is nothing less than marvelous, it opens unprecedented and limitless opportunity.

206. How, then, may we eliminate imperfect conditions?

By becoming conscious of our Unity with the source of all power.

207. What is one of the distinctive characteristics of the Master Mind?

He thinks big thoughts, he holds ideas large enough to counteract and destroy all petty and annoying obstacles.

208. How do experiences come to us?

Through the Law of Attraction.

209. How is this law brought into operation?

By our predominant mental attitude.

210. What is the issue between the old regime and the new?

A question of conviction as to the nature of the Universe. The old regime is trying to cling to the fatalistic doctrine of Divine election. The new regime recognizes the divinity of the individual, the democracy of humanity.

PART TWENTY-TWO

In Part Twenty-two you will find that thoughts are spiritual seeds, which, when planted in the subconscious mind, have a tendency to sprout and grow, but unfortunately the fruit is frequently not to our liking.

The various forms of inflammation, paralysis, nervousness and diseased conditions generally, are the manifestation of fear, worry, care, anxiety, jealousy, hatred and similar thought.

The life processes are carried on by two distinct methods; first, the taking up and making use of nutritive material necessary for constructing cells; second, breaking down and excreting the waste material.

All life is based upon these constructive and destructive activities, and as food, water and air are the only requisites necessary for the construction of cells, it would seem that the problem of prolonging life indefinitely would not be a very difficult one.

However strange it may seem, it is the second or destructive activity that is, with rare exception, the cause of all disease. The waste material accumulates and saturates the tissues, which causes autointoxication. This may be partial or general. In the first case the disturbance will be local; in the second place it will affect the whole system.

The problem, then, before us in the healing of disease is to increase the inflow and distribution of vital energy throughout the system, and this can

only be done by eliminating thoughts of fear, worry, care, anxiety, jealousy,
hatred, and every other destructive thought, which tend to tear down and
destroy the nerves and glands which control the excretion and elimination of
poisonous and waste matter.

"Nourishing foods and strengthening tonics" cannot bestow life, because
these are but secondary manifestations to life. The primary manifestation of
life and how you may get in touch with it is explained in the Part which I
have the privilege of enclosing herewith.

1. Knowledge is of priceless value, because by applying knowledge
we can make our future what we wish it to be. When we realize
that our present character, our present environment, our present
ability, our present physical condition are all the result of past methods of thinking, we shall begin to have some conception of the
value of knowledge.

2. If the state of our health is not all that could be desired, let us
examine our method of thinking; let us remember that every
thought produces an impression on the mind; every impression is a
seed which will sink into the subconscious and form a tendency; the
tendency will be to attract other similar thoughts and before we
know it we shall have a crop which must be harvested.

3. If these thoughts contain disease germs, the harvest will be sickness, decay, weakness, and failure; the question is, what are we
thinking, what are we creating, what is the harvest to be?

4. If there is any physical condition which it is necessary to change,
the law governing visualization will be found effective. Make a
mental image of physical perfection, hold it in the mind until it is
absorbed by the consciousness. Many have eliminated chronic ail-
ments in a few weeks by this method, and thousands have overcome

and destroyed all manner of ordinary physical disturbances by this method in a few days, sometimes in a few minutes.

5. It is through the law of vibration that the mind exercises this control over the body. We know that every mental action is a vibration, and we know that all form is simply a mode of motion, a rate of vibration. Therefore, any given vibration immediately modifies every atom in the body, every life cell is affected and an entire chemical change is made in every group of life cells.

6. Everything in the Universe is what it is by virtue of its rate of vibration. Change the rate of vibration and you change the nature, quality and form. The vast panorama of nature, both visible and invisible, is being constantly changed by simply changing the rate of vibration, and as thought is a vibration we can also exercise this power. We can change the vibration and thus produce any condition which we desire to manifest in our bodies.

7. We are all using this power every minute. The trouble is most of us are using it unconsciously and thus producing undesirable results. The problem is to use it intelligently and produce only desirable results. This should not be difficult, because we all have had sufficient experience to know what produces pleasant vibration in the body, and we also know the causes which produce the unpleasant and disagreeable sensations.

8. All that is necessary is to consult our own experience. When our thought has been uplifted, progressive, constructive, courageous, noble, kind or in any other way desirable, we have set in motion vibrations which brought about certain results. When our thought has been filled with envy, hatred, jealousy, criticism or any of the other thousand and one forms of discord, certain vibrations were set in motion which brought about certain other results of a

different nature, and each of these rates of vibration, if kept up, crystallized in form. In the first case the result was mental, moral and physical health, and in the second case discord, inharmony and disease.

9. We can understand, then, something of the power which the mind possesses over the body.

10. The objective mind has certain effects on the body which are readily recognized. Someone says something to you which strikes you as ludicrous and you laugh, possibly until your whole body shakes, which shows that thought has control over the muscles of your body; or someone says something which excites your sympathy and your eyes fill with tears, which shows that thought controls the glands of your body; or someone says something which makes you angry and the blood mounts to your cheek, which shows that thought controls the circulation of your blood. But as these experiences are all the results of the action of your objective mind over the body, the results are of a temporary nature; they soon pass away and leave the situation as it was before.

11. Let us see how the action of the subconscious mind over the body differs. You receive a wound; thousands of cells begin the work of healing at once; in a few days or a few weeks the work is complete. You may even break a bone. No surgeon on earth can weld the parts together (I am not referring to the insertion of rods or other devices to strengthen or replace bones). He may set the bone for you, and the subjective mind will immediately begin the process of welding the parts together, and in a short time the bone is as solid as it ever was. You may swallow poison; the subjective mind will immediately discover the danger and make violent efforts to eliminate it. You may become infected with a dangerous germ; the subjective will at once commence to build a wall around the infected area and destroy the infection by absorbing it in the white blood corpuscles which it supplies for the purpose.

12. These processes of the subconscious mind usually proceed without our personal knowledge or direction, and so long as we do not interfere the result is perfect, but, as these millions of repair cells are all intelligent and respond to our thought, they are often paralyzed and rendered impotent by our thoughts of fear, doubt, and anxiety. They are like an army of workmen, ready to start an important piece of work, but every time they get started on the undertaking a strike is called, or plans changed, until they finally get discouraged and give up.

13. The way to health is founded on the law of vibration, which is the basis of all science, and this law is brought into operation by the mind, the "world within." It is a matter of individual effort and practice. Our world of power is within; if we are wise we shall not waste time and effort in trying to deal with effects as we find them in the "world without," which is only an external, a reflection.

14. We shall always find the cause in the "world within"; by changing the cause, we change the effect.

15. Every cell in your body is intelligent and will respond to your direction. The cells are all creators and will create the exact pattern which you give them.

16. Therefore, when perfect images are placed before the subjective, the creative energies will build a perfect body.

17. Brain cells are constructed in the same way. The quality of the brain is governed by the state of mind, or mental attitude, so that if undesirable mental attitudes are conveyed to the subjective they will in turn be transferred to the body; we can therefore readily see that

if we wish the body to manifest health, strength and vitality this must be the predominant thought.

18. We know then that every element of the human body is the result of a rate of vibration.

19. We know that mental action is a rate of vibration.

20. We know that a higher rate of vibration governs, modifies, controls, changes, or destroys a lower rate of vibration.

21. We know that the rate of vibration is governed by the character of brain cells, and finally,

22. We know how to create these brain cells; therefore,

23. We know how to make any physical change in the body we desire, and having secured a working knowledge of the power of mind to this extent, we have come to know that there is practically no limitation which can be placed upon our ability to place ourselves in harmony with natural law, which is omnipotent.

24. This influence or control over the body by mind is coming to be more and more generally understood, and many physicians are now giving the matter their earnest attention. Dr. Albert T. Shofield, who has written several important books on the subject, says, "The subject of mental therapeutics is still ignored in medical works generally. In our physiologies no references is made to the central controlling power that rules the body for its good, and the power of the mind over the body is seldom spoken of."

25. No doubt many physicians treat nervous diseases of functional origin wisely and well, but what we contend is that the knowledge

they display was taught at no school, was learned from no book, but it is intuitive and empirical.

26. This is not as it should be. The power of mental therapeutics should be the subject of careful, special and scientific teaching in every medical school. We might pursue the subject of maltreatment, or want of treatment, further in detail and describe the disastrous results of neglected cases; but the task is an invidious one.

27. There can be no doubt that few patients are aware how much they can do for themselves. What the patient can do for himself, the forces he can set in motion are as yet unknown. We are inclined to believe that they are far greater than most imagine, and will undoubtedly be used more and more. Mental therapeutics may be directed by the patient himself to calming the mind in excitement, by arousing feelings of joy, hope, faith, and love; by suggesting motives for exertion, by regular mental work, by diverting the thoughts from the malady.

28. For your exercise this week concentrate on Tennyson's beautiful lines "Speak to Him, thou, for He hears, and spirit with spirit can meet, Closer is He than breathing, and nearer than hands and feet." Then try to realize that when you do "Speak to Him" you are in touch with Omnipotence.

29. This realization and recognition of this Omnipresent power will quickly destroy any and every form of sickness or suffering and substitute harmony and perfection. Then remember there are those who seem to think that sickness and suffering are sent by God; if so, every physician, every surgeon and every Red Cross nurse is defying the will of God and hospitals and sanitariums are places of rebellion instead of houses of mercy. Of course, this quickly reasons itself into an absurdity, but there are many who still cherish the idea.

30. Then let the thought rest on the fact that until recently theology has been trying to teach an impossible Creator, one who created beings capable of sinning and then allowed them to be eternally punished for such sins. Of course the necessary outcome of such extraordinary ignorance was to create fear instead of love, and so, after two thousand years of this kind of propaganda, Theology is now busily engaged in apologizing for Christendom.

31. You will then more readily appreciate the ideal man, the man made in the image and likeness of God, and you will more readily appreciate the all-originating Mind that forms, upholds, sustains, originates, and creates all there is.

> *All are but parts of one stupendous whole, Whose body nature is, and God the soul.*

> *Opportunity follows perception, action follows inspiration, growth follows knowledge, eminence follows progress. Always the spiritual first, then the transformation into the infinite and illimitable possibilities of achievement.*

PART TWENTY-TWO:
STUDY QUESTIONS WITH ANSWERS

211. How may sickness be eliminated?
By placing ourselves in harmony with natural law, which is Omnipotent.

212. What is the process?
A realization that man is a spiritual being and that this spirit must necessarily be perfect.

213. What is the result?

A conscious recognition of this perfection—first intellectually, then emotionally—brings about a manifestation of this perfection.

214. Why is this so?

Because thought is spiritual and therefore creative and correlates with its object and brings it into manifestation.

215. What natural law is brought into operation?

The law of vibration.

216. Why does this govern?

Because a higher rate of vibration governs, modifies, controls, changes, or destroys a lower rate of vibration.

217. Is this system of mental therapeutics generally recognized?

Yes, there are literally millions of people in this country who make use of it in one form or another (and obviously many more worldwide).

218. What is the result of this system of thought?

For the first time in the world's history every man's highest reasoning faculty can be satisfied by a demonstrable truth which is now fast flooding the world.

219. Is this system applicable to other forms of supply?

It will meet every human requirement or necessity.

220. Is this system scientific or religious?

Both. True science and true religion are twin sisters; where one goes, the other necessarily follows.

PART TWENTY-THREE

In the Part which I have the honor to transmit herewith you will find that money weaves itself into the entire fabric of our very existence; that the law of success is service; that we get what we give, and for this reason we should consider it a great privilege to be able to give.

We have found that thought is the creative activity behind every constructive enterprise. We can therefore give nothing of more practical value than our thought.

Creative thought requires attention, and the power of attention is, as we have found, the weapon of the superman. Attention develops concentration, and concentration develops Spiritual Power, and Spiritual Power is the mightiest force in existence.

This is the science which embraces all sciences. It is the art which, above all arts, is relevant to human life. In the mastery of this science and this art there is opportunity for unending progression. Perfection in this is not acquired in six days, nor in six weeks, nor in six months. It is the labor of life. Not to go forward is to go backward.

It is inevitable that the entertainment of positive, constructive and unselfish thoughts should have a far-reaching effect for good. Compensation is the keynote of the universe. Nature is constantly seeking to strike an equilibrium.

Where something is sent out something must be received; else there should be a vacuum formed.

By observance of this rule you cannot fail to profit in such measure as to amply justify your effort along this line.

1. The money consciousness is an attitude of mind; it is the open door to the arteries of commerce. It is the receptive attitude. Desire is the attractive force which sets the current in motion and fear is the great obstacle by which the current is stopped or completely reversed, turned away from us.

2. Fear is just the opposite from money consciousness; it is poverty consciousness, and as the law is unchangeable we get exactly what we give; if we fear we get what we feared. Money weaves itself into the entire fabric of our very existence; it engages the best thought of the best minds.

3. We make money by making friends, and we enlarge our circle of friends by making money for them, by helping them, by being of service to them. The first law of success then is service, and this in turn is built on integrity and justice. The man who at least is not fair in his intention is simply ignorant; he has missed the fundamental law of all exchange; he is impossible; he will lose surely and certainly; he may not know it; he may think he is winning, but he is doomed to certain defeat. He cannot cheat the Infinite. The law of compensation will demand of him an eye for an eye and a tooth for a tooth.

4. The forces of life are volatile; they are composed of our thoughts and ideals and these in turn are molded into form; our problem is to keep an open mind, to constantly reach out for the new, to recognize opportunity, to be interested in the race rather than the goal, for the pleasure is in the pursuit rather than the possession.

5. You can make a money magnet of yourself, but to do so you must first consider how you can make money for other people. If you have the necessary insight to perceive and utilize opportunities and favorable conditions and recognize values, you can put yourself in position to take advantage of them, but your greatest success will come as you are enabled to assist others. What benefits one must benefit all.

6. A generous thought is filled with strength and vitality, a selfish thought contains the germs of dissolution; it will disintegrate and pass away. Great financiers are simply channels for the distribution of wealth; enormous amounts come and go, but it would be as dangerous to stop the outgo as the income; both ends must remain open; and so our greatest success will come as we recognize that it is just as essential to give as to get.

7. If we recognize the Omnipotent power that is the source of all supply we will adjust our consciousness to this supply in such a way that it will constantly attract all that is necessary to itself and we shall find that the more we give the more we get. Giving in this sense implies service. The banker gives his money, the merchant gives his goods, the author gives his thought, the workman gives his skill; all have something to give, but the more they can give, the more they get, and the more they get the more they are enabled to give.

8. The financier gets much because he gives much; he thinks; he is seldom a man that lets anyone else do his thinking for him; he wants to know how results are to be secured; you must show him; when you can do this he will furnish the means by which hundreds or thousands may profit, and in proportion as they are successful will he be successful. Morgan, Rockefeller, Carnegie and others did not get rich because they lost money for other people; on the contrary, it is because they made money for other people that they become the wealthiest men in the wealthiest country on the globe.

9. The average person is entirely innocent of any deep thinking; he accepts the ideas of others, and repeats them, in very much the same way as a parrot; this is readily seen when we understand the method which is used to form public opinion, and this docile attitude on the part of a large majority who seem perfectly willing to let a few persons do all their thinking for them is what enables a few men in a great many countries to usurp all the avenues of power and hold the millions in subjection. Creative thinking requires attention.

10. The power of attention is called concentration; this power is directed by the will; for this reason we must refuse to concentrate or think of anything except the things we desire. Many are constantly concentrating upon sorrow, loss and discord of every kind; as thought is creative it necessarily follows that this concentration inevitable leads to more loss, more sorrow and more discord. How could it be otherwise? On the other hand, when we meet with success, gain, or any other desirable condition, we naturally concentrate upon the effects of these things and thereby create more, and so it follows that much leads to more.

11. How an understanding of this principle can be utilized in the business world is well told by an associate of mine:

12. "Spirit, whatever else it may or may not be, must be considered as the Essence of Consciousness, the Substance of Mind, the reality underlying Thought. And as all ideas are phases of the activity of Consciousness, Mind or Thought, it follows that in Spirit, and in it alone, is to be found the Ultimate Fact, the Real Thing, or Idea."

13. This being admitted, does it not seem reasonable to hold that a true understanding of Spirit, and its laws of manifestation, would be about the most "practical" thing that a "practical" person can hope to find? Does it not seem certain that if the "practical" men of the world could but realize this fact, they would "fall all over them-selves" in getting to the place in which they might obtain such knowledge of spiritual things and laws? These men are not fools; they need only to grasp this fundamental fact in order to move in the direction of that which is the essence of all achievement.

14. Let me give you a concrete example. I know a man in Chicago whom I had always considered to be quite materialistic. He had made several successes in life; and also several failures. The last time I had a talk with him he was practically "down and out," as com-pared with his former business condition. It looked as if he had indeed reached "the end of his rope," for he was well advanced into the stage of middle-age, and new ideas came more slowly, and less frequently to him than in former years.

15. He said to me, in substance: "I know that all things that "work out" in business are the result of Thought; any fool knows that. Just now, I seem to be short on thoughts and good ideas. But, if this "All-Mind" teaching is correct, it should be possible for the indi-vidual to attain a 'direct connection' with Infinite Mind; and in Infi-nite Mind there must be the possibility of all kinds of good ideas which a man of my courage and experience could put to practical use in the business world, and make a big success thereof. It looks good to me; and I am going to look into it."

16. This was several years ago. The other day I heard of this man again. Talking to a friend, I said: "What has come of our old friend X? Has he ever gotten on his feet again?" The friend looked at me in amazement. "Why," said he, "don't you know about X's great success? He is the Big Man in the '_____ Company' (naming a concern which has made a phenomenal success during the last eigh-teen months and is now well known, by reason of its advertisements, from one end of the country to another, and also abroad). He is the man who supplied the BIG IDEA for that concern. Why, he is about a half-million to the good and is moving rapidly toward the million mark; all in the space of eighteen months." I had not connected this man with the enterprise mentioned; although I knew of the wonderful success of the company in question. Investigation has shown that the story is true, and that the above stated facts are not exaggerated in the slightest.

17. Now, what do you think of that? To me, it means that this man actually made the "direct connection" with Infinite Mind—Spirit—and, having found it, he set it to work for him. He "used it in his business."

18. Does this sound sacrilegious or blasphemous? I hope not; I do not mean it to be so. Take away the implication of Personality, or Magnified Human Nature, from the conception of "The Infinite," and you have left the conception of an Infinite Presence-Power, the Quintessence of which is Consciousness—in fact, at the last, Spirit. As this man, also, at the last, must be considered as a manifestation of Spirit; there is nothing sacrilegious in the idea that he, being Spirit, should so harmonize himself with his Origin and Source that he would be able to manifest at least a minor degree of its Power. All of us do this, more or less, when we use our minds in the direction of Creative Thought. This man did more, he went about it in an intensely "practical" manner.

19. I have not consulted him about his method of procedure, though I intend doing so at the first opportunity, but he not only drew upon the Infinite Supply for the ideas which he needed (and which formed the seed of his success), but he also used the Creative Power of Thought in building up for himself an Idealistic Pattern of that which he hoped to manifest in material form, adding thereto, changing, improving its detail, from time to time—proceeding

from the general outline to the finished detail. I judge this to be the facts of the case, not alone from my recollection of the conversation a few years ago, but also because I have found the same thing to be true in the cases of other prominent men who have made similar manifestation of Creative Thought.

20. Those who may shrink from this idea of employing the Infinite Power to aid one in his work in the material world, should remember that if the Infinite objected in the least to such a procedure the thing could never happen. The Infinite is quite able to take care of itself.

21. "Spirituality" is quite "practical," very "practical," intensely "practical." It teaches that Spirit is the Real Thing, the Whole Thing, and that Matter is but plastic stuff, which Spirit is able to create, mold, manipulate, and fashion to its will. Spirituality is the most "practical" thing in the world—the only really and absolutely "practical" thing that there is!

22. This week concentrate on the fact that man is not a body with a spirit, but a spirit with a body, and that it is for this reason that his desires are incapable of any permanent satisfaction in anything not spiritual. Money is therefore of no value except to bring about the conditions which we desire, and these conditions are necessarily harmonious. Harmonious conditions necessitate sufficient supply, so that if there appears to be any lack, we should realize that the idea or soul of money is service, and as this thought takes form, channels of supply will be opened, and you will have the satisfaction of knowing that spiritual methods are entirely practical.

We have discovered that premeditated, orderly thinking for a purpose matures that purpose into fixed form, so that we may be absolutely sure of the result of our dynamic experiment.

—FRANCIS LARIMER WARNER

PART TWENTY-THREE:
STUDY QUESTIONS WITH ANSWERS

221. What is the first law of success?

Service.

222. How may we be of the most service?

Have an open mind; be interested in the race rather than the goal, in the pursuit rather than possession.

223. What is the result of a selfish thought?

It contains the germs of dissolution.

224. How will our greatest success be achieved?

By a recognition of the fact that it is just as essential to give as to receive.

225. Why do financiers frequently meet with great success?

Because they do their own thinking.

226. Why do the great majority in every country remain the docile and apparently willing tools of the few?

Because they let the few do all their thinking for them.

227. What is the effect of concentrating upon sorrow and loss?

More sorrow and more loss.

228. What is the effect of concentrating upon gain?

More gain.

229. Is this principle used in the business world?

It is the only principle which is ever used, or ever can be used; there is no other principle. The fact that it may be used unconsciously does not alter the situation.

230. What is the practical application of this principle?

The fact that success is an effect, not a cause, and if we wish to secure the effect we must ascertain the cause, or idea or thought by which the effect is created.

Nurture your mind with great thoughts; to believe in the heroic makes heroes.

—DISRAELI

PART TWENTY-FOUR

Enclosed you will find Part Twenty-four, your final lesson of this course.

If you have practiced each of the exercises a few minutes every day, as suggested, you will have found that you can get out of life exactly what you wish by first putting into life that which you wish, and you will probably agree with the student who said: "The thought is almost overwhelming, so vast, so available, so definite, so reasonable and so usable."

The fruit of this knowledge is, as it were, a gift of the Gods; it is the "truth" that makes men free, not only free from every lack and limitation, but free from sorrow, worry and care, and, is it not wonderful to realize that this law is no respecter of persons, that it makes no difference what your habit of thought may be, the way has been prepared.

If you are inclined to be religious, the greatest religious teacher the world has ever known made the way so plain that all may follow. If your mental bias is toward physical science, the law will operate with mathematical certainty. If you are inclined to be philosophical, Plato or Emerson may be your teacher, but in either case, you may reach degrees of power to which it is impossible to assign any limit.

An understanding of this principle, I believe, is the secret for which the *ancient Alchemists vainly sought, because it explains how gold in the mind may be transmuted into gold in the heart and in the hand.*

1. When the scientists first put the Sun in the center of the Solar System and sent the earth spinning around it, there was immense surprise and consternation. The whole idea was self-evidently false; nothing was more certain than the movement of the Sun across the sky, and anyone could see it descend behind the western hills and sink into the sea; scholars raged and scientists rejected the idea as absurd, yet the evidence has finally carried conviction in the minds of all.

2. We speak of a bell as a "sounding body," yet we know that all the bell can do is to produce vibrations in the air. When these vibrations come at the rate of sixteen per second, they cause a sound to be heard in the mind. It is also possible for the mind to hear vibrations up to the rate of 38,000 vibrations per second. When the number increases beyond this, all is silence again; so that we know that the sound is not in the bell, it is in our own mind.

3. We speak and even think of the Sun as "giving light." Yet we know it is simply giving forth energy which produces vibrations in the ether at the rate of four hundred trillion a second, causing what are termed light waves, so that we know that we call light is simply a form of energy and that the only light there is, is the sensation caused in the mind by the motion of the waves. When the number increases, the light changes in color, each change in color being caused by shorter and more rapid vibrations; so that although we speak of the rose as being red, the grass as being green, or the sky as being blue, we know that the colors exist only in our minds, and are the sensations experienced by us as the result of the vibrations of light waves. When the vibrations are reduced below four hundred trillion a second, they no longer affect us as light, but we experience

the sensation of heat. It is evident, therefore, that we cannot depend upon the evidence of the senses for our information concerning the realities of things; if we did we should believe that the sun moved, that the world was flat instead of round, that the stars were bits of light instead of vast suns.

4. The whole range then of the theory and practice of any system of metaphysics consists in knowing the Truth concerning yourself and the world in which you live; in knowing that in order to express harmony, you must think harmony; in order to express health you must think health; and in order to express abundance you must think abundance; to do this you must reverse the evidence of the senses.

5. When you come to know that every form of disease, sickness, lack and limitation is simply the result of wrong thinking, you will have come to know "the Truth which shall make you free." You will see how mountains may be removed. If these mountains consist only of doubt, fear, distrust or other forms of discouragement, they are none the less real, and they need not only to be removed but to be "cast into the sea."

6. Your real work consists in convincing yourself of the truth of these statements. When you have succeeded in doing this you will have no difficulty in thinking the truth, and as has been shown, the Truth contains a vital principle and will manifest itself.

7. Those who heal diseases by mental methods have come to know this truth, they demonstrate it in their lives and the lives of others daily. They know that life, health and abundance are Omnipresent, filling all space, and they know that those who allow disease or lack of any kind to manifest themselves have as yet not come into an understanding of this great law.

8. As all conditions are thought creations and therefore entirely mental, disease and lack are simply mental conditions in which the person fails to perceive the truth; as soon as the error is removed, the condition is removed.

9. The method for removing this error is to go into the Silence and know the Truth; as all mind is one mind, you can do this for yourself or anyone else. If you have learned to form mental images of the conditions desired, this will be the easiest and quickest way to secure results; if not, results can be accomplished by argument, by the process of convincing yourself absolutely of the truth of your statement.

10. Remember, and this is one of the most difficult as well as most wonderful statements to grasp . . . remember that no matter what the difficulty is, no matter where it is, no matter who is affected, you have no patient but yourself; you have nothing to do but to convince yourself of the truth which you desire to see manifested.

11. This is an exact scientific statement in accordance with every system of Metaphysics in existence, and no permanent results are ever secured in any other way.

12. Every form of concentration, forming Mental Images, Argument, and Auto-suggestion are all simply methods by which you are enabled to realize the Truth.

13. If you desire to help someone, to destroy some form of lack, limitation or error, the correct method is not to think of the person whom you wish to help; the intention to help them is entirely sufficient, as this puts you in mental touch with the person. Then drive out of your own mind any belief of lack, limitation, disease, danger, difficulty or whatever the trouble might be. As soon as you have succeeded in doing this the result will have been accomplished, and the person will be free.

14. But remember that thought is creative and consequently every time you allow your thought to rest on any inharmonious condition, you must realize that such conditions are apparent only, they have no reality, that spirit is the only reality and it can never be less than perfect.

15. All thought is a form of energy, a rate of vibration, but a thought of the Truth is the highest rate of vibration known and consequently destroys every form of error in exactly the same way that light destroys darkness; no form of error can exist when the "Truth" appears, so that your entire mental work consists in coming into an understanding of the Truth. This will enable you to overcome every form of lack, limitation or disease of any kind.

16. We can get no understanding of the truth from the world without; the world without is relative only; Truth is absolute. We must therefore find it in the "world within."

17. To train the mind to see Truth only is to express true conditions only, our ability to do this will be an indication as to the progress we are making.

18. The absolute truth is that the "I" is perfect and complete; the real "I" is spiritual and can therefore never be less than perfect; it can never have any lack, limitation, or disease. The flash of genius does not have origin in the molecular motion of the brain; it is inspired by the ego, the spiritual "I" which is one with the Universal Mind, and it is our ability to recognize this Unity which is the cause of all inspiration, all genius. These results are far reaching and have effect upon generations yet to come; they are the pillars of fire which mark the path that millions follow.

19. Truth is not the result of logical training or of experimentation, or even of observation; it is the product of a developed consciousness. Truth within a Caesar, manifests in a Caesar's deportment, in his life and his action; his influence upon social forms and progress. Your life and your actions and your influence in the world will depend upon the degree of truth which you are enabled to perceive, for truth will not manifest itself in creeds, but in conduct.

20. Truth manifests itself in character, and the character of a man should be the interpretation of his religion, or what to him is truth, and this will in turn be evidenced in the character of his possession. If a man complains of the drift of his fortune he is just as unjust to himself as if he should deny rational truth, though it stand patent and irrefutable.

21. Our environment and the innumerable circumstances and accidents of our lives already exist in the subconscious personality which attracts to itself the mental and physical material which is congenial to its nature. Thus our future being determined from our present, and if there should be apparent injustice in any feature or phase of our personal life, we must look within for the cause, try to discover the mental fact which is responsible for the outward manifestation.

22. It is this truth which makes you "free" and it is the conscious knowledge of this truth which will enable you to overcome every difficulty.

23. The conditions with which you meet in the world without are invariably the result of the conditions obtaining in the world within, therefore it follows with scientific accuracy that by holding the perfect ideal in mind you can bring about ideal conditions in your environment.

24. If you see only the incomplete, the imperfect, the relative, the limited, these conditions will manifest themselves in your life; but if you train your mind to see and realize the spiritual ego, the "I" which is forever perfect and complete, harmonious, wholesome, and healthful conditions only will be manifested.

25. As thought is creative, and the truth is the highest and most perfect thought which anyone can think, it is self-evident that to think the truth is to create that which is true and it is again evident that when truth comes into being that which is false must cease to be.

26. The Universal Mind is the totality of all mind which is in existence. Spirit is Mind, because spirit is intelligent. The words are, therefore, synonymous.

27. The difficulty with which you have to contend is to realize that mind is not individual. It is omnipresent. It exists everywhere. In other words, there is no place where it is not. It is, therefore, Universal.

28. Men have, heretofore, generally used the word "God" to indicate this Universal, creative principle; but the word "God" does not convey the right meaning. Most people understand this word to mean something outside of themselves; while exactly the contrary is the fact. It is our very life. Without it we would be dead. We would cease to exist. The minute the spirit leaves the body, we are as nothing. Therefore, spirit is really all there is of us.

29. Now, the only activity which the spirit possesses is the power to think. Therefore, thought must be creative, because spirit is creative. This creative power is impersonal and your ability to think is your ability to control it and make use of it for the benefit of yourself and others.

30. When the truth of this statement is realized, understood, and appreciated, you will have come into possession of the Master Key, but remember that only those who are wise enough to understand, broad enough to weigh the evidence, firm enough to follow their own judgment, and strong enough to make the sacrifice exacted, may enter and partake.

31. This week, try to realize that this is truly a wonderful world in which we live, that you are a wonderful being that many are awakening to a knowledge of the Truth, and as fast as they awake and come into a knowledge of the "things which have been prepared for them" they, too, realize that "Eye hath not seen, nor ear heard, neither hath it entered into the heart of man," the splendors which exist for those who find themselves in the Promised Land. They have crossed the river of judgment and have arrived at the point of discrimination between the true and the false, and have found that all they ever willed or dreamed, was but a faint concept of the dazzling reality.

> Though an inheritance of acres may be bequeathed, an inheritance of knowledge and wisdom cannot. The wealthy man may pay others for doing his work for him, but it is impossible to get his thinking done for him by another or to purchase any kind of self-culture.
>
> —S. SMILES

PART TWENTY-FOUR:
STUDY QUESTIONS WITH ANSWERS

231. Upon what principle does the theory and practice of every system of Metaphysics in existence depend?

Upon a knowledge of the "Truth" concerning yourself and the world in which you live.

232. What is the "Truth" concerning yourself?

The real "I" or ego is spiritual and can therefore never be less than perfect.

233. What is the method of destroying any form of error?

To absolutely convince yourself of the "Truth" concerning the condition which you wish to see manifested.

234. Can we do this for others?

The Universal Mind in which "we live and move and have our being" is one and indivisible; it is therefore just as possible to help others as to help ourselves.

235. What is the Universal Mind?

The totality of all mind in existence.

236. Where is the Universal Mind?

The Universal Mind is omnipresent, it exists everywhere. There is no place where it is not. It is therefore within us. It is "The World within." It is our spirit, our life.

237. What is the nature of the Universal Mind?

It is spiritual and consequently creative. It seeks to express itself in form.

238. How may we act on the Universal Mind?

Our ability to think is our ability to act on the Universal Mind and bring it into manifestation for the benefit of ourselves or others.

239. What is meant by thinking?

Clear, decisive, calm, deliberate, sustained thought with a definite end in view.

240. What will be the result?

You will also be able to say, "It is not I that doeth the works, but the 'Father' that dwelleth within me, He doeth the works." You will come to know that the "Father" is the Universal Mind and that He does really and truly dwell within you, in other words, you will come to know that the wonderful promises made in the Bible are fact, not fiction, and can be demonstrated by anyone having sufficient understanding.

Temples have their sacred images, and we see what influence they have always had over a great part of mankind; but, in truth, the ideas and images in men's minds are the invisible powers that constantly govern them; and to these they all pay universally a ready submission.

—JONATHAN EDWARDS

ABOUT THE AUTHOR

Born in 1866, Charles F. Haanel achieved success as both a business-man and an author, rising to top positions at numerous corporations in his native St. Louis throughout his life. Often called the "Father of Personal Development," Haanel was among the earliest writers to popularize the "Law of Attraction." Haanel originally published *The Master Key System* as a correspondence course in 1912, before collecting the lessons and publishing them as a single volume in 1917. Haanel retained membership in many influential groups, such as the American Society for Psychical Research, and went on to write *Mental Chemistry* and *The New Psychology*. He died in 1949.

LOOK FOR THESE PROSPERITY FAVORITES
FROM TARCHER/PENGUIN

Think and Grow Rich by Napoleon Hill
The landmark guide by the champion wealth-builder
of all time—now revised and updated for the
twenty-first century.   ISBN 978-1-58542-433-7

As a Man Thinketh by James Allen
The beloved classic on the creative potential of the
human mind—available in a beautiful early rep-
lica edition.   ISBN 978-1-58542-564-8

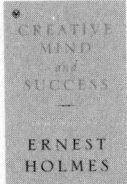

Creative Mind and Success by Ernest Holmes
A slender volume of immense power on the mental
principles to success, by the author of *The Science
of Mind*.   ISBN 978-1-58542-608-9

Your Magic Power to Be Rich! by Napoleon Hill
The ultimate all-in-one prosperity bible, featuring updated editions of Hill's great works *Think and Grow Rich, The Magic Ladder to Success,* and *The Master-Key to Riches.*   ISBN 978-1-58542-555-6

Relax into Wealth by Alan Cohen
One of today's top life coaches explores the hidden key to success: Being yourself.
ISBN 978-1-58542-563-1

The Circle by Laura Day
The treasured guidebook that shows how the power of one simple wish can transform your entire life.   ISBN 978-1-58542-598-3

If you enjoyed this book, visit

www.tarcherbooks.com

and sign up for Tarcher's e-newsletter to receive
special offers, giveaway promotions, and
information on hot upcoming releases.

TARCHER
PENGUIN

Great Lives Begin with Great Ideas

Connect with the Tarcher Community

• • •

Stay in touch with favorite authors!
Enter weekly contests!
Read exclusive excerpts!
Voice your opinions!

Follow us

 Tarcher Books

 @TarcherBooks

If you would like to place a bulk order
of this book, call 1-800-847-5515.